D0399138

BRITISH INDUSTRY

Economics

Editor

SIR ROY HARROD
F.B.A.

Student of Christ Church, Oxford,
and Fellow of Nuffield College

BRITISH INDUSTRY

CHANGE AND DEVELOPMENT IN
THE TWENTIETH CENTURY

J. H. Dunning
Professor of Economics
in the University of Reading

&

C. J. Thomas
Senior Lecturer in Economic Statistics
in the University of Southampton

HUTCHINSON UNIVERSITY LIBRARY
LONDON

UNIVERSITY OF VICTORIA
LIBRARY
Victoria, B C.

HUTCHINSON & CO *(Publishers)* LTD
178–202 Great Portland Street, London W1

London Melbourne Sydney
Auckland Bombay Toronto
Johannesburg New York

First published 1961
Reprinted 1961
Second (revised) edition 1963
Reprinted 1966

The paperback edition of this book is sold
subject to the condition that it shall not, by way
of trade or otherwise, be lent, re-sold, hired out,
or otherwise circulated without the publisher's
prior consent in any form of binding or cover
other than that in which it is published and
without a similar condition including this condition being imposed on the subsequent purchaser

*Cover design of paperback edition by courtesy
of Imperial Chemical Industries Ltd*

© J. H. Dunning and C. J. Thomas 1961 and 1963

*This book has been set in Times, printed in Great Britain
on Smooth Wove paper by Anchor Press, and
bound by Wm. Brendon, both of Tiptree, Essex*

CONTENTS

TABLES

7

INTRODUCTION

Many factors combine to influence a country's industrial structure. This book discusses some of the major changes and developments which have taken place within British industry during recent years. It is a study of the interaction between the more important variables affecting technological progress and the pattern of economic activity.

The economist is concerned both with the ways in which scarce resources are allocated within a community at any given moment of time, and the effect which such an allocation has on the rate of growth of the national product. Though it is sometimes argued that he should take technological factors as data, he is in fact much concerned with how these may both influence and be influenced by economic considerations, e.g. a changing price structure or redistribution of incomes.

The last half-century has brought with it many changes which have made their impact on British industry. Twelve years have been taken up by war, yet these have produced technological discoveries of lasting and far-reaching significance. There have been periods of prolonged depression in trade and comparatively stagnant technology; there have been others of full employment and rapid innovation. Our period of coverage begins with the introduction of a new technology based on the internal combustion engine and electrical power; it ends on the threshold of the age of atomic power, with the discovery and exploitation of a wide range of new industrial materials. In the interim a social revolution has been accomplished, bringing with it a changing pattern of consumer wants, while the emergence of new industrial nations has fundamentally affected the basis and composition of Britain's external trade. Chapter I traces the main implications of these developments on the size and composition of U.K. industrial output, and Chapter II

9

their impact on the size-structure, ownership patterns and location of industry.

Of the variables influencing industrial progress in the twentieth century we have chosen three as worthy of particular consideration. The first is that of energy and power. In the past there has been a very close relationship between an industrial country's living standards and its consumption of energy: periods of intensive economic expansion have usually been accompanied by large increases in fuel usage, and discoveries of new sources of energy have often heralded revolutions in industrial techniques and processes. At the same time it is only in the course of the past fifty years that the sources of industrial fuel have become so diverse and flexible. Chapter III analyses the ways in which Britain's fuel needs have been, and are being met, and indicates future prospects. Secondly, an industrial country's prosperity is being increasingly influenced by its ability to innovate. Again, there is reason to suppose that a close link exists between a country's rate of expansion and its ability to undertake and benefit from research and development. Not only is research a contributory factor to progress: in the case of the United Kingdom in her present economic circumstances it may be thought essential for the maintenance of living standards. Yet, once more, the development of organized research is essentially a twentieth-century phenomenon. Chapter IV discusses the various agents which have contributed towards its extension within industry.

A third element affecting industrial progress, and one which is closely allied to the previous two, has its genesis in the search for new materials. The rapid growth of world population and living standards during the twentieth century has meant that many traditional materials have become near-exhausted and others increasingly expensive to produce, at a time when the pressure on all kinds of land for the growing of foodstuffs is increasing. It is thus of particular significance that during the last twenty years a wide variety of substitute materials of mineral derivation have been discovered, while equally important advances have taken place in the field of industrial metallurgy. At the same time changes in the relative costs of factors of production on the one hand, and widening markets on the other, have induced more capitalistic production techniques. Automation is best-known amongst these and is briefly treated in Chapter V.

Chapters VI and VII deal with two non-technical influences affecting industrial development in the twentieth century. First, we outline the pronounced changes which have taken place in the role of the State in economic affairs and the many ways in which industry has been directly or indirectly affected. Second, international economic developments. How have the trends in world trade affected British industry? The U.K. exports nearly 40% of her manufacturing output and is no less reliant on the imports of essential raw materials. Chapter VII discusses the changing composition of British exports and the implications the technical developments described above are having on her imports. The problems of securing a balanced economy are outlined and there is a final section on the recent developments in European economic integration.

The reader will appreciate the selective nature of the variables we have chosen to discuss. Others are mentioned in the course of argument but are not discussed at any length. First, little attention has been paid to the social revolution of the twentieth century and its impact on tastes and habits; secondly, we have been forced to ignore the various factors affecting productivity save those of research and development; thirdly, only passing reference has been made to the various problems involved in the transference from a policy of *laissez-faire* to that of a controlled economy.

Finally, in a book of this length it has not been possible to deal in any detail with the development of particular industries. We have, however, noted in passing the more important features of the fuel and power industries in Chapter III and the man-made fibres, plastics and petro-chemical industries in Chapter V. These are incomplete accounts but may form a useful basis for further reading.

This book has been written for those who wish to obtain a descriptive background of some of the more important technical developments in British industry over recent years as viewed from their effect on the economy as a whole. It is not a volume about the economics of industry as such—but rather on the economic implications of the more important technological events. It pretends neither to deal with such crucial problems as pricing and investment policy, nor to suggest cures for some of the problems raised. It is, nevertheless, hoped that it will prove useful to the first and second year Economics undergraduate as well as having an appeal to those interested in British industrial development in general.

We are very grateful to Miss D. M. Marshallsay, B.A., A.L.A., for compiling the Index and for her invaluable assistance at every stage in the preparation of this book. The manuscript was expertly typed by Mrs P. Powell and Mrs P. Dunn of our Department; their cheerful and patient help has been greatly appreciated. Finally, we wish to acknowledge permission from the Editor of the *Indian Journal of Economics* to reprint material by the authors now included in Chapter IV.

NOTE TO REVISED EDITION

For this edition we have sought to bring up-to-date as many of our statistics as possible. Several modifications have also been made to the text, particularly Chapters II, IV and VII, in the light of developments of the past eighteen months or so.

We are indebted to Mr J. Parker, B.SC (ECON.), of the Department of Economics for his help in preparing the edition.

J.H.D.
C.J.T.
June 1962

THE CHANGING PATTERN OF INDUSTRIAL OUTPUT, 1914–60

British industry in 1914

THE outbreak of the First World War brought to an end a century of unprecedented, and virtually uninterrupted, expansion in British industrial output. It was a century during which both population and living standards quadrupled, and the economic structure of the country as a whole underwent a number of profound changes. At the end of the Napoleonic wars 34% of the employed population in England and Wales was still engaged in agricultural and fishing activities, and only one-seventh of the total domestic food consumption was imported. Although by this time the United Kingdom had already experienced the initial phases of the new machine era—textile manufactures, for example, accounted for 67% of British exports in 1820—in most major respects her industrial framework was immature, unstable and highly specialized. Few of the main technological innovations of the previous 50 years had yet been exploited on any scale. Coal output was then only 15 million tons per year and pig-iron production less than a million tons; the application of steam power and the new mechanical devices was being handicapped by a deficiency of skilled engineers, both to produce and to operate the necessary machinery and machine tools; industrial chemistry was in its infancy; there were no railways or steamships and few good roads; the transformation of the banking system and the capital market had yet to be accomplished; and over half the exports of the United Kingdom were composed of indigenous products or manufactures based on them.

During the years which followed, however, the United Kingdom became the most highly industrialized country in the world and by

1914 was dependent on her manufacturing exports to finance three-quarters of her consumption of raw materials (apart from coal) and one-half her food. As the obstacles to her industrial progress were gradually overcome and a technology especially favourable to her economic environment evolved, the rate of industrial growth accelerated. In the nineteenth century the output of manufacturing industry increased fourteenfold, whereas the proportion of the working population employed in agriculture and fishing fell to only 8%. The relative importance of the tertiary industries, viz. transport, commerce and distribution, rose proportionately to the decline of agriculture. Between them, coal, textiles and metal-based products accounted for three-quarters of all British exports in 1913.

From the viewpoint of world industrial growth the period between 1815 and 1914 may be divided into two main phases: up to 1876, and 1877 onwards. During the first phase the rate of British industrial expansion averaged 3 to 4% per annum, or twice that of the eighteenth century. By 1860 the United Kingdom had achieved complete industrial supremacy and was supplying half the world's output of coal and manufactured goods. Twenty years later her economy reflected an almost complete fulfilment of the principles of free competition and the international division of labour, and her dependence on retained imports as a proportion of net national income was now 33%. One of the unique features of this period of rapid change and growth was that conditions enabled Britain to consolidate her initial lead and take the fullest advantage of technological advancements, improvements in transport and communications, and the liberalization of trade, unhampered by the threat of foreign competition.

In contrast, the latter phase is best remembered, first, for the emergence and growth of the United States and Germany as major competitive powers, both of whom, now politically unified and protected by high tariff walls (and often aided by State subsidies), were able to challenge Britain's early monopoly; and secondly, for the development of a new technology which was not only less suited to the structure of the United Kingdom's resources than that which it replaced, but which strongly favoured the economy of her main competitors. In consequence the rate of British industrial growth after 1880 fell to less than 2% per annum whereas that of Germany rose to 3·9% and that of the U.S. to 4·8%. During these years the United Kingdom ceased to be the workshop of the world. By 1900 she had been replaced by the U.S. as the largest supplier of coal and metal products and by Germany as the chief producer of industrial chemicals; between the years 1876 and 1913 her share of world trade in manufactured goods fell from 38 to 27%; and over the period as a whole the rate of increase in her manufacturing exports was only one-half that of the previous half-century.

Nevertheless, with a rapidly expanding home market, the U.K. labour force and absolute level of output increased steadily. At the outbreak of the First World War British shipyards still supplied 61% of the world's total tonnage of shipping. Coal output had doubled between 1880 and 1913 and exports quadrupled, and over the same period the production of pig-iron and steel rose from 10 million tons to 18 million tons. In the cotton industry the number of spindles and looms in use increased by 45% between 1885 and 1914, while the yardage of piece goods exported in the quinquennium 1909–13 was nearly half as much again as it had been in 1880–4. The demand for engineering products both at home and overseas also expanded rapidly after the turn of the century.

Yet, if the past could be looked upon with pride and the present seemed prosperous enough, the future gave little room for complacency. For, when viewed retrospectively, there is little doubt that the industrial structure of the United Kingdom in 1914 was seriously maladjusted in relation to world economic trends; the seeds of the depression which was to follow a decade later had already been firmly sown. On the one hand, the products in which her industries had excelled in the past were now being increasingly supplied by her former customers; on the other, her technological ability in the newer and expanding trades was, in general, inferior to that of her main industrial competitors—Germany and the United States. Her economy was over-specialized both as regards her manufacturing output and the markets it served. In 1907, for example, when the first comprehensive Census of Production was taken, the staple trades of coal-mining, iron and steel, and textiles accounted for no less than 46% of the total 'value added by manufacture' of British industry, gave employment to nearly a quarter of the gainfully occupied population and supplied 70% of all British exports. The newer industries of motor vehicles, electrical goods, chemicals, artificial silk and certain types of machinery were responsible for only 6·5% of the net output, 5·2% of the labour force and less than 2·0% of the manufacturing exports. Unfortunately, comparative figures for Germany and the U.S. do not exist, but such information as is available strongly suggests that their economies were more successful in adapting themselves to the demands of the new technology. In 1912, for example, the motor-car industry in the U.K. produced some 25,000 vehicles, as compared with an American output of 485,000; her share of the world's manufacture of all kinds of electrical products was 13·0%, whereas that of Germany was 31·9% and that of the U.S. 28·9%. Germany was also then the leading supplier of rayon goods and in 1914 produced 3,500 tons of a world output of 11,000 tons.

To some extent, of course, the above trends were inevitable, as Britain could not have expected permanently to maintain her absolute industrial supremacy of the previous century. At the same time, the inability of this country effectively to cushion the depression of the 1920's reflected not only the inadequacy of the newer industries to fill the gap left by the disrupted markets for the basic products, but also the neglected state of the staple trades, as shown in their manufacturing techniques and capital equipment. In 1918, for example, it was pointed out that the efficiency of the British iron and steel industry was 'very far behind that of its competitors in the U.S. and Germany'.[1] Britain had invented basic steel but had neglected to recognize its commercial possibilities; she had been the first to produce solid-drawn weldless steel tubes but had let the initiative pass to Germany; as early as 1879 she was experimenting in electrical metallurgy but by 1900 the lead was in American hands. Again, though still the foremost supplier of heavy chemicals, the United Kingdom lagged seriously behind in the rapidly developing field of synthetic organic chemicals: in 1913, for example, she was forced to import no less than nine-tenths of her annual consumption of synthetic dyes and dyestuffs from the Continent. Likewise, by virtue of her superior production techniques, the U.S. had outstripped the U.K. as the world's major manufacturer of glass products. There appeared to be less grounds

[1] *Iron and Steel Trades.* Departmental Committee. Report; 1918, Cd 9071, xiii.

for criticism in the textile, shipbuilding and engineering industries. A report on conditions in the textile trades, published in 1918,[1] commented that 'the machinery and plant are on the whole highly efficient'. In the engineering industry, though, it must be recalled that U.S. capital and expertise played a major part in pioneering a number of new products and manufacturing techniques, and was primarily responsible for the early growth of the sewing, printing and typesetting, match-making, office and boot and shoe machinery trades in Britain.

A variety of causes have been suggested to explain the United Kingdom's comparative decline as an industrial power. Of these some were undoubtedly the product of extraneous forces, others a reflection of internal economic weaknesses and inflexibilities. Thus, although many of the major innovations of the late nineteenth century originated from this country, economic and social conditions often favoured their more speedy commercial exploitation elsewhere. For example, much of the credit for the pioneering steps in motor engineering and the development of the internal combustion engine is due to the U.K. and Continental Europe, but because of the ideal circumstances then facing the American industry—such as a large standardized market, an abundance of motor fuel, the inadequacy of competitive transport, a high income per head and the presence of Henry Ford, a master in the field of industrial organization—the United States was the first country to shepherd the motor-car industry successfully from its experimental stage into large-scale production. Likewise, many of the early discoveries of the electrical manufacturing industry were of British genesis, but the industrial structure then prevailing was inherently less adaptable to their commercialization than was that of other countries. Whereas, for example, in the United States and Germany there was a preference for centralized administrative units and concentrated production, any movement in this direction in the United Kingdom was condemned as being contrary to the principles of *laissez-faire* and unrestricted competition. Finally, in contrast to the U.S., where the economy was geared to meet the needs of the new technology and innovations were highly rewarded, U.K. business men were hampered by tradition while restrictive legislation, e.g. in respect of the electrical and motor-car industries,

[1] *Textile Trades.* Departmental Committee. Report; 1918, Cd 9070, xiii.

and indifferent and expensive patent procedure often completely
paralysed the exploitation of new inventions and techniques.[1]

At the same time, it must be remembered that the industrial
prosperity of the British economy was then hardly in question.
Why launch out on the uncertainty associated with new products,
sources of power, manufacturing methods etc. when the old ones
were serving the country so well? Unlike his American counterpart,
the British industrialist, faced with a smaller and less standardized
market and an abundance of cheap coal and labour, had not the
same incentive either to use highly mechanized production techniques or to substitute electrical power for steam power. Again,
almost without exception the newer industrial nations practised a
policy of economic nationalism from the start and gave strong
tariff protection to their infant industries, and in some cases financial
aid as well. Britain, on the other hand, at this time found her overseas investment opportunities more attractive than the prospects at
home: between 1870 and 1913, 40% of all the United Kingdom's
investments were directed to the Dominions, South America and
the United States, principally at the expense of domestic capital
formation.

In 1914, then, the United Kingdom, though still a major industrial power, was structurally maladjusted in relation to the
world economic trends then emerging. Even in the basic industries
progress towards the adoption of the new technology was haphazard
and slow, though it was now becoming all too obvious that, unless
the U.K. industrialist was prepared to modernize his methods and
re-equip his plant, his goods were in danger of being priced out of
the export market, either by the cheaper mass-produced substitutes
of the U.S. or by the better quality and technically superior
products of Germany. But the memory of the past and the prosperity
of the present were sufficient to stifle any forebodings about the
future. The United Kingdom was still the world's financial centre
and chief supplier of invisible exports, and, with the balance of
payments position looking as healthy as it had done for some years
past, there was little immediate sign of the misfortune which was to
befall British industry within the very near future.

[1] For further particulars see *Electrical Trades*. Departmental
Committee. Report; 1918, Cd 9072, xiii.

1919-30 : the decline in industrial output

A position of industrial expansion and rising exports gave place to one of chronic depression and heavy unemployment within less than a decade. After the war there was a short restocking and speculative boom which lasted for eighteen months. Shipbuilding capacity, for example, was greatly enlarged to replace the shipping lost during the war and by March 1921 the total tonnage under construction was 40% above that immediately before 1914. In the same way the iron and steel industry, which had been profoundly stimulated by the demand for munitions during the war years, was supplying 33% more steel in 1920 than in 1913. Speculation was particularly rife in the Lancashire cotton industry, where some 238 mills comprising 42% of the total spinning capacity changed hands between 1919 and 1920. But prosperity was short-lived. From 1921 onwards the industrial position steadily deteriorated and, though by 1924 the absolute decline in output had been halted, recovery over the next five years was only in the order of 12%—less than one-half the rate of growth experienced by Germany, France or the U.S. Indeed, not only was Britain replaced by the United States as the world's chief exporter of manufactured goods in these years, she was selling less, compared with before the war, than any other European country save Russia. In spite of a favourable movement in the terms of trade and an increase in productivity of 35% between 1913 and 1929, the *total* volume of manufacturing output rose by only 12%. Since the size of the working population was also growing during these years, this was accompanied by an increase in unemployment, the total volume of which had reached 1·5 million or 12·2% of the working population by 1929. Of this figure, two-fifths was concentrated within the staple trades of coal-mining, iron and steel, shipbuilding and textiles which had been the most seriously affected of all by the reduction in overseas demand.

The fortunes of the cotton industry, for example, in spite of a considerable increase in domestic consumption, suffered a dramatic and almost continuous decline during the inter-war period. In 1907, 88·9% of its total output of £126 million was exported and over one-half this amount went to Far Eastern markets. However, because of the growing self-sufficiency of India as a cotton producer and the increasing competition from the Japanese industry, Britain's exports to this area fell by 38% between 1913 and 1925. India alone, who at one time bought from Britain nearly three times the yardage of cotton piece goods she produced herself, slashed her imports from this country by 57%, while China, who had imported 55% of her cotton goods from the United Kingdom in 1913 and only 18% from Japan, reversed this relationship and in 1926 purchased only 30% of her supplies from Lancashire and 58% from Japan. In all, total production of British cotton piece goods fell from 8·0 million square yards in 1912 to 3·3 million square yards in 1930, while the U.K.'s share in world cotton exports dwindled from 68% to 44%. Similarly, the increased tariffs levied on woollen imports by Australia and the Americas together with the growing self-sufficiency of Far Eastern markets reduced the exports of the industry by one-third between 1924 and 1929.

In the iron and steel industry, the growth of domestic production (usually under tariff protection) in former Continental and Asiatic markets was perhaps the main factor responsible for a 15% fall in U.K. exports during the 1920's, though excess capacity[1] and obsolescent plant, the changing emphasis of demand away from wrought-iron and acid steel, and financial weaknesses must also be held partly responsible. Between 1913 and 1929, while the output of British iron and steel products fell by 24%, Continental capacity rose by 16% and that of the U.S. by 30%. By this time both France and Germany had completely reconstructed their destroyed works on the most modern lines and Belgium had rationalized and integrated her industrial structure. German recovery was also aided by a depreciating currency and a Government subsidy, while India in an effort to build up her own industry raised her tariffs on imported iron and steel products from 1% in 1913 to up to 30% in 1924.

The fall in coal exports from 94 million tons in 1913 to 77 million tons in 1929 was due to four main reasons: first, the fact that productivity in coal-mining was increasing much more rapidly in other parts of the world than in the United Kingdom; secondly, the opening up of a number of new mines in the Netherlands, Spain and the Far East who had previously relied on the

[1] In 1925 the U.K. was using only 44·5% of pig-iron capacity and 58% of her steel-making capacity. Between 1923 and 1927 some 45 blast furnaces closed down. See C. L. Mowat, *Britain Between the Wars, 1918–1950*, Methuen, 1955.

U.K. for their coal supplies; thirdly, the greater economy of fuel utilization; and fourthly, the growing substitution of competitive fuels for coal. Thus, while the world consumption of coal remained almost constant between 1913 and 1924, that of petroleum trebled, the output of lignite nearly doubled and new sources of hydro-electric power were developed in the U.S., Scandinavia, Italy, Germany and France.

One important explanation for the growth in oil consumption was the development of the oil-fired ship. In 1914 96·6% of the world's mercantile tonnage was coal-fired; by 1932 the proportion had fallen to 60% and by 1939 to 54%. The considerable fluctuations in the fortunes of the British shipbuilding industry after the war were, however, not so much a result of the more rapid adoption of the oil motor ship by her competitors as of the comparative stagnation of world trade and the protection and subsidies given by foreign governments to their shipyards. The importance of this latter consideration is illustrated by the fact that, whereas the output from British shipyards in 1929 was only 79% of its pre-war level, that of foreign shipbuilding had risen by 19%. On the other hand, British shipping still retained much of its pre-war pre-eminence. In 1929, for example, it accounted for 47% of the entire seaborne trade of the world.

Even more striking was the failure of the U.K. to grasp the opportunities offered by the growing world trade in the newer industrial commodities at this time. The results of an enquiry published by the German economist Schlote in 1938[1] showed that of the total manufacturing exports of the U.K., U.S.A. and Germany in 1929, those in which world trade had expanded the most rapidly (viz. by more than 150%) since 1913 accounted for 28·6% of U.S. exports, but only 4·5% of German exports and 4·3% of British exports. On the other hand, those manufactures which had expanded the least rapidly (viz. by less than 75%) in international markets accounted for 17·1% of U.S. exports and 27·3% of German exports, but for no less than 42·1% of British exports. Such figures clearly illustrate the declining role of the U.K. as a leading exporter of manufactured goods and the difficulties she was experiencing in

[1] Quoted by W. A. Lewis, *Economic Survey*, p. 78. For a different interpretation of the role of the new industries in the inter-war years see H. W. Richardson, 'The New Industries between the Wars', *Oxford Economic Papers*, Vol. 13, no. 3, October 1961.

her attempts to adjust her economy to the changes in world taste. By and large, the internal economic climate of the 1920's was neither favourable to a speedy commercialization of new ideas nor conducive to the expansion of new industries, and in a number of cases the innovations of British scientists were exploited to greater effect by other countries, for example, the carbon-tetrachloride fire-extinguisher and the transfer-machining of motor-cars.

At the same time, it would be wrong to imply that there were no important technological advances in British industry during this period. Both the war and its aftermath provided a considerable impetus to innovatory development, not only in a variety of specialized spheres, e.g. wireless and telecommunications, ship propulsion, automatic welding and hull design, the new stainless steels and synthetic chemicals,[1] but more generally in the beginnings of organized co-operative research and the growing intervention of the State in industrial affairs. The imposition of the McKenna import duties in 1915, for example, was largely responsible for the tenfold increase in the numbers employed in the U.K. motor vehicles industry between 1913 and 1929 and the expansion in the output of cars and commercial vehicles from 34,000 to 238,000. During this same period the volume of imported motor vehicles and parts as a proportion of home production fell from 80 to 40%. Yet, even so, the reluctance of most vehicle producers to limit their range of bodies and engines, the lack of uniformity in the design of components and the inability of the machine tool industry to supply the necessary tools and equipment precluded any widespread adoption of flow production techniques, and so hindered Britain in her bid to gain a substantial share of the expanding export market for cars. In addition, the existing system of vehicles' taxation, by favouring the production of the small high-speed engine, restricted the export opportunities of U.K. manufacturers, because it was the high-powered large-bore engine which foreign countries were mostly demanding. Thus, it was not surprising that in 1929 U.S. motor vehicle exports were ten times those of Britain and equal to twice her entire domestic output.

Notable increases in the production of electrical equipment were also recorded during these years but again they were less

[1] For further details see R. Sayers, 'The Springs of Technical Progress', *Economic Journal*, June 1950.

pronounced than in the U.S. and Germany. For example, in 1924, only 49·7% of the total power consumed by all branches of British industry was electrically generated as compared with 73% in the United States and 67% in Germany a year later. There were three main reasons why the adoption of electrical power was less wide-spread in Britain: first, the relative cheapness of conventional coal-produced steam power in this country; secondly, the reluctance of the staple trades to experiment with new sources of energy, or their lack of capital to do so; and thirdly, the structure of the electricity supply system itself which, by its multiplicity of small generating plants each employing their own frequencies and supplying different voltages, was becoming increasingly inadequate to meet the needs demanded of it. Not until the Central Electricity Board was created in 1926 and the National Grid System put into operation was this problem in any way solved. Meanwhile the total value of all electrical products rose from £14 million in 1907 to £69 million in 1924 and £88 million in 1930: the numbers employed increased from 85,000 in 1911 to 165,000 in 1925.

Within the confines of the electrical equipment industry itself, many new and self-contained trades were fast evolving, of which perhaps the most important was that concerned with the production of radio and telecommunications equipment. National broad-casting first began in London on 14 November 1922. Although the origins of wireless telegraphy date back to the turn of the century, it was the First World War which provided the major impetus to develop the wireless transmission valve. By 1930 the number of wireless receiver licences had reached the 3 million mark and the annual turnover of the radio industry had risen to nearly £30 million. Innovations were hardly less spectacular in the electric lamp, lamp apparatus and generating equipment trades; yet in spite of these, and the improved structure of the electrical industry since its unification during the First World War, the rate of growth was less impressive than that in other countries. Germany, for example, employed 250,000 people in the production of electrical equipment in 1925 and could boast of an export market twice the size of that of the British, while the U.S. industry was five times as large and considerably more advanced from the technological viewpoint. As for her engineering exports in general, although these expanded in volume by 35% between 1913 and 1930, Britain's share in world trade dropped from 30·4% to 25·6% as that of the U.S. rose from 25·9% to 37·6%. Again, this was chiefly because those products in which the United Kingdom had specialized in the past, e.g. boiler and boiler-house plant, prime movers and textile machinery, were faced with static or slowly rising markets, while those now developing in the United States, e.g. agricultural machinery and machine tools, were increasingly demanded.

Advances in the chemical and artificial textile industries during this period were largely conditioned by the imposition of protective tariffs on the one hand and the rationalization of the industry's production structure on the other. The Dyestuffs (Import Regulation) Act (1920) and the Safeguarding of Industries Act (1921) imposed import duties varying from 10 to 25% on dyestuffs, synthetic organic chemicals (and their intermediaries) and fine glass, while as a result of the rayon custom and excise duties of 1925 the proportion of imported to home-produced rayon fell from 40% in 1924 to 2½% in 1931. At the same time, between 1920 and 1938, the capital employed in the chemical industry was trebled, the number of research chemists and the amount spent on research quadrupled and the total weight of fine chemicals produced increased almost elevenfold. Employment rose from 128,000 in 1907 to 178,000 in 1930 and 194,000 in 1935. By 1929 Britain was producing an output of rayon filament yarn over seven times greater than that of 1913, but world output was increasing even faster and in this particular field she was never able to win for herself a reputation comparable to the one she had once enjoyed in cotton and wool textiles. Other major technical advances in chemistry during the 1920's included the production of acetate rayon dyestuffs and synthetic alcohol, shortly to be followed by the innovation of synthetic resin adhesives, polythene and polymethyl methacrylate, a number of specialized fertilizers and the conversion of coals and tars into hydrocarbon oils.

The causes underlying Britain's industrial difficulties during this period were many and varied. Outside her control were the shifts in world consumption away from the exports in which she had traditionally specialized, the slowing down of population growth, the widespread growth in economic nationalism, fluctuating exchange rates, the rapid industrialization of the Far East and the increasing importance of both the U.S. and Germany as competitive powers. But much of the responsibility, if not for the occurrence of the depression, then for its severity and lengthy duration, must be placed on internal economic circumstances. Of these, the most important were perhaps the rigidity of the U.K. industrial structure and its inability to absorb unemployment in the export industries by expanding home consumption, the backward outlook and intensive individualism amongst British employers, the lack of aggressiveness in foreign-sales policies, a prolonged period of labour disputes, the hesitations and inconsistencies of national economic policy, the over-valuation of the pound consequent upon return to the gold standard in 1925[1] at too high an exchange parity, the shortage of investment capital and the excessive burden of taxation. Indeed, the situation was only rescued from disaster by the favourable movement of the terms of trade and the continued high earnings derived from invisible exports. Undoubtedly Britain's failure to adjust her economy speedily to the changes demanded of it was due to widespread belief that the decrease in exports was essentially temporary and cyclical in origin, whereas in fact it reflected a long-term shift in tastes. Industrial reorganization and the adoption of more efficient production techniques were thus retarded, while at the same time there was only a limited movement of resources from the declining staple trades to the newer industries, since these were mainly located in different parts of the country and required different types of skill.

Furthermore, the size-structure of the basic trades was itself unfavourable for meeting the challenge of overseas competition. One of the consequences of recent technological developments had been to increase the advantages of large-scale production and the highly capitalized firm. But in Britain most production units were small and parochial. They neither possessed the necessary capital to undertake research or engage in any large-scale investment programmes, nor were willing to co-ordinate their activities or standardize their product range. The Liberal Industrial Enquiry[2]

[1] Announced by Winston Churchill in his budget speech of 1925. In support of this measure the Government argued that the discrepancy between the level of U.S. and U.K. prices was only $2\frac{1}{2}\%$ in favour of the former: in fact, as it turned out, the difference was nearer 10%, and there followed a period of high interest rates, deflation and unemployment.

[2] *Britain's Industrial Future*, being the Report of the Liberal Industrial Enquiry, London, 1928.

of 1928 in referring to the 'unintegrated mass of independent atoms' which then comprised most of British industry argued that rationalization was the first prerequisite to recovery and that the competitive structure which now existed, however appropriate it might have been in an earlier era, was both wasteful and inexpedient.

Opinion was, in fact, gradually shifting to a new ideal of 'controlled' competition—already being practised with some success in the newer industries, e.g. rayon, aluminium, dyestuffs, motor vehicles, electricity supply, and in general supported by the Government. The need for united and consolidatory action was being increasingly expressed, yet as often as not jealousy and vested interests stood in the way of amalgamations while excess capacity, over-capitalization and heavy fixed charges made it difficult for the basic industries to set aside sufficient reserves to cover normal depreciation commitments let alone to finance renovations and improvements. Not only was the credit policy of the United Kingdom restrictive rather than expansionary at this time, but British banks, unlike their Continental or American counterparts, were unprepared to risk lending capital to industrial undertakings on a long-term basis.

What of the structure of individual industries? In 1926 it was reported by the Royal Commission on the Coal Industry that there were 1,400 collieries with 2,500 mines and that their average output was far below that of their more efficient Continental competitors. In the cotton industry there were more than 1,900 separate firms in the spinning and weaving sections, each highly specialized and individualistic in character and with a complete absence of any centralized control. Although in the iron and steel industry concentration had gone further, and vertical integration was more pronounced, the size of the typical U.K. plant or firm was still much less than that on the Continent and in America. Even on the eve of the Second World War the average annual output of a British blast furnace was only 40% of that of the American and two-thirds of that of the German. The lack of structural coherence within these and other basic industries meant that they were at a serious economic disadvantage as against the highly organized industries of their overseas rivals. Only by an elimination of surplus capacity, a revision of the financial structure and the introduction of technical improvements could Britain hope to recover something of her pre-war industrial strength.[1]

1930–9: a period of adjustment and slow recovery

Before the U.K. had time to emerge from her own particular industrial difficulties of the 1920's, she became involved in the international economic crisis of 1929–33. Originating primarily from the collapse of the U.S. economy, and spreading quickly overseas by credit contraction and withdrawals, falling prices and a curtailment of foreign trade, the impact of the slump was felt in varying degrees by all industrial countries. The U.K., however, was less severely affected than others, for example the U.S. and Germany, if only because her economy had made the least progress during the previous decade. But having previously lost export markets because of the changing *direction* of world demand, the U.K. now suffered from a fall in the *level* of world demand, principally because of reduced incomes of primary producers and the consequent contraction of trade in manufactured products.

Between 1929 and 1931 the volume of U.K. exports fell by 45% and that of industrial output as a whole by 16%. Unemployment had reached 19·9% of the insured population by 1930, with the proportion in the staple industries nearly double this amount. Subsequently, the position slowly improved as a result of the depreciation of sterling, the return of this country to protection, a lowering of interest rates, the provision of Government financial support for the staple trades and a more determined and concentrated attempt by British industry to rationalize its structure and raise its efficiency. By such means as these, the economic policy of the past, based on the gold standard, free competition and private enterprise, gave way to a managed currency and exchange control, an encouragement of monopolistic arrangements and the intervention of the State over a wide field of industrial enterprise.

Recovery started in 1933. In the previous year the numbers of unemployed had reached 3 million or 23% of the insured population, but thereafter there was a steady upward trend in industrial activity. A major cause of the recovery was the increase

[1] For further details see Ch. II, p. 43 et seq.

in housing investment and the building boom which developed later.[1] One authority attributes one-third of the increased employment in Britain at this time directly to this factor. Similarly, the general recovery of world trade, the expansion of the newer industries and that of the service industries (the labour force in which increased by 33% between 1929 and 1937), the reduction in interest rates, and the demands of the rearmament programme from 1935 onwards were important contributory factors. More doubt has been expressed as to how far the growth of restrictionist schemes contributed towards recovery, though it is generally agreed that in the iron and steel and tramp shipping industries rationalization which was backed by conditional State guarantees considerably improved efficiency. But while the Ottawa agreements and Imperial Preference Tariff of 1932 undoubtedly aided the development of certain newer (or infant) industries either directly, or indirectly by inducing American and other foreign firms to set up manufacturing units in this country, they also had their detrimental effects. The protection thereby afforded to the less efficient and backward industries served only to delay rather than to stimulate their recovery and reorganization.

During the 1930's the total British labour force rose by 17% and that within manufacturing industry by 8%. Industrial output increased by 23% between 1929 and 1937 but the volume of exports fell by a further 13%.[2] Thus whereas in 1929 exports were equal in value to 32% of net national income, by 1937 the corresponding figure was only 21%. If a loss of overseas markets had been the origin of Britain's difficulties, her recovery was principally due to a revival of domestic investment. Despite this, however, the situation of most of the staple industries failed to improve: only the steel industry had expanded.[3] As a whole the numbers employed in the basic trades, i.e. coal-mining, iron and steel, shipbuilding and textiles, fell from 2,264,000 in 1929 to 1,824,000 in 1939 and their

[1] The rate of house-building in the 1930's was more than double that of the previous decade. Reduced building costs, lower interest rates and easier mortgage facilities would appear to be the main reasons behind this increase in activity.

[2] The latter figure merely reflects the failure of exports to recover from the substantial fall of 35·5% between 1929 and 1932. In the subsequent 5 years however the volume of exports rose by nearly 27%.

[3] See C. L. Mowat, op. cit., pp. 444–5.

share of the total manufacturing labour force from 34·6 to 27·2%. Almost exactly counterbalancing this trend was an expansion of 450,000 in the labour force of the newer industries of motor vehicles, electrical engineering, scientific and industrial instruments, constructional engineering, heating and ventilating appliances, whose share of the manufacturing labour force rose from 8·6 to 15·1%. As a result of the growth of the working population, a rising real income, changing social habits, a cheap money policy and a large-scale slum-clearance programme, a third group of industries, e.g. food and drink, building, furniture and household appliance, clothing, chemical and the distributive trades, also recorded large increases in their labour force[1] in these years.

Once again, falling export markets were mainly responsible for the difficulties of the basic trades throughout the 1930's. Not only did the U.K.'s share of the world's output of shipping decline from an average of 51% in the years 1926–9 to 34% in 1937–8, but the total output forthcoming from British yards fell by 39% in spite of a doubling in the volume of foreign shipbuilding. The slump was particularly severe in the early years of the decade when the average annual output was only 45% of that of ten years previously and unemployment as high as 60% of the insured workers. Similarly, in the textile industry, exports of woollen goods slumped from 154 million yards in 1929 to 123 million yards in 1937, while with Japan expanding her overseas outlets at the expense of Lancashire, exports of U.K. cotton piece goods dwindled from 3,672 million yards to 1,921 million yards over the same period. Only partially did the substantial rise in domestic consumption help to compensate for these lost markets, and the numbers employed in the spinning and weaving sections fell from 356,000 in 1930 to 209,000 in 1938. Again, faced with a collapse of overseas investment outlets, iron and steel exports in 1937 were only 60% of those of 1929, though in this case the impetus of the building boom, the expansion of the motor-car industry and rearmament induced a remarkable recovery and total production was one-third greater at the end of the period than at the beginning. Finally, whereas economies in fuel consumption and the extension of the use of

[1] E.g. between 1929 and 1937 the numbers employed in transport and distribution rose by 18%, in the professions by 33% and in Government service by 22%.

electric power slightly reduced the internal demand for coal, the tonnage exported fell from 76·9 million in 1929 to 46·3 million in 1938. It is worth observing that all these trends occurred despite the various efforts to raise productivity and rationalize the structure of these industries. For example, in 1935, output per manshift in U.K. coal-mines was still only 60% of that of the average Continental mine.

Yet in other directions the situation was more encouraging. In 1937 the output of motor vehicles from U.K. factories was twice that of 1929; rayon production expanded from 52 million lb. in 1929 to 115 million lb. in 1937; the production of electricity more than doubled, employment in the electrical equipment industry increased by 150% and the British share of electrical exports rose from 26·3% in 1929 to 28·6% in 1937. With the expansion of the building industry, the non-ferrous metal trades also developed rapidly, e.g. the output of aluminium in 1938 was four times that of 1924, and a number of new industries, e.g. supplying canned foodstuffs, refrigerators and industrial instruments, sprang into being. The British machine tool industry, shielded by a protective tariff of 20% *ad valorem* and stimulated by the growth of the motor-car industry, the rearmament programme and large contracts placed by the U.S.S.R., was revived and production increased by 75% in the 1930's. Against such progress, however, development in the aircraft industry was exceedingly slow. In 1918 the U.K. was the largest supplier of aircraft and airframes in the world, but after the war the initiative quickly passed to Germany, partly because of the greater financial support given by the German Government and partly because the excessive variety of aircraft and components produced by the U.K. industry tended to keep up production costs. In 1936 the U.K. industry only employed 36,000 people and produced a gross output of £10 million.

Throughout the 1930's the terms of trade continued to move in Britain's favour thus enabling her real income to increase despite the continued fall in exports. At the start of the Second World War Britain was gradually adapting her industrial structure and regaining her economic strength. While the inter-war years, with unemployment averaging 12% of the insured labour force, could hardly be called prosperous, it would be unwise to underestimate the importance of the many technological advances of the period, the extent to which the shape and direction of the economy changed, the new attitude towards the role of the State in industrial affairs and the repercussions consequent on the abandonment of the gold standard and substitution of exchange management for free trade. Any reasoning which suggests that the U.K. economy stagnated in this period is clearly only valid when viewed in the light of earlier and, more particularly, subsequent developments or when related to industrial growth in the U.S. during these years, which was 60% above that of this country.

1939–60: the new technological revolution

In no period within our survey have circumstances been so conducive to industrial change and technological progress as during the past two decades. Industries dependent upon scientific advances for their prosperity have increased in importance, whereas those based on traditional techniques have declined. Moreover, the whole balance of industrial power has shifted and, in consequence, the inter-relationships between individual trades have been revolutionized. Of the developments none has had more far-reaching significance than the emergence of the oil refining and nuclear energy industries in which over £1,000 million was invested between 1945 and 1960. Only second in importance to the new power supplies have been the changes wrought by the advent of many new industrial raw materials, the rapid innovatory strides of the aircraft, electronics and chemical industries and the tremendous expansion of the motor-car industry. It is not surprising that the amount spent on research and development over the period has increased out of all recognition.

Bare statistics hardly tell the full story, since many of the basic industries have also prospered for the greater part of the post-war period and their share of the total output and labour force is today not much less than it was in 1938. Some 193 million tons of coal were mined in 1960, compared with 227 million tons in 1938. Steel output has risen by 133% over the same period to its present figure of over 24 million tons. In both industries the productivity of the labour force has risen substantially. The shipbuilding industry has also been prosperous for most of the post-war period with the tonnage of shipping launched in the years 1954–8 being one-third more than in the corresponding period before 1939. Only the older textile industries have recorded a continuous decline. Thus, at the end of 1960 fewer than 200,000 people were employed in the cotton industry compared with 414,000 before the war, while cotton exports, which in 1913 accounted for one-quarter of all Britain's exports, fell to under 2% in 1960.[1]

The reasons for these developments have been manifold. Quite apart from any question of technological innovation, the reconstruction boom following the Second World War, the rising cost and scarcity of labour and the redistribution of consumer incomes would have been sufficient to maintain a high level of demand for the products of the basic industries for at least the greater part of the post-war period. But undoubtedly, and especially in recent years, technological advance in the newer capital-using industries has been the chief cause of the large increases in the capacity of the basic industries. Thus, the prosperity of British shipyards for most of the period since 1945 has been largely due to the expansion of the petroleum refining industry both in this country and overseas. Between 1952 and 1960 nearly one-half of the gross merchant tonnage launched in Britain took the form of oil tankers. Similarly, the huge constructional programmes for petroleum refineries, atomic power stations, chemical and electricity generating plant and the rapid growth of all branches of the metal industries have meant a continual pressure on the iron and steel industry to increase its output. Finally, the demand for more power has itself not only ensured (until recently) the prosperity of the coal industry but has induced developments in other fields as well.

Overall, the volume of industrial production in the United Kingdom rose by 78% between 1938 and 1960. In marked contrast to the situation before the war, the rate of increase in exports has been even more pronounced,[2] and the United Kingdom is now not only sending abroad as large a proportion of her manufacturing output as at any time in the present century, but is also more heavily dependent on imports of raw materials to supply her manufacturing

[1] Indeed in 1958, the U.K. recorded the first adverse balance of overseas trade in cotton cloth since the rise of the cotton mill industry in this country. See W. G. Pilkington, 'Cotton under Scrutiny', *District Bank Review*, Dec., 1959.

[2] Taking 1938 = 100, the volume of manufacturing exports in 1961 was 222.

industries. These developments are a reflection partly of the overall movement since before the war of the terms of trade against the industrial countries,[1] partly of technological developments within industry and partly of the rising level of international trade in both manufactured and primary products. When considering both the rapid expansion of industrial products in world trade and the intensive competition of the U.S., Germany and Japan, the importance to the U.K. of maintaining an adequate rate of technological advancement is greater than it has ever been. Yet, though her share of the world's manufacturing exports has continued to decline— from 23·8% in 1938 to 15·9% in 1961—the place of the newer industrial exports is much more favourable than before the war; in 1960, for example, the motor-car industry accounted for one-sixth of all U.K. manufacturing exports and could claim to occupy a position in the U.K. economy not far short of that of the cotton textiles industry before the First World War. In 1938 Britain's exports of newer industrial products, e.g. aircraft, refined petroleum, synthetic fibres etc., were equivalent to one-thirtieth of those of the U.S.; by 1948 this country's share had risen to one-third and by 1959 to nearly three-fifths.

Once again, there is no one single explanation for the rapid technological innovation which has taken place since 1939 and for the many new products, manufacturing processes and materials which have emerged. Perhaps the greatest impetus was provided by the Second World War itself and the subsequent defence programme, which were both direct causes of such developments in atomic power, aircraft and electronics as are now being increasingly put to peaceful uses. Without the Government-sponsored research and defence contracts in these fields, not only might the horizons now opening up have been slower to appear, but it is more than likely that those countries which possess that type of economy best able to bear the heavy initial overhead costs would have forged ahead. For instance, nearly three-fifths of the U.K.'s research expenditure in 1958 was allocated to these three industries of which the State was responsible for about three-quarters. Again, partly as a result of the war, the cost and demand structure of the economy has

[1] Again, taking 1938=100, the U.K. terms of trade in 1951 were 139. Although there has been a marked improvement since that date, the corresponding figure for 1960 was 106.

B

undergone a marked change. Full employment and rising labour costs, a shortage of most kinds of materials, redistribution of income, the greater prominence of the State in economic affairs and a persistent shortage of foreign exchange (particularly $) have meant a shift in the values placed upon certain resources and their allocation. Such a situation has led both to the creation of new British industries for the manufacturing of all kinds of labour-saving and productivity-raising machinery, e.g. mechanical hand-ling equipment, agricultural implements, office machinery, earth-moving equipment etc., and to the increased demand of the domestic consumer for products which at one time were chiefly the province of the higher income groups. For example, more than twice as many new motor-cars were bought in 1960 as in 1938, over 5 times the number of electric washing machines and 13 times the number of refrigerators. At the same time, the need for new sources of energy, coupled with the balance of payments situation and continual dis-turbances in the Middle East, provided the stimulus for the develop-ment of the petroleum refining industry in this country, whereas the search for new materials and spontaneous innovations in the chemi-cal and metallurgical industries has made possible a whole new complex of products and materials, ranging from the newer syn-thetic fibres and plastics on the one hand to the new drugs and medicinal preparations on the other. As a result of these trends, the engineering and motor vehicle industries' share of the total manufacturing labour force has increased from 21·0% in 1935 to 33·1% in 1957 and that of the chemical industry from 3·3% to 4·7%.

An important feature of the above developments, which will be discussed further in the following chapter, is that they have led to a closer interdependence both between the different branches of industry and between science and technology. This is most clearly seen in the emergence of new 'hybrid' industries, i.e. those of dual parentage, e.g. petro-chemicals, electronic engineering, chemical metallurgy etc.; but perhaps of equal significance is the extent to which the successful commercialization of a new process or product now depends upon the interchange of knowledge between pre-viously independent industries. Automation is a good example: the machine tool, industrial instruments and electronic industries are each involved in production of automatic machinery. At one time the textile industry had virtually no connections with the chemical industry; nowadays with man-made fibres accounting for one-third of all textile production the two industries are very much inter-related. Similarly, the building of a modern chemical plant or petroleum refinery is so complex an operation that only a specialist in the relevant design techniques can undertake it effectively. Without the close co-operation between the radio engineer and the plastics chemist the electronics industry as we know it today would be an impossibility. The efficiency of a great variety of trades, especially those highly mechanized, is dependent on adequate measuring and control techniques supplied by the instruments industry, which itself relies upon the latest discoveries in electronics to perfect its products. The development of new methods of communication and the extension of mechanized office work is also partially determined by innovations in the electronics industry, while another branch of the electrical equipment industry is supplying new products to the domestic consumer, notably television sets, washing machines and steam irons which have been purchased out of the rising incomes enjoyed by the greater part of the population.

In many instances the United Kingdom has been aided in its post-war developments by the technology of other countries. Hence, through the establishment of an increasing number of U.S.-financed firms in this country and the conclusion of many thousands of licensing agreements between U.S. and British firms, industrial development has been advanced more speedily and probably more efficiently than it would otherwise have been. Over the period as a whole, due partly to advances in technology, partly to more intensive mechanization caused by rising labour costs[1] and partly to the high level of demand for defence goods, the ratio of producer to consumer goods manufactured has risen from 7 : 5 in 1935 to 9 : 5 in 1960 and the proportion of capital goods exported (including motor-cars) from 2% to 25%. The high level of demand for defence goods has been partly responsible for this former trend, as more than 1 million people are still engaged on defence contracts for the Government.

[1] For example, the development of synthetic materials has often meant an increase in capital intensity and a decrease in the use of land and labour.

TABLE 1

DISTRIBUTION OF THE EMPLOYED POPULATION. MAIN INDUSTRIAL GROUPS 1907–57[1] UNITED KINGDOM

Trade	Numbers (000)					Percentages				
	1907	1924	1935	1948	1957	1907	1924	1935	1948	1957
Mining and quarrying	965	1,281	842	826	845	17·6	20·9	13·6	11·0	9·6
Treatment of non-metalliferous mining products	226	209	259	277	307	4·1	3·4	4·2	3·7	3·5
Chemical and allied trades	128	178	207	338	417	2·3	2·9	3·3	4·5	4·7
Metal manufacture	407	402	362	525	567	7·4	6·6	5·8	7·0	6·4
Engineering, shipbuilding, electrical goods	286	741	857	1,583	2,022	5·2	12·1	13·8	21·0	22·9
Vehicles	83	252	449	707	904	1·5	4·1	7·2	9·4	10·2
Metal goods not elsewhere specified	166	203	274	402	472	3·0	3·3	4·4	5·3	5·3
Precision instruments	70	72	70	107	136	1·3	1·2	1·1	1·4	1·5
Textiles	1,253	1,262	1,044	830	929	22·9	20·6	16·8	11·0	10·5
Leather	55	48	59	58	61	1·0	0·8	1·0	0·8	0·7
Clothing	757	474	528	476	542	13·8	7·7	8·5	6·3	6·1
Food, drink, tobacco	464	440	524	578	588	8·5	7·2	8·4	7·7	6·7
Manufactures of wood and cork	239	138	206	218	268	4·4	2·2	3·3	2·9	3·0
Paper and printing	326	343	403	404	535	6·0	5·6	6·5	5·4	6·0
Other manufacturing industry	47	96	135	201	243	0·9	1·6	2·2	2·7	2·7
All trades	5,470	6,139	6,216	7,531	8,834	100	100	100	100	100

[1] It has not been found possible to bring this table further up to date, owing to the changes in the Standard Industrial Classification which took place in 1958. Figures have been rounded.

Source: Censuses of Production: group coverage adjusted to render data as comparable as possible.

Conclusion

Surveying the past half-century of industrial development, what then are the main changes which have taken place? First, as illustrated in Table 1, the composition of industrial output is far more diversified today than 50 years ago. This is partly a reflection of a

TABLE 2

RELATIVE SIZE OF MAIN INDUSTRIAL GROUPS BY NUMBERS EMPLOYED 1907–57[1] UNITED KINGDOM

(1907 = 100)

Trade	1907	1924	1935	1948	1957
Mining and quarrying	100	132	87	86	87
Treatment of non-metalliferous mining products	100	93	114	123	136
Chemical and allied trades	100	139	162	264	326
Metal manufacture	100	99	89	129	139
Engineering, shipbuilding, electrical goods	100	259	300	553	707
Vehicles	100	303	541	851	1,090
Metal goods not elsewhere specified ..	100	122	165	242	284
Precision instruments	100	103	100	152	194
Textiles	100	101	83	66	74
Leather	100	87	107	105	110
Clothing	100	63	70	63	72
Food, drink, tobacco	100	95	113	124	127
Manufactures of wood and cork ..	100	58	86	91	112
Paper and printing	100	105	124	124	164
Other manufacturing industry ..	100	205	289	430	517
All trades	100	112	114	138	161

[1] Data derived from Table 1.

normal trend that as incomes rise new products have to be devised to satisfy new wants, partly the result of the diminution or cutting off of existing sources of supply which has encouraged the development of substitutes, and partly the result of two world wars and their aftermath which have given so much impetus to the development of new techniques and materials from which this country has especially benefited. Yet it is interesting to note that only the textiles, clothing and coal-mining industries have experienced an *absolute* decline in their total labour force over the period—the first two primarily because of their unduly high dependence on the export market before the First World War, the third partly because of the operation of the law of decreasing returns and labour and other supply difficulties, and partly because of the growing importance of oil as a competitive source of power. In contrast, however, the products of the iron and steel and shipbuilding industries are as much in demand as they ever were. Naturally the relative share of these industries in the national output has fallen but the long-term trend is still in favour of their growth.

Secondly, one must observe the marked change in the attitude of the State to its role in industrial affairs and the entirely different economic climate within which industry produces today as compared with fifty years ago. This theme will be taken up further in Chapter VI.

Thirdly, just as the third decade of the present century brought with it a marked change in official economic policy and thought, the succeeding decades may well be remembered by historians as the starting point of a new technological revolution, based on the discovery of new sources of power and synthetic materials, and bringing with it closer interdependence both between science and industry and between the different sections of industry. The implications of some of the changes will be examined in more detail in the subsequent chapters of this book.

II

DEVELOPMENTS IN INDUSTRIAL
STRUCTURE, OWNERSHIP AND LOCATION

Trends in size-structure and industrial concentration

(a) Up to 1914

Despite a number of important mergers and monopolistic arrangements which were concluded at the turn of the last century and the growing scepticism in both business and academic circles of the universal desirability of unregulated competition, the U.K. industrial structure continued to be dominated by a multiplicity of small, independent and highly individualistic business units right up to the First World War. In the staple industries of coal-mining, iron and steel, shipbuilding and textiles, the small family enterprise remained the typical unit of control, and even in the newer trades, where output tended to be more highly concentrated and the pattern of ownership more diverse, the philosophy of the competitive ideal still prevailed. Until the late 1870's, in fact, there was an almost complete absence of any important monopolistic arrangements in British industry or any attempt by the State to intervene in the course of economic affairs.

There were various reasons for such an industrial organization and for firms not being larger or more integrated. First, most attempts to conclude monopolistic agreements would almost certainly have been rendered ineffective by overseas competition, since there was virtually no tariff protection for the British industrialist; secondly, a large proportion of the output of British industry was exported and the need to cater for widely differing tastes and specifications made firms reluctant to adopt any policy of standardization or to surrender their independence by combining with other producers; thirdly, in most industries the existing state of technology was such that the optimum scale of production was comparatively small, while the ease with which new competitors could establish themselves precluded existing producers from charging monopolistic prices; and fourthly, belief in the expediency of *laissez faire* and the dislike of any form of trade restraint was both in line with current academic thought and upheld in common law right up to the last quarter of the nineteenth century.

In certain directions, however, there was a definite movement towards larger production units and the concentration of output. For example, it soon became clear that free competition was totally inapplicable in the case of gas, electricity, water and other enterprises of a public nature, while in some of the newer industries, e.g. those supplying electrical equipment, rayon and non-ferrous metals, maximum productive efficiency was conditional upon a highly capitalized plant being operated at full or near-full capacity. This not only meant that the initial costs of entry were often sufficiently large to shield existing manufacturers from outside competition, but also that the total market for any particular product could be adequately satisfied by a small number of firms. Indeed, in certain of the well-established trades as well, e.g. the boot and shoe, match-making, paper, flour-milling, and iron and steel industries, the rate of technological development was now exceeding that of market growth, a fact which both induced amalgamation among competitors and squeezed out inefficient firms or forced their absorption by larger concerns. These trends in their turn facilitated joint action by producers to restrict competition. Finally the rise of the limited joint stock company and the improvement of loan facilities, while making possible a larger and readier flow of business finance, also tended to favour the expansion of established concerns.

Such collective agreements as were concluded before 1914 were principally between firms making similar products,[1] though the actual circumstances leading to their formation varied. For example, one group of trusts formed in the late nineteenth century was confined to those industries where foreign competition, because

---

[1] i.e. *horizontal* agreements. There was little impetus for *vertical* integrations, i.e. between firms engaged in different stages of the same manufacturing processes, in these years, as most raw materials were easily available at competitive prices and adequate markets were not difficult to secure.

of differences in freight charges, product quality or materials availability, was absent or ineffective. Of these, the Portland Cement Trust, the Industrial Spirit Company and the Wall Paper Manufacturers were the most significant. In other cases the possibility of destructive competition or a prolonged price war from overseas competitors induced amalgamations. Thus to meet the threat presented by the establishment of the American Tobacco Company in this country, thirteen U.K. tobacco manufacturers merged in 1901 to form the Imperial Tobacco Company. In the same year a period of bitter competition between the two match producers, Bryant & May (U.K.) and the Diamond Match Company (a U.S. subsidiary manufacturing in this country), ended when the former concern surrendered 54·5% of its equity capital to the latter in exchange for its goodwill, property rights and assets. By way of contrast, depressed market conditions and the desire to avoid cut-throat competition led to the birth of such combinations as the Salt Union (1888), J. & P. Coats Ltd (1890), the United Alkali Company (1891) and the British Cotton & Wool Dyers (1895). In shipping and meat distribution mergers concluded at the turn of the century were financed by American capital; the International Mercantile Marine Company and the United States Beef Trust are two cases in point.[1]

(b) The First World War and after

The First World War provided a considerable impetus to the growth of industrial combines: competition was suppressed in the national interest while the Government encouraged the setting up of a number of representative industrial bodies to facilitate negotiations in such matters as the allocation of materials, import and export licensing, the provision of loan capital and so on. In 1916 the Federation of British Industries was established and by the end of the war there were probably more than 500 manufacturers' trade associations in existence. In every direction, collective control replaced isolated action and official support was given both to the unification movement in the chemical, electrical engineering and other industries and to the modernization of firms' equipment and the standardization of their products. Moreover, since the more efficient firms were those most highly favoured with Government

[1] For further particulars see R. Evely and I. M. D. Little, *Concentration in British Industry*, C.U.P., 1960, p. 115 ff.

contracts, it is not surprising that they should have gradually enlarged their size and acquired a dominant share of the market.

The remarkable growth of monopolistic arrangements during the war led the Ministry of Reconstruction to appoint a Standing Committee in 1918 to investigate in detail the scope and implications of their activities. In its report a year later, which concluded that 'in every important branch of industry in the U.K. there is an increasing tendency to the formation of trade associations and combinations',[1] the Committee listed no less than 93 varieties of combinations. It recommended that the Board of Trade, through a specially appointed tribunal, should investigate the operation of any organization of which there had been complaint and suggest any remedy thought necessary. The individual reports of some thirty sub-committees, appointed to examine conditions in particular industries, confirmed that 'free competition no longer governs the business world'. Yet, as another committee had earlier recognized, the replacement of competition by co-operation and amalgamation was in some cases not only desirable but practically inevitable under modern conditions.[2] Similarly, a number of the departmental reports of this same committee contrasted unfavourably the looseness and lack of organization of many British industries with the strongly centralized structure of their U.S. and German counterparts.

The previous chapter has already partly described the impact made by the inter-war depression on the organization of British industry. The difficulties of the basic industries were aggravated by their inefficient competitive structure, extreme specialization, diffused responsibility and their inherent and persistent dislike of centralized control. In addition, the over-capitalization and inadequate financial reserves of most firms prevented the undertaking of any comprehensive reorganization or re-equipment programme, so that, unlike their more 'cartel-minded' competitors who were increasingly penetrating British export markets, they were unable to benefit from the latest economies of research, manufacturing and marketing. In the cotton industry, for example, a partial inventory of capital assets taken in 1930 revealed that up to 75% of the spinning and weaving machinery was twenty years old or

[1] *Trusts*. Committee. Report, p. 2; 1918, Cd 9236, xiii.
[2] *Commercial and Industrial Policy*. Committee. Final Report; 1918, Cd 9035, xiii.

more, while in the coal-mines only 19% of coal was being cut by machinery in 1924 compared with a U.S. proportion of nearly 70%. The Balfour Committee, reporting in 1929, was in no doubt that a reorganization of industrial structure was the first prerequisite for recovery. In particular, it stressed the need for an 'enlargement of the industrial unit both by growth and the regrouping of units through consolidation or other forms of association, so as to obtain the full benefits of large-scale production, elimination of waste, standardization, and simplification of practice. . . .'[1] All this, however, would necessarily involve the surrendering of the authority of the individual firm to that of the industry as a whole— the substitution of association for isolation.[2]

Yet the response of industry was slow. Though the traditional weapons of free competition were proving increasingly inappropriate for the much-needed eradication of chronic excess capacity, any pressure towards unification was resisted, partly because the depression was thought to be only temporary and partly because business leadership was backward and uninspired. Early attempts at amalgamation, such as those made in the cotton and ship-building industries, failed because they were insufficiently supported, incoherent and unco-ordinated. Gradually, however, sometimes as the result of direct and active intervention by the State, this traditional antagonism to collective action was overcome and, in turn, every basic industry was affected.

(c) The trend towards rationalization

Rationalization, the term by which much of the reorganization of U.K. industry in the inter-war years was popularly known, has been defined as 'an industrial combination not to secure monopolistic advantages but to secure economies of production and distribution' or 'a process necessary to produce higher organization rather than to confer monopolistic advantages'. Both definitions clearly indicate that such agreements tend to be defensive rather than aggressive and, in so far as the aim of each of the inter-war reconstruction schemes was to raise industrial efficiency by a

[1] *Industry and Trade.* Committee. Final Report, p. 297; 1928–29, Cmd 3282, vii. Quoted in A. E. Lucas, *Industrial Reconstruction and the Control of Competition*, 1937, p. 37.
[2] A. E. Lucas, op. cit., p. 29.

concerted effort to eliminate excess capacity, improve production methods, introduce systematic work specialization and encourage the economies of concentrated management, distribution and research, this would seem to be an adequate description. The actual form and extent of rationalization varied according to individual circumstances, but there were four features common to the majority of schemes adopted.

(i) In all cases, an attempt was made to regulate output, fix prices and guard distributive channels by decentralization of sales and by such means as boycotts, exclusive dealing, price maintenance etc.

(ii) In almost every case there was some effort to raise productive efficiency by curtailing excess capacity and replacing obsolete equipment. While some experiments involved the amalgamation of individual production units without much central control, others required a rigid subordination of the participating firms to collective action. In only a few cases, however, was there any complete financial unification; most contracts between the firm and the centralized body representing the industry were of a loose and terminable character.

(iii) The combinations were primarily *horizontal* rather than *vertical* by nature.

(iv) The majority of the schemes for industrial reconstruction and self-government were supported, directly or indirectly, conditionally or unconditionally, by the Government.

It is outside the scope of this book to examine in detail the individual schemes adopted[1] but a brief summary of the more important developments is perhaps desirable. In the coal-mining industry several regional attempts such as the Five Counties Scheme[2] were made in the late 1920's to control and institute marketing schemes, but it was only when the Government took direct legislative action through the Coal Mines Act of 1930 that the problem was tackled from a national viewpoint. This Act (and subsequent amending legislation in 1934 and 1936) not only forced adherence to a systematic scheme of regional quota allocations and price

[1] For further details see particularly A. E. Lucas, op. cit., Chs. II–VIII.
[2] For further details see, for example, G. C. Allen, *British Industries and Their Organization*, 4th ed., 1959, Ch. III.

control, but also established a Coal Mines Reorganization Commission, with the task of promoting amalgamations and reorganization schemes within the industry. Owing, however, to the reluctance of the Commission to invoke its coercive powers and the unwillingness of the individual mine-owners to combine voluntarily, little progress was made and the international position of the coal industry continued to deteriorate. A fresh attempt to resolve this problem was made in 1938 by the creation of a new Coal Commission with powers to reduce the number of collieries and effect compulsory reorganization, but this legislation had scarcely been put to the test when war broke out.

In the cotton industry piece-meal and unco-ordinated efforts to rid the industry of its surplus capacity and to introduce short-time working eventually gave way to the formation in 1929 of the Lancashire Cotton Corporation Limited. This amalgamation of more than 200 mills, backed financially by the Bank of England operating through the Bankers' Industrial Development Company and the Securities Management Trust, aimed to acquire up to one-fifth of the existing capacity of the spinning section. To accomplish this a Surplus Spindles Board was created to buy and sterilize the redundant spindles, and a reconstruction levy was imposed by law in 1936. Yet, although between 1929 and 1937 the total number of spindles in operation was reduced by 31%, the other sections of the industry continued to remain burdened with excess capacity and it was not until the passing of the Cotton Industry (Reorganization) Act (1939), which created the necessary machinery for industry-wide technical reorganization, that this deficiency was properly remedied. Even so, judged by the standards and methods of other countries, the equipment of the Lancashire industry was inefficient and antiquated. In 1946 only 5% of the weaving looms in use were automatic compared with 95% in U.S. industry.

In the shipbuilding industry little was done to heed an earlier governmental committee's[1] recommendation for a more effective organization until the formation by the Shipbuilding Conference in 1930 of the National Shipbuilders' Security Ltd. The purpose of this privately organized company, to which some 47 firms representing over 90% of British shipbuilding capacity subscribed shares,

[1] *Shipping and Shipbuilding Industries.* Departmental Committee. Report; 1918, Cd 9092, xiii.

was to buy up and dismantle redundant and obsolete yards and to resell the sites with restrictions on their further use for shipbuilding. By means of a reconstruction levy which provided the security for an immediate loan from the Bankers' Industrial Development Co. Ltd, the company was able to reduce productive capacity by about one-third between 1930 and 1939, though, as with other schemes of this type, this was only achieved at the expense of imposing an additional burden on the surviving firms. Moreover, since the misfortunes of the shipbuilding industry were mainly of external origin, any attempt to eliminate competition and stabilize prices was bound to worsen rather than improve the industry's share in international markets. Only partly did the economies made possible by more specialized and concentrated production save the situation.

Rationalization was even more protracted in the iron and steel industry. It was not until 1932, when, on the recommendation of the Import Duties Advisory Committee, a $33\frac{1}{3}\%$ tariff was imposed on a wide range of iron and steel products,[1] conditional upon a scheme of reorganization being prepared and put into force, that the industry began to improve its efficiency. To further this end, a co-ordinating body, the British Iron and Steel Federation, was formed in 1934, but in spite of spending £50 million on technical improvements its function was primarily one of production control and price fixing. For example, a year after its formation the Federation reached an agreement with the European Steel Cartel for the control of world trade in iron and steel products. Similarly, after a period of bitter competition in rates, the Government intervened in tramp shipping and granted a subsidy under the British Shipping (Assistance) Act of 1935, on condition that some kind of centralized self-government was undertaken by the industry; in the same year Parliament also authorized a drastic scheme of control in the herring industry.

A series of private experiments was also made to improve the size-structure and to release excess capacity in the flour-milling and wool-combing trades, while a further wave of amalgamations, many international in scope, took place in the match, electrical equipment, sewing cotton and textile machinery trades. Finally the centralization of sales and the growth of trade associations (76

[1] Raised to 50% in 1934.

were registered between 1920 and 1939) did much to unify the structure of certain specialized branches of the engineering, chemical and textile industries.

Unfortunately, it is impossible to assess the results of these developments statistically, because not until the 1935 Census of Production were there any officially published comprehensive data on the size-structure of U.K. industry. A certain amount of information is, however, available for a number of individual trades. For example, in 1924 there were 2,480 coal-mines belonging to 1,480 undertakings; by 1944 these numbers had been reduced, either by closure or amalgamation, to 1,630 and 740 respectively. In the iron and steel industry the average annual output per blast furnace rose from 48,000 tons in 1929 to 83,000 tons in 1937[1] and by 1935 75% of the total output of iron and steel was concentrated in the hands of the 20 largest firms. Similarly, between 1929 and 1934 the total number of spindles in the Lancashire cotton industry was reduced from 56 million to 44 million, and after the formation of the Surplus Spindles Board in 1936 capacity was further curtailed in the next 3 years to 39½ million.

The movement towards self-government and a more concentrated pattern of output was not solely confined to the depressed industries. An oligopolistic or monopolistic size-structure was also evolved in some of the newer trades. Protected by patents and favoured by Government legislation, the dyestuffs, soap, sugar beet and air transport industries all became more centralized, while technological advances led to an increase in the typical size of the business unit in the motor-car, rayon, aluminium and electrical equipment industries. Thus, between 1922 and 1939 the number of vehicle manufacturers fell from 88 to 33 (in 1939 the 6 largest producers accounted for nine-tenths of the total production) and that of rayon suppliers from 20 in 1928 to 11 in 1939. In this period, too, the structure of the electricity supply industry was reorganized.

Perhaps, however, the most significant merger of the inter-war years was that which resulted in the formation of the Imperial Chemical Industries Ltd in 1926. Nobel Industries Ltd, Brunner, Mond & Co. Ltd, United Alkali Co. Ltd and British Dyestuffs

---

[1] The figures for German and U.S. blast furnaces were 123,000 tons and 210,000 tons respectively.

Corporation Ltd were the constituent firms. The fundamental objectives underlying this rationalization, which gave the new combine control of more than one-third of the entire output of chemical products in the country, were:

(i) to promote the efficiency of chemical operations by appropriate reorganization and sufficient centralization, and to reduce manufacturing costs, thus helping to improve the competitive position of U.K. industry in home and overseas markets,

(ii) to pool resources and to strengthen the activities of the constituent companies concerned so as to allow the undertaking of construction and development schemes beyond the reach of the individual companies and

(iii) to strengthen their activities by the co-ordination of research and technical knowledge.[1]

A year earlier another important combination, the Distillers Company, was also formed. This embraced firms responsible for over 80% of the whisky output and an even greater proportion of yeast and industrial alcohol in this country. In certain of the smaller and specialized branches of the engineering industry, e.g. in the lift, sewing machine and weighing machine sections, output also became increasingly concentrated within the hands of one or two firms.

(d) The Census of Production, 1935

On the basis of new statistical data contained in the 1935 Census of Production and additional information provided by the Board of Trade, Messrs. Leak and Maizels published the first comprehensive study of the size-structure of firms within British industry in 1945.[2] They considered the distribution of businesses by numbers of persons employed both in manufacturing industry as a whole and within individual industries. In amplification of these data, they also presented for the first time certain information concerning the inter-relationships between the larger firms in British industry. The broad conclusions of this study may now be briefly summarized.

[1] Association of British Chemical Manufacturers. Report on the Chemical Industry, 1949, p. 7.
[2] H. Leak and A. Maizels, 'The Structure of British Industry', *Journal of the Royal Statistical Society*, 1945, Vol. CVIII, Parts 1–2.

In 1935 there were 302 trades and subdivisions of trades (249 after allowing for duplication) classified within 15 broad industrial groups. The size distribution of firms (defined as 'the aggregate of establishments trading under the same name') comprising these groups is shown in Table 3. Of the 53,217 firms thus classified rather more than one-half employ less than 50 persons whereas

TABLE 3

DISTRIBUTION OF FIRMS BY NUMBERS EMPLOYED
1935

Size (Persons employed)	Firms No.	%	Total persons employed No.	%
11– 24	17,609	33·1	304,113	4·2
25– 49	14,147	26·6	491,696	6·8
50– 99	9,459	17·7	656,237	9·1
100– 199	5,814	10·9	808,848	11·2
200– 299	2,218	4·2	539,770	7·5
300– 499	1,690	3·1	644,623	9·0
500– 749	865	1·6	527,855	7·3
750– 999	405	0·8	350,909	4·9
1,000–1,999	612	1·2	844,349	11·7
2,000–4,999	297	0·6	915,579	12·7
5,000 and over	101	0·2	1,119,078	15·5
Total	53,217	100	7,203,057	100

Source: H. Leak and A. Maizels, op. cit., p. 144, Table I.

only 1 firm in 25 has a labour force of 500 or more. However, while the former group only employ 11% of the total numbers employed, the latter account for 52% of the total. In order to assess the degree of concentration of employment within a particular industrial group or trade, the authors calculated the total number employed by the 3 largest business units[1] as a percentage of that of the group or trade as a whole. Thus for the 15 omnibus groups, this degree of 'tripoly' averaged out at 26%, varying from 48% for chemicals, 44% for public utilities and 43%

[1] A business unit is defined as a 'single firm or aggregate of firms owned or controlled by a single company and employing 500 people or more, control being defined as ownership of more than half the capital (or voting power) of each firm'.

for engineering, to 4% for building and 10% for mines and quarries and timber. Within these broad groups the degree of concentration also differed markedly. Though two-thirds of those employed were to be found in trades or subdivisions of trades where the degree of concentration was below 30%, in some 69 trades the concentration percentage was 50% or over and in 33 trades 70% or over. Of these latter, 8 were in the chemicals and allied group, 6 in the engineering, shipbuilding and vehicles group and 5 each in the food, drink, tobacco and miscellaneous manufacturers' groups. More specifically, the figure for manufactured fuel was 95%, sewing machines and boot-and-shoe-making machinery 93%, wallpaper 90%, matches 89%, sugar and glucose 83%, dyes and dyestuffs 82%, petroleum 82%, rayon manufacturing 80%, rubber tyres and tubes 76%.[1] The largest 200 firms alone provided nearly one-third of the aggregate employment. Of the 2,280 firms employing more than 500 workers, 27% operated more than 1 manufacturing unit and rather more than one-half of these were multi-product in character. Some 63 business units were among the 3 largest in more than 1 trade, and 7 including I.C.I., Vickers, Lever Bros and G.E.C. in 4 trades or more.

The inter-connections between the different manufacturing trades were also examined and 6 main groups, viz. coal-mining, non-metalliferous mining, iron and steel (smelting and rolling), mechanical engineering, chemicals and textile finishing, were shown to be focal points. For example, some 89 business units employing 84% of the total labour force of iron and steel blast furnaces and coke and by-products trades were also engaged in coal-mining activities; business units in the iron and steel industry accounted for 63% of the total employment in the tin-plate industry; and in its turn the chemical group had important associations with the iron and steel, blast furnace, coke and by-products, metalliferous mining, textile finishing trades and so on. Firms in the mechanical engineering industry were shown to have important interests in the wrought-iron and steel tubes, chemicals, carriage and wagon-building trades, while there are also close inter-relationships between the non-metalliferous mining and cement trades and motor vehicles and aircraft trades.

[1] Concentration percentages were also given in respect of net output and in most cases these were slightly higher than the employment figures.

By 1939, then, the U.K. industrial structure was mixed in character. Throughout the previous twenty years there had been a gradual modification of competitive principles and a movement towards the concentration of business output within the hands of a comparatively few producers. First, the basic industries, faced with falling markets, out-dated in organization and technology and financially weak, were forced to sacrifice their stubborn individualism for collective and centralized control; secondly, there was the increased inducement given to rationalization schemes and mono-polistic arrangements by tariff protection and Government legis-lation; thirdly, the trend of business and academic opinion was in favour of large-scale business units, regulated competition and enlightened self-government in industry; and fourthly, the techno-logical developments of the era and the natural evolution of in-dustrial growth combined to induce a market structure composed of a few dominant firms and a large number of smaller concerns. However, in some of the more traditional industries, such as clothing, boots and shoes, building, cutlery and pottery, the small competitive firm continued to remain the typical business unit.

(e) The impact of a changing technology on industrial organization
The economic and technological developments of the last two decades have profoundly affected the size-structure and organiza-tion of British industry and the inter-relationships between firms. Depression, a limited rate of technological advance and indifferent trading conditions have given way to full employment, a new industrial revolution and a seller's market. The increased scope of Government intervention has had its repercussions on both the direction and organization of industrial activity, while the external trade situation has directly promoted the establishment of many new industries of overseas (and particularly United States) parentage in this country. Entry conditions into established industries have tended to become more difficult with increasing capital require-ments and a more complex patent problem.

The results of these trends have been varied. First, the structure of industry is more oligopolistic today than it was before the war. Industries are being increasingly dominated by a few large firms which supply the bulk of the output between them. The exceptions are where a wide diversity of specialized products is produced or

where the rate of growth of demand has exceeded that of technological achievement, e.g. as in the machine tools and pharmaceutical
industries. Secondly, there has been an expansion in the number
and scope of multi-product companies: the specialist producer is
in general a less frequent phenomenon than 25 years ago. Thirdly,
the traditional boundaries between industries have become increasingly blurred as new ventures, jointly financed by firms of
different industrial parentage, have been set up. New hybrid occupations have risen as a direct result of scientific developments with
which more than one branch of industry has been directly concerned. Thus one has the establishment of such enterprises as
British Nylon Spinners Ltd, owned by Courtaulds Ltd and
Imperial Chemical Industries, and British Petroleum Chemicals,
financed equally by the Distillers Company and the Anglo-Iranian
Oil Company Ltd. In many other instances the discovery and
exploitation of new products, new materials and new production
techniques have given rise to new organizational relationships
between previously independent firms.

At the root of the majority of these structural changes have
been the technological advances within the chemical industry on
the one hand, and the engineering and electronics industries on the
other. For instance, the development of the various synthetic raw
materials has not only meant that the chemical industry is now the
supplier of many products which were previously the province of
e.g. the textile, timber, metal, leather and rubber industries, but also
that its rate of technical progress is likely to have a marked effect on
that of its customers; for instance, any innovation in the field of
petro-chemicals may well have important repercussions on the
development of paints and plastics manufactures at a later stage in
the production chain This has encouraged a closer vertical integration between firms and the setting up of jointly financed companies.
On the other hand it has often been the case that technological
advances, e.g. the discovery of new types of materials, have enabled
the secondary producer to be more self-sufficient in his manufacturing processes. Thus, many electrical equipment producers who previously purchased wooden or metal components from specialized
suppliers now operate their own plastic-moulding plants. Indeed, it
sometimes happens that where there is a certain amount of capacity
to spare after internal wants have been satisfied the manufacturer

enters into other fields and competes with specialist producers.

A firm which has reached market capacity in one line of business can expand only by diversifying its output. This is usually accomplished within the confines of the firm itself, but in some cases the expanding firm may prefer to purchase a company already producing the proposed new product range.[1] Take-over bids have become far more frequent in recent years and there are now twice the number of business units operating more than one factory as before the war. Some 65% of all firms employing more than 500 people are multi-plant. Of these perhaps the best known is Unilever Ltd, a holding company which controls 500 operating subsidiaries, at home and abroad, supplying a wide variety of manufactures including soap products, vegetable oils and fats, ice-cream, sausages, frozen foods, fish, soups, perfumes and so on. The Distillers Co. Ltd is a whisky-and-gin combine with 105 affiliated companies active in the bio-chemicals, plastics, alloys and industrial alcohol fields. The ramifications of Imperial Chemical Industries Ltd, now the most highly capitalized manufacturing company in the country, are equally wide and its products range from explosives, dyestuffs, sulphuric acid and caustic soda to terylene, plastics materials, pharmaceutical products and paints. In the engineering and metal products industries Tube Investments Ltd operate 70 factories and employ over 40,000 people. It is linked with virtually all of Britain's principal industries through supplying such products as steel tubes, electrical equipment, paint, bicycles, aluminium alloy products and so on. The interests of Vickers Ltd and its subsidiaries extend to ships, armaments, aircraft, printing machinery, paint and food processing plant, railway vehicles, scientific instruments, rubber, cellulose and plastics materials and ink. The three giants of the electrical equipment industry—the Associated Electrical Industries Ltd, General Electric Company Ltd and English Electric Ltd—not only produce every conceivable type of electrical apparatus but are also involved in the aircraft, marine propulsion, transport equipment and heavy industrial machinery industries as well.

[1] A recent case in point is that of Courtaulds, which until 1958 was a specialist producer of man-made fibres, but since then has spread its interests, mainly by the acquisition of other companies, into the field of paints, plastics, wood pulp, engineering, packaging and finished textiles.

But in addition to these cases of *lateral* expansion, there have been others of *vertical* integration. Such an extension of interests may be backwards or forwards in character: the acquisition in 1953–4 of several car body companies by the major vehicle assemblers is an example of the former and that of various baking interests by Spillers Ltd, a flour-milling concern, in 1954 and subsequently, of the latter. Of course, for a considerable time now the interests of some of the larger U.K. companies, e.g. Dunlop, Unilever, Pilkington and Courtaulds, have extended far and wide, but in recent years technological developments have given added impetus to firms to gain control both over sources of supply and over market outlets. Thus, in the former case the suppliers in question may be deficient in the technical expertise necessary to fulfil efficiently the contracts placed with them. To overcome this difficulty, the purchasers, assuming they possess the necessary knowledge, may consider it profitable to purchase the share capital of their suppliers outright and treat them as an integral part of their organization. There has also been a similar tendency to integrate forwards. This is partly because new uses have been found for existing end products (thus we see chemical and oil companies interested in the development of the plastics and synthetic fibres industries) and partly because the selling of many durable goods and products today is being increasingly influenced by the service and maintenance facilities offered by the wholesale or retail distributor in question. Thus it is often in the interest of companies in, for example, the motor-car, office equipment and chemical engineering industries to operate their own outlets.[1] Yet despite these examples, the large specialist firm still exists: the Imperial Tobacco Co. Ltd, for example, is the fourth largest U.K. manufacturing company.

These developments have been accompanied by the growing importance of research and development as a factor influencing industrial progress. This has mainly tended to increase the larger firm's advantage over its smaller competitor. Thus we have had the merger of the Austin Motor Co. Ltd and Morris Motors Ltd in 1952 to form the British Motor Corporation in the belief that

[1] Again, in 1952, 33 brewery companies each owned over 500 houses and together accounted for nearly 50% of the total number of houses; *vide* R. S. Edwards and H. Townsend, *Business Enterprise*, 1958. In the distribution of petroleum four out of five garages are 'tied' to one or other of the major oil companies.

unified control would not only lead to more efficient production but would also concentrate research facilities and be particularly beneficial to manufacturing and assembly abroad. Virtually the same reasons were given when Courtaulds purchased the share capital of its main competitor British Celanese in 1957. In other industries—notably aircraft, chemical and industrial instruments— the movement towards concentration was accelerated during the war when the number of trade associations rose to 2,500 and the Government placed its contracts mainly with larger firms.[1] Save in those industries where the methods of production are still comparatively uncomplicated or where a highly specialized product is being supplied, the role of the small firm is increasingly becoming that of a feeder to the larger concern. The atomic power, man-made fibres, petroleum refining, motor-car and electrical equipment industries are now also completely dominated by a few highly capitalized companies: widening markets, standardization of products and simplification of manufacturing processes have tended to increase the optimum output of individual *plants*, while horizontal, vertical and lateral integration have all combined to enlarge the average size of the *firm*.

Not only has the size-structure of firms been affected, but the traditional competitive techniques as well. In oligopolistic industries price competition has tended to be more and more supplanted by centralized agreements and resale price maintenance, with competition being directed to product quality and design and the accompanying advertising and service facilities. At the same time, technological advances of the capital-using kind have continued to enlarge the size of the establishment at which maximum efficiency is attained; and with such speed and intensity that this has inevitably led to a fall in the number of competitors.

Financial unification is, however, only one of the ways in which the economies associated with new techniques can be achieved. The growth of cross-licensing and patent agreements, particularly as between British and American firms, have been very numerous

---

[1] In the last two years or so a number of other important mergers have taken place, particularly in the aircraft industry where three main groups—British Aircraft Corporation, Hawker Siddeley and Western Aircraft—now dominate the airframe side, and Rolls-Royce and Bristol-Siddeley the engine side. Short Brothers and Harland remains an important independent company.

since 1945, while sometimes an entirely new company is jointly sponsored by two firms in apparently unrelated industries to produce a specialized item in which both are interested. Since the war, for example, a number of important Anglo-American-financed companies have been established in the paper, engineering, electronics, aircraft, chemical and atomic energy fields. With the technological complexity and high capital costs of modern industry, it is sometimes necessary to pool knowledge between a number of interested firms. Thus, no less than 11 companies at present make up the United Sulphuric Acid Corporation, established in 1951 at the Government's instigation; 5 rubber tyre companies hold a financial interest in International Synthetic Rubber Co. Ltd set up in 1958; and 5 separate co-operative groups, comprising firms in the nuclear energy, engineering and constructional industries, are responsible for building power plant for the Central Electricity Generating Board.[1] All this, of course, has not only meant an increase in the ramifications of ownership but an extension in the number and variety of interlocking directorates: in 1956, for example, the directors of the 9 largest firms in the steel industry held between them 673 directorships in other branches of industry. Similarly, the chemical industry, chiefly through I.C.I. and Unilever directorates, is closely associated with the joint-stock banks and with firms in the petroleum, coal and engineering industries. In all, 33 of the largest firms in this country are linked through interlocking directorates with one or more of the joint-stock banks.

The pattern of growth since 1939 has been such that many of the newer products and technical developments have emanated from established firms in peripheral industries, either directly by an extension of their own manufacturing activities or indirectly through the setting up of specialist subsidiaries. For example, the modern electronics industry has principally evolved out of the domestic radio industry on the one hand and the electrical equipment industry on the other; new and independent companies of external origin have grown up since the war, but these are the exception rather than the rule. Likewise, most of the important post-war advances in the field of plastics, petro-chemicals and the newer man-made

[1] For further particulars see Edwards and Townsend, op. cit., pp. 259–62.

fibres have arisen from established firms in the chemical, oil and rayon industries. Except in industries where foreign firms have played a significant role, such as office machinery, pharmaceutical products and oil refining, the difficulty in raising new capital, the existing tax structure, the high initial costs of entry and the immediate advantage enjoyed by firms already producing in related fields have limited the growth of new businesses, except those of a deliberately specialized character. Marshall's famous analogy of the trees in the forest is less applicable today than at the time when he was writing; rather the small trees which grow are off-shoots of the larger and well-established trees, or are the latter's main suppliers of specialist component parts or materials.

Unfortunately, such trends as have been described are veiled in the official statistics which only give information about the size of *establishments*. However, Table 4 illustrates the main changes which have taken place in this latter direction since 1935. As a whole, it would appear that the competitive structure has been very little affected. On the other hand, we see that, while the total number of establishments in U.K. industry has risen by 12·7% between 1935 and 1961 and those employing less than 100 persons by 6·5%, those with a labour force of 500 or more are 83·5% more numerous. As already indicated, these forces are more the reflection of the rapid technological developments which have occurred since 1939 than of the related trend towards a more concentrated structure of business ownership and control. They are also a feature of the changing pattern of industrial output in as much as the trades which have expanded the fastest since the war are also those in which output is most concentrated in the larger firms.[1]

The other information which is available about the trend of business concentration in this country is that published in 1956 by Hart and Prais in the *Journal of the Royal Statistical Society*,[2] and that by Messrs Little and Evely in their book *Concentration in British Industry*.[3] The former study limited its scope to the market valuation of the net assets of some 2,150 public joint-stock companies engaged in mining, manufacturing and distribution as quoted on the

[1] See G. C. Allen, *The Structure of Industry in Britain*, Longmans Green, 1961, p. 62
[2] P. Hart and S. Prais, 'The Analysis of Business Concentration', *Journal of the Royal Statistical Society*, 1956, Vol. 119, Part 2.
[3] C.U.P., 1960.

TABLE 4

SIZE DISTRIBUTION OF ESTABLISHMENTS BY NUMBERS EMPLOYED IN FACTORY TRADES 1935, 1952 AND 1961

Size (No. of employees)	Establishments						Persons employed (000's)					
	1935		1952		1961		1935		1952		1961	
	No.	%	No.	%	No.	%	No.	%	No.	%	No.	%
11—24	16,490	33·7	17,441	30·8	12,571	22·8	279	5·4	299	4·2	222	2·7
25—49	12,542	25·6	14,730	26·0	14,704	26·7	438	8·5	517	7·2	523	6·4
50—99	8,582	17·6	10,473	18·5	12,774	23·2	602	11·7	731	10·2	897	11·0
100—499	9,750	19·9	11,543	20·4	12,213	22·1	2,015	39·0	2,398	33·4	2,552	31·2
500—999	1,047	2·1	1,471	2·6	1,693	3·1	719	13·9	1,011	14·1	1,163	14·2
1,000 and over	533	1·1	980	1·7	1,206	2·1	1,106	21·4	2,224	30·9	2,821	34·5
Total	48,944	100·0	56,638	100·0	55,161	100·0	5,159	100·0	7,180	100·0	8,178	100·0

Source: *Annual Abstract of Statistics*, No. 84, 1935–46. *Ministry of Labour Gazette*, December, 1952, April 1962.

London Stock Exchange. It is, of course, true that these firms probably employ more than 50% of the industrial labour force, but because they account for less than 5% of the total number of U.K. firms, changes in their size distribution are not necessarily a good guide to the size trend of industry as a whole. For example, Hart and Prais show that the concentration of market assets fell slightly between 1939 and 1950: it seems, however, that one of the reasons for this was the considerable number of new firms of small to medium size converting themselves into public companies. As a whole, the authors found that for the period 1885–1950 there was only a slight increase in the concentration of firms. For example, the largest 5% of quoted companies controlled 55% of the total net assets in 1950 compared with 65% in 1939, whilst the smallest 30% controlled 2% of the net assets in 1950 and 6% in 1885. A fair degree of symmetry is apparent in the size distribution throughout the years, though the range of dispersion varied between industries, being least in the boot and shoe industry and greatest in the chemical trade.

The authors concluded that the two factors having the most important effect on the size distribution of firms were (i) the extent to which new firms entered the market and existing producers left and (ii) the sizes of existing firms. On the whole it was found that the first consideration tended to dilute rather than accentuate the degree of concentration and that in the second case the major influence was the change in the sizes of existing firms—either by amalgamation or in the normal course of growth. Between 1896 and 1950 some 218 firms were apparently involved in amalgamation, the number remaining after merger being 93. Most amalgamations were between two or more unquoted companies which then became quoted, or between unquoted and quoted companies; they have been most numerous since 1939, but over the period as a whole the normal growth of firms would appear to be a more dominant cause of their increasing size. In all, the number of quoted companies rose from 60 in 1885 to 2,103 in 1950, while the average (arithmetic mean) market valuation increased from £125,000 to £1,400,000 and the median from £150,000 to £1,350,000. These figures, of course, take no account of changing money values over the period, but even allowing for this factor, the movement towards more highly capitalized business units is unmistakable.

The other enquiry worth mentioning briefly is that which has been concerned with analysing the statistical data contained in the 1951 Census of Production in respect of the size of business units and the degree of industrial concentration. In their book Messrs. Little and Evely sought to bring up-to-date the statistics compiled by Leak and Maizels some 15 years earlier, and to analyse the main changes in concentration which had taken place since 1935. In 1951 there were 17 main industrial groups and 348 separate trades and subdivisions of trades, of which 219 were considered suitable for further analysis.[1] Like the earlier survey, the authors measured the degree of business concentration by expressing the employment of the 3 largest business units in a particular trade as a percentage of the total employed by that trade. In addition, however, by relating the concentration ratios so derived to the total number of business units and their relative size, they were able to obtain a reasonably accurate picture of the competitive structure of U.K. industry.[2] On the face of it, the conclusions reached in both cases were very similar: whereas, for example, Leak and Maizels produced an overall employment concentration ratio of 26%, Little and Evely arrived at a figure of 29%. How far, however, this slight increase is indicative of a more highly concentrated business structure, and how far of changes in definition, exclusiveness and specialization, it is difficult to say.

A frequency distribution of the 219 trades examined by their employment concentration ratio in 1951 is given in Table 5, which also gives a somewhat broader grouping of the same ratios to the total numbers employed in each group. Clearly, as this table shows, by far the greater proportion of those employed in British industry are still to be found in industries where the three largest firms account for less than one-third of the total labour force: in only 50 trades is the employment concentration ratio 67% or over. As regards changes in the size-structure of trades, in only 27 of the 219

[1] For example, all trades where the proportion of the output of the principal products was less than two-thirds of the total output were excluded.

[2] Thus, the combination of high concentration, a small number of units and a large size inequality suggests the trade in question is dominated by one or two large concerns. Trades consisting of a few units roughly equal in size, and with high or medium concentration are likely to be oligopolistic by nature and so on. See *Concentration in British Industry*, p. 10.

trades studied does there appear to have been any increase in the concentration ratio between 1935 and 1951.[1] These included mineral oil refining, coke ovens, razors, watches and clocks, building bricks, drugs and pharmaceutical preparations, china and porcelain, cinematograph film printing and bread and flour confectionery. In 14 trades, of which the biscuit, wall-paper, match, boots and

TABLE 5

DISTRIBUTION OF 219 TRADES
BY EMPLOYMENT CONCENTRATION 1951

Degree of employment concentration %	Number of trades		Concentration category	Number of trades	Total employment	
	No.	%			(000's)	%
1– 10	19	8·7				
11– 20	37	16·9	Low	100	3,784	63·4
21– 30	43	19·6				
31– 40	26	11·9				
41– 50	23	10·5	Medium	69	1,545	25·9
51– 60	20	9·1				
61– 70	13	5·9				
71– 80	18	8·2	High	50	636	10·7
81– 90	17	7·8				
91–100	3	1·4				
Total	219	100·0		219	5,965	100·0

Source: I. M. D. Little and R. Evely, 'Some aspects of the structure of British industry', Tables III and IV, *Proceedings of the Manchester Statistical Society*, Feb. 1958.

shoes and carpet industries are the main examples, the concentration ratio actually fell over this period of time. In general, Little and Evely do not believe that it is possible to say definitely whether or not business concentration has risen or fallen since 1935. Their general conclusions as to the present-day structure of industry would, however, appear to bear out what has so far been said in this chapter:

[1] It is perhaps worth noting that since 1951 several important mergers have occurred in the motor-car, agricultural machinery, aircraft, chemical, man-made fibres and brewery industries.

'To sum up, one can say that the most important structural type of British industry is where there is a low concentration as a result of a few giants surrounded by a host of pygmies. The next most important is the more nearly competitive type, where firms are many and there are no extreme disparities in size. The third most important is again where there is one or more giants among the pygmies with the giant or giants controlling more than one-third of the output. These three categories account for about 85% of the total employment.'[1]

Examples of the trades which conform to the first type include iron and steel (melting and rolling), radio apparatus and gramophones, drugs and pharmaceutical preparations and bread and flour confectionery. Business units in the pottery, boots and shoes, most types of clothing, cutlery, building, toilet preparations and perfumery trades are of the second variety and those within the third group include motor-cars, mineral oil refining, rubber tyres, watches and clocks, tobacco, valves and cathode-ray tubes and aircraft manufacture and repair.

Sources of finance

An adequate and readily available supply of industrial finance has always been an essential prerequisite for an expanding economy.

While several sources of loan finance exist, their availability to potential borrowers depends on many factors such as the age and credit-worthiness of the borrowing concern, the character of its business and the period for which credit is required. In point of fact, undistributed profits and other forms of internal finance still provide the greater part, probably two-thirds, of the new capital expansion undertaken by established companies, whatever their size. In addition, however, public joint-stock companies can draw upon the facilities of the new issue market,[2] a course which is also

---

[1] Little and Evely, 'Some aspects of the structure of British industry', p. 14, *Proceedings of the Manchester Statistical Society*, Feb. 1958.
[2] Between 1954 and 1961 some £2,505 million was raised in this way by U.K. concerns.

open to the larger private company, if its business is sufficiently prosperous and if it desires to convert itself into a public corporation. The smaller private company and the limited partnership are faced with rather more difficulties owing to their relatively weaker security status; and this applies equally in the short run since the joint-stock banks—who are normally the chief providers of working capital for industry—will usually lend or grant overdrafts only on the basis of first-class collateral. An entirely new business is usually started by a single person or group of persons who will supply the initial capital out of their own resources (or those of a 'backer'), but who for working capital rely on trade credit from suppliers of components or raw materials, and who may rent their machinery and equipment or acquire it by hire purchase.[1]

The inadequacy of medium- to long-term loan-capital facilities for small and medium-sized businesses was both recognized and criticized by the Committee on Finance and Industry in 1931 (the Macmillan Committee) and since that date special efforts have been made to ensure that the growth of such concerns (who, so often, are the pioneers of new products, processes and techniques) should not be impeded for want of financial aid. As a consequence, during the 1930's, several new specialist institutions appeared on the scene such as Credit for Industry Ltd, Bankers' Industrial Development Co. Ltd, Charterhouse Industrial Development Company and the Special Areas Reconstruction Co., the capital of which was subscribed by the commercial banks, insurance companies and other members of the money market. In addition, the scope of existing agencies, e.g. the United Dominions Trust Ltd, was greatly widened.[2]

In 1945 these measures were strengthened by the formation of two further institutions, viz. the Industrial and Commercial Finance Corporation (I.C.F.C.) and the Finance Corporation for Industry (F.C.I.). The first of these bodies was specifically designed to provide intermediate or long-term finance for the smaller and medium-sized industrial or commercial businesses where the amounts involved (ranging from £5,000 to £200,000) would not justify or even possibly

[1] For further information on the significance of these forms of finance see *Studies in Company Finance*, ed. by B. Tew and R. F. Henderson, C.U.P., 1959.

[2] For further particulars see N. MacCrae, *The London Capital Market*, 1955, Ch. IX.

permit the making of a public issue of capital.[1] Its authorized
and issued share capital was £15 million subscribed by the London
clearing banks and Scottish banks in proportion to their size and it
could also borrow up to a further £30 million from the same
sources. By 31 March 1961 the I.C.F.C. had made available some
£74 million to about 1,000 enterprises. In the last five years roughly
one in five applications for funds has been successful[2] in a wide
range of industries. By way of contrast the F.C.I. was set up to assist
in the provision of development finance (in amounts of £200,000
and upwards) to firms in the major basic industries for a period of
time (usually one to five years) where neither normal bank accom-
modation nor the financing of a new issue is a practicable proposition. Its nominal capital is £25 million contributed as follows: 40%
by insurance companies, 30% by trust companies and 30% by the
Bank of England. In addition the F.C.I. is empowered to borrow a
further £100 million from the joint-stock banks, thus making its
total resources £125 million. By 31 March 1961 the Corporation
had granted loans of more than £200 million to firms in the steel,
chemical, oil, textiles, shipping and engineering industries. A particularly important contribution of the F.C.I., if not a very profitable
one, was its investment of £10 million in the new enterprise, Petro-
Chemicals Ltd, an interest subsequently relinquished, when the firm
reached financial independence, to the Shell Chemical Company.

Another source of medium-term credit (specifically designed to
nelp raise efficiency in the smaller firm) is that made available by
the U.S. (and administered by the Board of Trade) under the
Conditional Aid Scheme.[3] This has enabled a revolving loan fund
of £100,000 to be set up from which firms in the engineering,
clothing, plastics and printing industries have already benefited.
With similar intentions in view, the National Union of Manufacturers founded in 1953 a managerial advisory service for small-scale
industry; subsequently, a further grant enabled the service to
recruit three industrial engineers to spend short periods with

[1] For comments on the current difficulties in this connection, see
Working of the Monetary System. Committee. Report, paras. 229–33;
1958–9, Cmnd 827, xvii.

[2] J. Bates, 'The Macmillan gap—thirty years after', *The Banker*, July
1961, p. 470.

[3] For further particulars see *Expenditure of Counterpart Funds derived
. . . under . . . the Mutual Security Act of 1952*; 1952–3, Cmd 8776, xxx.

member firms. Finally, in January 1957, the National Union of Manufacturers Advisory Service was officially constituted. It employs at present five senior industrial engineers to give advice and assess the potentialities of a firm and five work-study officers and cost accountants for resident work in firms. The service is specifically planned to give help to those firms employing 30–150 employees with a sales turnover of £50,000–£250,000.

Complementing the above sources of finance there has been, in recent years, a considerable increase in the scope of both hire-purchase facilities, particularly in respect of machinery or vehicles, and mortgage loans on property, the latter made available principally by insurance companies. Another type of assistance is that provided by the Government under the Local Employment Act, 1960, to firms setting up factories in specified areas of high unemployment.[1] In the field of research and development, the Government-sponsored National Research Development Corporation is helping to finance the development of inventions originating from public or private sources, if these are considered likely to further the public interest. Exports are aided by various forms of credit guarantees.[2] The State also controls the National Film Finance Corporation, while in the private sphere the Ship Mortgage Finance Co. Ltd (an association of shipbuilding concerns and various insurance and other City interests) grants loans by way of first mortgage on British-built ships. Air Finance Ltd is another privately sponsored body, formed in 1953 to help finance U.K. aircraft exports by making short-term loans to purchasers to cover up to 40% of the purchase price.[3] To ease the situation of those small family businesses whose shareholders are faced with paying high estate duties, the Estate Duties Investment Trust Ltd (EDITH)—an associate of the I.C.F.C.—was registered in 1952 with a capital of £1 million and substantial overdraft facilities. Up to the end of March, 1962, it had invested £3·1 million in 100 companies in this way.

Undoubtedly, the net effect of all these various measures has been to help remedy an important gap in our financial system. At the same time, the Radcliffe Committee still felt the need for a

---

[1] For further particulars see p. 75.
[2] See pp. 200–1.
[3] See H. Rose, *The Economic Background to Investment*, C.U.P., 1960, p. 283.

C

new Government-sponsored institution which could assist small businesses in the commercial exploitation of new inventions and innovations of promise. The function of such a body—the name proposed is the Industrial Guarantee Corporation—would be to offer guarantees to the various existing financial institutions who themselves would put up the money, so as to cover an agreed proportion of the loan.[1] Even supposing, however, that a scheme of this kind were adopted its impact would at best be only marginal. For in spite of the proliferation of institutions now available for the finance of small business only a very small proportion—probably about 3%—of the private companies in this country have made serious applications for assistance. Moroever, of these applications the proportion refused has been extremely high—the most common reason cited being the applicant's failure to show a long or prosperous history of trading. Yet such a state of affairs itself presupposes the past investment of long-term capital. Here, then, lies the crux of the inherent problem which is faced by most small firms and which is as real today as it was 30 years ago.

Finally, the steadily increasing flow of foreign (and in particular United States) capital into this country over recent years must be mentioned. This has considerably aided the development of, for instance, the motor-car, office and agricultural machinery, pharmaceutical products, industrial instruments and oil refining industries. In fact, between 1950 and 1957, investment by U.S.-controlled firms in Britain accounted for nearly 15% of all net fixed capital formation in U.K. manufacturing industry.

Ownership patterns

One of the consequences of the developments so far described in this chapter has been that the structure of ownership and the effective control of industrial affairs have gradually become more centralized. In 1957–8 the six main public corporations alone employed some 1·9 million people, owned net assets worth £4,698 million and had a combined turnover of £2,474 million.[2] The nationalization of the coal-

[1] Cmnd 827, op. cit., paras. 948–52.
[2] R. Harris and M. Solly, *A survey of large companies*, Institute of Economic Affairs, 1959.

mining, gas, electricity, internal transport and civil aviation industries, and the Bank of England, and the acquisition by the State of
the share capital of Cable and Wireless Ltd has meant that many
hundreds of firms which were previously separately controlled are
now concentrated under one ownership. The co-operative societies
have also extended their interests. For the rest of the economy, the
number of public joint-stock companies has fallen from some 14,500
in 1939 to 10,900 in 1960 and that of private companies risen from
145,000 to 368,000. Between them, these incorporated businesses
accounted for nearly 90% of the gross income of manufacturing
traders in 1955 (approximately £3,500 million): the largest 2,500
firms accounted for some 55% of this latter figure. And, as we have
seen, capital is highly concentrated, the largest 200 U.K. corporations probably owning one-third of the total net assets in the private
sector of U.K. industry.[1]

As regards the distribution of equity capital within manufacturing industry, whereas the *number* of shareholdings held by private
individuals outnumber those in the hands of investment houses,
bank, insurance companies and other business ventures by over 4 to
1, the *value* of their combined stake is considerably less significant.
Nevertheless, in a survey recently conducted by the Institute of
Economic Affairs into the financial and administrative structure of
the 120 largest British public companies, it was found that in 91
cases individuals held a majority shareholding.[2] The role of the
institutional investor, however, was seen to be growing and in some
industries they are the most important shareholders. For example,
in an analysis of ordinary shares of 11 denationalized steel companies (which in 1956 accounted for 70% of the total privately produced crude steel output of the country) it was shown that the 5%
largest shareholders, who then owned 56% of the total capital, were
almost exclusively insurance companies, investment trusts and other
institutional investors.[3]

Again, in his book *Ownership of Industry* (1951), Mr. H. Parkinson recalls that the 5% largest equity shareholders in a sample of

[1] It is estimated that the 40 largest exporting companies account for
30% of all manufacturing exports. See *The Economist*, 23 July 1960, p. 389.
[2] Harris and Solly, op. cit., p. 20.
[3] In spite of the fact that the typical holding in a steel company is 150
shares.

30 companies owned over 50% of the total capital. A relatively small proportion of shareholders could therefore control the operation of any business by virtue of their dominant voting power. Indeed, since the vast majority of shareholders do not attend meetings (nor vote by proxy), it follows that if the above illustration is representative of industry as a whole the *de facto* financial control of the country's manufacturing assets could well be in the hands of 3% or less of the total shareholders. Of these, according to Parkinson, a family or group of families or an outside company is likely to have the largest stake, and the directors of the enterprise immediately concerned the smallest. At the same time, it would seem that the concentration of ownership has decreased since before the war. According to Professor Sargant Florence, the average proportion of the votes held by the 20 largest voteholders in publicly quoted industrial, commercial and brewery companies, with a capital of £3 million or more in 1951, fell from 30% in 1936 to 19% in 1951.[1] This fall in vote concentration was most pronounced among the faster growing companies, and affected the personal investor considerably more than the company or institutional investor. Like Parkinson, Sargant Florence found that the proportion of shares owned by the directors of the company in question was usually very small indeed;[2] he also discovered that the divorce between ownership and control was positively correlated with the size of firm. On the other hand, companies with a high vote concentration were more likely to be under the financial control of their directors (by virtue of their ownership of shares) than those with a medium or low vote concentration.[3]

Trends in industrial location

Prior to the First World War the geographical distribution of industry in the U.K. gave little cause for concern. Interest in the subject was confined to the major considerations governing a business man's choice of factory location and the possible effects

[1] *Ownership, Control and Success of Large Companies*, Sweet & Maxwell, 1961.
[2] 2·3% for all size public companies, excluding breweries, in 1951.
[3] P. S. Florence, op. cit., p. 124 ff.

which that location might have on his subsequent costs of production. Within this broad setting the relative merits of the specialization and diversification of industry were discussed. No real attention was paid to the consequences of the locational pattern of industry from the viewpoint of the economic well-being of either a particular region or of the country as a whole. A *laissez-faire* philosophy, full employment and an expanding economy on the one hand and the locational immobility of the older industries on the other would seem to have accounted for this absence of any integrated location policy. The economies of the various geographical regions developed alongside their main industries and the distribution of the industrial population simply reflected this fact. The locational attraction of the coalfields, most of which were sited on or near the coast and close to iron-ore deposits, explains why the basic industries, dependent on steam for motive power, ferrous metals for fabrication and good ports for their export outlets, clustered in a limited geographical area before 1914. In consequence, in 1907, 60% of the insured population in manufacturing industry was concentrated in four main areas: (i) South Wales, (ii) the North East coast of England, (iii) Lancashire and (iv) mid-Scotland.

As long as these areas remained prosperous and the demand for the products of the basic trades was maintained at a high level, then it mattered little whether or not the newer industries of the period were locating their factories in other parts of the country. Consequently, the depression of the 1920's was all the more devastating in its effects. Though no part of the economy escaped heavy unemployment, the London and Midlands areas were at least partially buttressed by the growth of the newer and expanding industries, while London itself was still the centre of the international finance and business market.[1] Unlike the basic industries, the newer trades were less influenced by purely technical considerations in their choice of site. No longer was the location of a particular basic material the chief deciding factor. Most of

[1] For example, in 1923 the numbers employed in the five main declining industries (coal mining, cotton textiles, shipbuilding, ship repairing and iron and steel) as a proportion of the total insured population was only 1·1% in London and 12·3% in the Midlands area; it was as high as 24·3% in Scotland, 35·8% in Lancashire, 49% in the North and 59·1% in Glamorgan and Monmouthshire. See *Distribution of the Industrial Population*, Royal Commission Report, App. 2; 1939–40, Cmd. 6153, iv.

the newer industrial products then being developed used a wide variety of materials and bought-out parts which were not only of ubiquitous origin but were not appreciably changed in weight during manufacture. This meant that other determinants, in particular that of a large and concentrated market, were more likely to influence the final choice of location. Thus, with the added flexibility and efficiency of modern forms of transport, it was not surprising that the motor-car, light engineering, electrical apparatus, photographic equipment, scientific instruments and the rapidly growing service trades should make London and the Midlands their main choice of location. Whereas, for example, the number of insured workers in the traditional manufacturing areas rose by 4·6% in the period 1923–37, that in the Midlands area and London and the Home Counties increased by 35·5%.

Just as her industrial organization had been inadequate to meet the economic changes demanded of it after 1918, so the geographical immobility of resources impeded the achievement of a balanced pattern of industrial location without the aid of centralized action. The problem was, in fact, self-perpetuating. Because of the economic difficulties of the traditional areas of industry, the newer and expanding trades were unwilling to locate their plants there, while those men and women who migrated to seek employment elsewhere were mainly the younger and more enterprising members of the community, which only worsened, rather than relieved, the plight of those who remained. Moreover, the high cost of providing relief for the large numbers of unemployed was reflected in the form of increased local rates which added to the burden of businesses already hard-pressed.

Eventually the Government was forced to take direct action. By 1932 the average rate of unemployment in the depressed areas had risen to 38% of the insured population compared with $22\frac{1}{2}$% for the country as a whole. In West Cumberland it was as high as 46% and in South Wales 41%, and in every case the position for male workers was relatively worse than that for females. In addition there was serious *under*-employment in the main industries of these regions as a good deal of short-time was worked. Between 1932 and 1938, for every 10 factories established in the Midlands and London areas, only one was set up in the depressed areas: over the inter-war period as a whole, while more than half a million people migrated *to* the London area, 400,000 moved *away* from the North East coast and South Wales.[1]

Such attempts as were made to remedy the situation were first concerned with encouraging labour to move out of the depressed areas. Thus, the Industrial Transference Board was established in 1928 to give financial aid to families wishing to migrate to the more prosperous centres, and various training schemes were implemented for young workers. It was soon recognized, however, that this was only a partial solution to the problem and that, in future, attention ought to be given to the problem of attracting new industries into the areas of heavy unemployment rather than encouraging labour to move out. In 1934 the Special Areas Act was passed in order to set up the Commissioners for Special Areas. Their principal task was to facilitate the economic development and social improvement of areas in Central Scotland, South Wales, West Cumberland and on the North East coast, then the chief sufferers from unemployment. In such localities the Government established Trading Estates on which factories were built and let to manufacturers. In 1937 an amending Act was passed by which the Commissioners were also empowered to contribute towards the rents, income tax and rates of industrial undertakings for a period of up to five years. In addition, the Special Areas Reconstruction Association was formed in 1936 to grant loans to small firms wishing to establish plants in the Special Areas, and supplementary aid was provided by the Nuffield Trust and other private or semi-public bodies. In all, loans of nearly £5 million were made available to industrialists between 1934–9 and Government rearmament contracts were also directed to firms in these regions.

By 1939 some 12,000 people were employed in Government-owned factories in the Special Areas. Nevertheless, their economies were still highly unbalanced. The distribution of industrial employment was such that 60·4% was concentrated in those industries, e.g. coal-mining, shipbuilding, iron and steel etc., which were declining or expanding less than the national average for all industry, and only 29·2% in those industries, e.g. motor-cars, electrical

---

[1] As a whole the population of Great Britain rose by 6·3% between 1923 and 1937. But, whereas in London and the Home Counties it increased by 16·4% and in the Midlands by 10·4%, in Lancashire it fell by 0·2%, in the North by 3·5% and in Glamorgan and Monmouthshire by 11·2%.

goods etc., which were expanding more than the national average. The number of women employed per 100 men in these areas was 25 compared with the national average of 37. Unemployment was still 18% of the insured population and double that for the rest of the U.K. economy, and what improvement there had been since the beginning of the decade was largely due to the substantial rate of migration from those regions and the smaller rate of population growth there than in the rest of the country.

In 1937 the Barlow Commission was appointed. By now it was becoming increasingly recognized that the problems of any particular depressed area could not be effectively tackled unless they were related to distribution of industry and employment policy as a whole. The Commission had as its terms of reference the causes and effects of the present distribution of industrial population in Great Britain and, more particularly, the consideration of the social, economic or strategic disadvantages which arise from the concentration of industries in large towns or in particular areas of the country. Its report, published in 1940, strongly recommended that consideration should be given to means by which the geographical structure of industry might be redeveloped, decentralized and dispersed.[1] The importance attributed to the subject was later emphasized in the White Paper on Employment Policy of 1944 which proposed measures to check the development of unemployment in particular industries and areas. These measures, it stated, would be an integral part of the Government's post-war policy of maintaining a high and stable level of employment. In other words, the Government now accepted responsibility for minimizing structural maladjustments and inflexibilities by a policy which both encouraged the mobility of labour and controlled the location of industry.

To further this aim, the Distribution of Industry Act was passed in 1945, scheduling four 'Development' Areas[2] (the successors of the pre-war 'Special' Areas) and laying down the powers by which the Board of Trade and the Treasury could assist new firms

[1] For further details see *Distribution of the Industrial Population*. Royal Commission. Report; 1939–40, Cmd 6153, iv.

[2] i.e. North Eastern, West Cumberland, South Wales and Monmouthshire and Central Scotland. South Lancashire and Wrexham were added in 1946, Merseyside and the Highlands in 1949 and North East Lancashire in 1953.

to establish factories or branch units in the areas. Thus the Board of Trade might build factories and purchase land, make loans to industrial estate companies, reclaim derelict land and provide factories for improved basic services, e.g. transport, power, lighting etc. Additional concessions which might be granted to the individual firms included subsidized rents, cheap service facilities, increased raw material quotas and special allocations of houses for key workers.

It was also intended that the Government should be given authority to prohibit the construction of factories in areas where 'serious disadvantages would arise from further industrial development', but legislation was never passed to this effect. Instead, every industrialist who wished to erect buildings over 10,000 square feet in area was required to furnish the Board of Trade with particulars of his proposed plans, while under the Town and Country Planning Act, 1947, applications to local authorities for industrial buildings of over 5,000 square feet have had to be accompanied by an Industrial Development Certificate stating that the 'development in question can be carried out consistently with the proper distribution of industry'. Legislation specifically designed to disperse people and industry from congested urban areas was provided by the New Towns Act, 1946, and its complement, the Town Development Act, 1952.[1]

These measures, coupled with the selective granting of building licences and the need for Treasury consent where a loan of £10,000 or more was required, have given the Government very substantial control over the siting of new factories since the war. In fact, 29% of the national industrial building undertaken between 1945 and 1955 was located in the Development Areas, although these areas account for only 18% of the total insured population in manufacturing industry. At the same time, it must be recalled that general economic conditions, e.g. the scarcity of labour and high housing costs in London and the Midlands, have made these regions relatively less attractive as industrial sites than they used to be, while the large pool of unskilled labour, low rents and cheap service facilities in the Development Areas have exerted a strong pull, particularly for branch plants of established firms whose main production units are located close to the centre of their industries' research activities.

[1] See p. 77.

Between the end of the war and mid-1957 the economies of the Development Areas increasingly prospered. By December 1956 their average unemployment rate had fallen to 2·0% compared with a national average of 1·4%; and at that time most of the difference was explained by the higher proportion of unemployables and older men out of work for a long period in the Development Areas. And although during 1958 and early 1959 the unemployment rate in these regions rose to 3·5% and the total manufacturing labour force is now only slightly in excess of that 10 years ago, the proportion of those engaged in the newer industries has steadily risen. Thus, while the numbers engaged in those industries which since the war have either declined or expanded less than the national average[1] have fallen to two-fifths of the total labour force, those in the industries expanding more than the national average have risen to nearly one-quarter. Moreover, although the newer industries still only account for 15% of the total employment, they have been responsible for 40 to 45% of the *increase* in employment between 1939 and 1957. For example, the electronics, aircraft manufacturing, synthetic fibres, light chemicals, office equipment and precision instrument industries between them enlarged their numbers by over 120,000. The Development Areas' share of the electrical goods, clothing and vehicle trades has expanded from 5·3 to 9·7%, whereas that of the mining and quarrying, building and contracting and metal manufacturing industries has contracted from 30·3 to 25·3%. The number of women per 100 men employed is now 48. In all, there are now some 44 Government Trading Estates on which 1,100 firms of all kinds at present provide employment for over 200,000 workers—more than 15 times the pre-war number.

At the same time, specialized pockets of unemployment both within the Development Areas and in other parts of the country, e.g. Cornwall, North East Suffolk and certain coastal belts of Devon, Kent, Yorkshire, Norfolk and Lincolnshire, have continued to cause anxiety; and it was to encourage further industry into these regions that a new act—the Distribution of Industry (Industrial Finance) Act—was passed in 1958. Under this legislation the Government was given power to extend its practice of making

[1] As measured by the rate of change in employment between 1939 and 1953.

grants or loans to industrialists wishing to set up factories in the scheduled Development Areas to apply also to those contemplating production in a wide range of new areas suffering from high and persistent unemployment.[1] At that time the places listed as qualifying for support, including those mentioned above and other parts of Scotland and Wales, employed 7% of the working population of the country but accounted for 17% of the unemployed. It was intended to review the list every six months, and in fact new areas were designated in February 1959 which increased the number of employees living in these regions by 3%. To advise and assist the movement of industry to these areas of unemployment the Government reconstituted and extended the powers of the Development Areas Treasury Advisory Committee (D.A.T.A.C.), a body which could now grant loans to firms setting up or expanding in the scheduled areas.

Finally, in April 1960, the Local Employment Act 1960 came into effect. This legislation supersedes all previous Government measures to deal with the problem of industrial location in areas of high unemployment though in fact it is more a consolidation and extension of such legislation. Industrial Development Certificates now have to be obtained by anyone wishing to establish industrial buildings of 5,000 square feet or more, and it is expected that the Board of Trade will exert its powers of refusing to grant certificates to those industrialists seeking to build factories in areas of low unemployment more strictly than in the past, while doing everything to steer industry into the new Development Districts scheduled under the Act. These Districts—the successors of the Development Areas—are defined as localities in which a high rate of unemployment exists or is expected and is likely to persist.[2] On the whole, their coverage, which is subject to review from time to time, is more concentrated and clearly demarcated than heretofore. One of the main features of the new legislation is its more positive financial inducements to firms contemplating setting up factories in the Development Districts. These include (i) the letting of Government-built factories at favourable terms, (ii) grants to firms

[1] Roughly defined as 4% or over of the insured labour force.
[2] For a full list of these areas, which employ 12% of the total labour force, see *Ministry of Labour Gazette*, April 1960. Their total unemployment in March 1960 amounted to 141,500, some 33% of the national figure.

building their own premises (a completely new measure), and (iii) on the advice of an independent committee, loans or grants to firms for the purposes of purchasing plant and equipment. In the first annual report on the operation of the Act, it was stated that the Board of Trade had offered some £50½ million in loans and grants for industrial projects in 1960 and had given approval for the building of 74 factories or extensions of factories, including several major projects envisaged by the leading motor-car manufacturers.

Quite apart from these localized problems of the post-war period, the industrial distribution of the U.K. population as a whole has undergone some important changes. As new and more easily transportable sources of power, e.g. electricity, petroleum and atomic energy, have been developed, and as there is an increasing substitution of the virtually ubiquitous synthetic materials for their more rigidly located natural equivalents, the choice of factory location has widened and has become more dependent on purely economic factors than heretofore. Thus the 'agglomerative' dis-economies of the traditional manufacturing areas, and in particular

TABLE 6

ESTIMATED NUMBER OF INSURED EMPLOYEES
BY REGION, GREAT BRITAIN,
MID-JUNE 1948 AND END-MAY 1961

Region	Number (000's)		Percentage increase from 1948 to 1961
	1948	1961	
London & South Eastern	5,073	5,670	11·7
Eastern & Southern	1,982	2,436	22·9
South Western	1,060	1,266	19·4
Midlands	1,960	2,238	14·2
North Midlands	1,369	1,565	14·3
East and West Ridings	1,774	1,885	6·3
North Western	2,892	3,003	3·8
Northern	1,219	1,302	6·8
Scotland	2,095	2,155	2·9
Wales	925	970	4·9
Great Britain	20,349	22,490	10·7

Source: *Ministry of Labour Gazette.*

the acute scarcity of labour and high rents of the London and Midlands areas, have led industrialists to seek elsewhere for sites fo their plants.

The overall trends in the pattern of industrial location since 1948 are shown in Table 6 opposite. The chief movement of the industrial population over the past thirteen years has clearly been away from the traditional areas of manufacturing towards Southern England and the Midlands, a fact which in turn reflects the changing emphasis of U.K. industrial output away from textiles, coal-mining and heavy engineering towards the newer trades of electrical engineering, light chemicals, aircraft, motor vehicles etc. Within these developments must be mentioned one of the boldest experiments of recent times, viz. the establishment of 15 New Towns, e.g. Crawley, Hemel Hempstead, Harlow, Corby, East Kilbride etc., which in 1961 had a combined population of 462,570. Eight of these were planned as industrial dispersion outlets from the London area and have expanded their residential population by over 226,000 since they were first scheduled between December 1946 and October 1949; some 56,463 are employed in the 362 new factories established since 1946. The remainder of the New Towns are associated with industrial trading estates in the South Wales, North East England and mid-Scottish development areas.[1] A number of other towns, mostly within 40–60 miles of London (e.g. Aylesbury, Swindon and Basingstoke), are expanding under the provisions of the Town Development Act 1952. In each case the aim is to accommodate people and industry from congested urban areas, the cost of expansion being shared between the receiving local authority, its county council and the authority 'exporting' people and industry.

It is still too early to judge the net result of these changes, but on the face of it the balance of the economy has been greatly stabilized. There is less dependence both of individual regions on particular industries and of particular industries on individual regions for their respective prosperities. Naturally, certain geographical areas remain more vulnerable than others to trade fluctuations, but the likelihood of their suffering from serious

[1] For further particulars of the role of industry in the New Towns see J. H. Dunning, 'Manufacturing Industry in the New Towns', *Manchester School of Economic and Social Studies*, Vol. XXVIII, No. 2, May 1960.

unemployment has been substantially reduced. Moreover, there is no real evidence that the Government's Distribution of Industry policy has seriously impaired the manufacturing costs of firms who have been induced to establish their factories in certain areas but would have preferred to go elsewhere.[1]

---

[1] See, for example, D. C. Hague and P. Newman, *Costs in Alternative Locations: the Clothing Industry*, Paper XV of N.I.E.S.R. C.U.P., 1952; and D. C. Hague and J. H. Dunning, 'Costs in Alternative Locations: the Radio Industry', *Review of Economic Studies*, 1954–5, XXII, no. 59; W. F. Luttrell, *Factory Location and Industrial Movement*, 2 vols. N.I.E.S.R., 1962.

III

ENERGY AND POWER
IN THE TWENTIETH CENTURY

Energy and living standards

The amount of power consumed by a country is an indication both of its industrialization and of its wealth. Each of the basic industrial developments in the United Kingdom since the middle of the eighteenth century has been closely associated with the discovery of new kinds of energy and improved methods by which it may be converted into motive power. Water, coal, electricity, mineral oil and now atomic energy—each has led to the creation of new industries, the exploitation of new production techniques and the introduction of new materials. Those countries with a plentiful

TABLE 7

NATIONAL INCOME AND FUEL AND POWER
CONSUMPTION 1960

	Population (m)	Income per capita (equivalent in £ p.a.)	Fuel consumption (equivalent per capita tons p.a.)
U.S.A.	180·7	816	8·65
Canada	17·8	550	7·77
Great Britain	52.5	387	5·04
Belgium	9·2	351	4·20
W. Germany	43·5	345	3·96
Netherlands	11·5	287	2·99
Italy	49·4	182	1·55
Japan	93·2	122	1·40
India	432·6	22	0·15

Source: A. Parker, 'Energy income and capital', *World Energy, Financial Times Survey*, September 1962.

and cheap supply of these resources have throughout the past 200 years raised their industrial stature relatively to that of their competitors. Today, as Table 7 shows, there is a close relationship between the amount of energy a country consumes and its living standards. The United States, with the highest *per capita* income is also the largest *per capita* consumer, whereas India with the lowest standard of living uses the least energy; Great Britain, with a *per capita* income approximately one-half that of the United States and 17 times that of India, has a consumption equal to 58% of the former and 33 times that of the latter. Moreover, this kind of relationship is likely to be even more marked in the future as the industrial applications of certain forms of power, e.g. coal and oil, are widening. Not only are these fuels being used for generating light, heat, power etc., but they are the basis of important synthetic materials, e.g. plastics and man-made fibres, which are assuming an increasingly important role in world industrial development.

The relationship between the growth in real national income and in energy consumption in the United Kingdom from 1870 to 1960 is illustrated in Table 8. Though, in the main, spurts of industrial growth have been accompanied by large increases of energy consumption, in recent years the average ratio between the 2 variables has ranged between 3 : 1 in the period 1930–40 and 2 : 1 since 1950.[1] In the former period the balance of the economy shifted away from the major coal-consuming industries, and there were considerable fuel economies as a result of technical advances in the generation of gas and electricity and improvements in boiler and furnace techniques. In the last decade, however, there has not only been a resurgence of industrial activity but also a reversal of the earlier trend, in that those industries with a fuel consumption above the average, e.g. iron and steel, chemicals and engineering, have been amongst those expanding the most rapidly.

As Table 9 shows, since the end of the war the large increase in energy consumption has been accompanied by a change both in the composition of the primary fuels used and in the relative role of primary and secondary energy: indeed, many industries today rely almost exclusively on the 'processed' fuels such as gas

[1] If one takes a different 10-year period the above relationships may differ slightly. Thus for the years 1945–54, the ratio between the rate of growth of national income and energy consumption works out at 1·33 : 1.

TABLE 8

TOTAL DOMESTIC FUEL CONSUMPTION AND NATIONAL INCOME, UNITED KINGDOM

Approximate average annual rates of change for intervals within the period 1870–1960

(Per cent change per annum)

	1870–1880	1881–1890	1891–1900	1901–1910	1911–1920	1921–1930	1931–1940	1941–1950	1951–1960
(1) *Fuel Consumption* ..	2·6	1·6	1·4	1·0	1·1	0·8	0·7	0·5	1·2
(2) *National income* ..	2·9	2·1	1·8	2·0	1·4	1·3	2·2	1·3	2·5
Ratio of (2) to (1) ..	1·1	1·3	1·3	1·9	1·2	1·5	3·1	2·5	2·1

Source: For period 1870–1950 data derived from Figure 1 in G. H. Daniel, 'Britain's Energy Prospects', *Journal of the Institution of Production Engineers*, February 1956, Vol. 35, pp. 76–93; 1951–60: National income data from A. R. Prest, 'National Income of the United Kingdom 1870–1946', *Economic Journal*, 1948, and Central Statistical Office publication *National Income & Expenditure 1961*. Fuel consumption data from E. A. G. Robinson, 'The Problems of Coal and Energy Policy', London & Cambridge Economic Service Bulletin, *Times Review of Industry*, March 1960. Ministry of Power, *Statistical Digest, 1960*. H.M.S.O., 1961.

TABLE 9

FUEL CONSUMPTION ANALYSED BY SECTOR OF CONSUMPTION 1946 AND 1960[1] UNITED KINGDOM

(million tons coal equivalent (c.e.) and index of consumption for 1960)

Consumption Sector	Coal and solid fuel 1946 c.e.	1960 c.e.	1960 (1946=100)	Oil 1946 c.e.	1960 c.e.	1960 (1946=100)	Electricity 1946 c.e.	1960 c.e.	1960 (1946=100)	Gas[2] 1946 c.e.	1960 c.e.	1960 (1946=100)	Total 1946 c.e.	1960 c.e.	1960 (1946=100)
Domestic	39·7	39·5	99	0·9	2·6	289	8·8	20·0	226	10·3	7·9	765	59·7	70·0	118
Iron and steel	22·5	22·3	99	0·2	4·1	2005	1·9	3·5	184	2·0	3·5	175	26·6	34·4	129
Collieries ..	10·6	5·0	47	—	—	—	1·3	2·6	199	0·1	—	—	12·0	7·6	64
Agriculture	0·5	0·4	80	1·3	1·6	123	0·1	1·2	109	—	—	—	1·9	3·2	174
Other industry	36·2	34·0	94	1·7	18·4	1008	9·9	24·6	248	3·0	5·3	176	50·8	82·4	162
Railways ..	15·3	9·0	58	—	0·4	*	1·1	1·1	100	—	—	—	16·4	11·0	67
Road transport	—	—	—	8·0	17·3	216	0·8	0·3	38	—	—	—	8·8	17·6	204
Air and water transport ..	1·4	0·6	43	0·8	4·8	601	—	—	—	—	—	—	2·2	5·4	246
Miscellaneous ..	16·2	13·6	84	0·4	5·6	1400	3·5	10·4	308	2·2	2·9	132	22·3	32·5	145
Totals	142·4	124·4	87	13·3	54·8	412	27·4	63·7	232	17·6	19·6	111	200·7	264·1	132

[1] Fuels used in the production of other fuels are excluded, only the coal equivalent of the secondary fuel finally consumed is shown.

[2] Includes coke oven gas and creosote/pitch mixtures (1·3 million tons in 1946 and 2·6 million tons in 1960).

* This figure not calculated since the consumption in 1946, in the range of 0·00—0·005 million tons is not known with sufficient accuracy.

Source: Derived from Ministry of Power *Statistical Digest*.

and electricity. Electricity, in particular, has been responsible for effecting a major industrial transformation. While at first this source of power was only readily available in or around the coal-fields, the development of the national grid system, largely completed before the Second World War, made possible the siting of industries in previously rural areas. Not only has electricity allowed a wider choice of location, but also a higher degree of mechanization, since electric motors can be placed almost anywhere and put to many uses for which bulky steam engines and other attendant mechanical systems for energy transmission are unsuitable.

As industry becomes more complex and living standards rise, larger supplies of both primary and processed fuels are necessary; however, it is only since the end of the Second World War that the United Kingdom has been under any real strain to meet her continually growing requirements. Before 1914 Great Britain was completely self-sufficient in her fuel supplies and, in spite of an increasing volume of mineral oil imported, she remained a significant net exporter right up to 1939. Throughout the next eighteen years there was an almost continuous shortage of all kinds of fuels,[1] with the rationing of coal to domestic consumers only coming to an end in early 1958. The past four years have seen a considerable easing of the situation due chiefly to the rapid increase in output from U.K. petroleum refineries and the stabilization of total energy requirements. To appreciate more fully the reasons for these developments and to assess their implications for the future, we shall discuss, first, the development and present-day structure of the main primary and secondary fuel industries, and secondly, a number of broader economic issues likely to affect the demand for and supply of energy and power in the course of the next two decades.

The British coal-mining industry

The British coal industry is today by far the largest industrial employer in the country and supplies some 74% of the country's energy requirements.

In 1800, 18 years after James Watt had invented the steam

---

[1] For example, by 1955 the value of coal imports had risen to £73·7 million, some £20·5 million *more* than coal exports.

engine, the output of coal was 10 million tons; 60 years later, by which time most of British industry had adopted the factory system of operation, it had risen to 80 million tons, an amount then equal to one-half the world supply. A period of rapid and intense industrial expansion brought the total to 225 million tons in 1900 and to a record figure of 287 million tons in 1913, of which 34% was exported.[1] For the next 30 years the trend moved in the opposite direction, not halting until 1945 when the output was 178 million tons. Subsequently production gradually recovered, reaching 224 million tons in 1957, but then swung downwards again to 194 million tons in 1960, due partly to the effects of the 1957–8 recession and the changing pattern of national output, but mainly to the increased efficiency of coal utilization, higher than average temperatures and the growing competition from oil.[2] The consumption of coal has in fact fallen more quickly than output with the consequence that stocks have accumulated. These amounted to some 23·6 million tons in December 1960.

Employment in coal-mining has also fluctuated. Throughout the nineteenth century it rose steadily and by 1913 had reached its peak of 1,100,000. During the next 25 years the labour force dwindled: in 1938 only 782,000 were employed and in 1946, 697,000. Then followed a period of increased recruitment, but this was only temporary and the labour force which had reached 724,000 in 1948 dropped again to 699,000 in 1958 and to 607,000 in 1960.

As we have seen in Chapter I, British coal-mining suffered an almost continuous decline in the inter-war period in sharp contrast to its earlier prosperity. The expansion of foreign production and the substitution of alternative fuels led to a marked fall in exports, while in spite of a rise of some 50% in industrial output between 1924 and 1937, the domestic consumption of coal rose by only 2%. The resultant difficulties of the industry were aggravated by falling productivity and poor industrial relations.

---

[1] The overseas earnings from the sale of British coal in these years were of even greater importance than their value indicates. The system whereby Britain was supplied with overseas products in exchange for coal meant that ships which brought foreign goods to these shores left laden with British coal. If there had been no coal exports a far larger proportion of shipping would, in fact, have had to leave British ports in ballast, with a consequent increase in freight rates.

[2] Between 1957 and 1960, while the inland consumption of coal *fell* by nearly 16 million tons, that of oil *rose* by 20 million tons.

Various attempts were made to rationalize the industry's structure during these years. First, immediately after the 1914-18 war, a Coal Industry Commission, under the chairmanship of Lord Sankey, was set up to investigate the economic situation of the industry and the causes of unrest among mineworkers. The members of the Commission reached divergent conclusions, and no important legislation emerged. Little more successful were the efforts of two Courts of Enquiry, in 1923 and 1924, and a Royal Commission in 1925 (this time under the chairmanship of Lord Samuel) to find a constructive solution to the problem. Eventually the Government was forced to take direct legislative action. In 1930—by which time the situation, aggravated by world depression, had greatly worsened and the industry was literally on the verge of financial collapse—the Coal Mines Act was passed. Its dual purpose was to reorganize the industry by encouraging the combination of mining companies and to promote the orderly co-operative marketing of coal.

In order to further this first aim a Coal Mines Reorganization Commission was set up to advance voluntary amalgamations in the industry, but because of its legal inability to resolve the conflict of interests between mine owners, its efforts were unrewarding. Over-capacity still remained, unemployment in the industry never fell below 100,000 and no single amalgamation was effected. A new attempt to solve these problems was made by the Coal Act of 1938, which replaced the Coal Mines Reorganization Commission by the Coal Commission, a body equipped with powers to effect compulsory reorganization of the industry. The coal owners, however, could still be obstructive and by September 1939, when war broke out, little progress had been made.

During the war coal exports virtually ceased and both the labour force and productivity greatly declined. The problem soon became one of supplying sufficient coal for urgent needs. In 1942 the Government used its emergency powers to take over control of the mines and in the same year acquired, as a result of the provisions of the 1938 Act, the mineral rights in coal, thus removing one of the main barriers to combination. The Ministry of Fuel and Power was created to co-ordinate fuel and power supplies and to promote efficiency in distribution and consumption.

With the post-war situation in mind, the Minister of Fuel and

Power appointed in 1944 a committee of mining engineers under the chairmanship of Mr (later Sir) Charles Reid to examine the techniques of coal production and to advise on methods for making the industry fully efficient. The report compared unfavourably recent trends in British mines with those on the Continent, and found that, whereas the average output per manshift in Dutch, Rhenish and Polish mines increased by 118%, 81% and 54% respectively in the period 1926–36, the corresponding British increase was only 14%. Such figures as these reflected the failure of the coal industry in this country to undertake any major technical improvements or to concentrate mining operations. One great obstacle in the way of full efficiency was the existence of a large number of ill-planned mines of inadequate capacity. Another was the under-mechanization of mines: by 1928 85% of the coal mined in the Ruhr was cut by machinery, compared with 42% in this country, and whereas one worker was employed for every 5 tons of saleable coal mined in Britain, in Holland it was one for every 20–25 tons and in the United States one for every 50 tons. The report, therefore, recommended modernization of layout and reorganization of production programmes on the basis of coal-fields, not individual mines, and argued that the conflicting interests of individual companies made some modification of the system of ownership necessary. And while the Committee did not actually specify the desirability of nationalizing the industry, the National Coal Board, formed three years later, clearly had the broad owner-ship characteristics that the Reid Committee envisaged.

The progress of the coal industry since 1947 is shown in Table 10. Output per manshift has steadily improved and is now higher than ever before.[1] Production of deep-mined coal rose from 175 million tons in 1945 to 214 million tons in 1954 but fell back to 186 million tons in 1960; a further 7 million tons of open-cast coal were also mined in this latter year. It can be seen that the rate of progress since the war has been small compared with that achieved by manu-facturing industry and the price paid has been a high one, for coal-mining is an extractive industry especially subject to the Law of Diminishing Returns.

As mining operations proceed, the more accessible coal de-posits are used up and costs of production rise. In consequence

[1] Output per manshift is now the highest in Europe.

TABLE 10

SELECTED COAL STATISTICS 1947-60

UNITED KINGDOM

	1947	1948	1949	1950	1951	1952	1953	1954	1955	1956	1957	1958	1959	1960
Coal production (mn. tons)[1] ..	197	209	215	216	223	227	224	224	222	222	224	216	205	193
N.C.B. output of deep-mined saleable coal (mn tons)	187	198	203	204	212	214	213	214	210	210	210	201	195	186
Employment (000s)	711	724	720	697	699	716	717	707	704	703	710	699	665	607
Percentage of output mechanically:														
cut	75	76	78	79	81	82	83	84	86	87	88	89	89	90
loaded	2·5	2·5	3·2	3·7	4·2	4·9	5·9	7·3	9·8	14·1	21·5	26·3	31	37
conveyed	75	78	82	85	87	88	89	90	91	92	94	94	94	94
cleaned	48	49	51	52	52	53	54	55	57	59	61	61	61	61
Output of saleable coal per manshift worked (tons) ..	1·09	1·12	1·17	1·21	1·22	1·21	1·22	1·23	1·23	1·23	1·23	1·26	1·33	1·40
Average output per man per year (tons)	263	273	282	293	303	299	296	303	299	299	296	288	294	306
Capital expenditure (£mn)	16	21	28	26	28	40	54	71	77	82	91	96	107	80

[1] Including production from licensed mines and open-cast.

Source: Ministry of Power *Statistical Digest*.

a constant output can be maintained only by sinking new pits or by reconstructing and modernizing existing mines.[1] At the same time production in the post-war period of full employment has been hampered by a shortage of manpower, and in order to make recruitment more attractive several large wage increases have been granted. The wage bill in coal-mining has, therefore, had a proportionately greater effect on the price of coal than corresponding wage increases would have on the cost of production of manufactured products.

Undoubtedly the inadequacy of coal supplies in the period 1945–57 was largely the outcome of neglected investment during the preceding decade when the existing capacity of the industry was more than adequate to meet current demands. The industry's capital position continued to deteriorate during the war years, so that when nationalization eventually took place in 1947 investment on a huge scale had to be undertaken to prevent a further decline in output. Partly as a result of such intensive reconstruction and capitalization, and partly due to the increased labour force, annual output rose over the next decade by 27 million tons. In 1950 the National Coal Board published the first of its long-term plans for the future of the industry.[2] Drawn up at a time when there was an acute scarcity of all types of fuel, the plan envisaged an increase in the total output of coal to 250 million tons by 1965. Due to changing circumstances, however, both on the supply and demand sides, this target has since been twice reduced, first in 1956 to 240 million tons,[3] and second in October 1959 to 210–215 million tons.[4]

---

[1] In actual fact the National Coal Board has estimated that an annual replacement of 4–5 million tons' capacity is necessary to maintain the present level of output and any expansion of capacity requires a further investment of £11 per ton. E. F. Schumacher, 'Britain's Coal', *National Provincial Bank Review*, November 1957, p. 11.

[2] *Plan for Coal*, N.C.B., 1950.

[3] *Investing in Coal*, N.C.B., 1956.

[4] See *Revised Plan for Coal*, N.C.B., 1959. Included in this figure is an estimated export market of 10 million tons. For further details of this latest plan, see p. 108.

The British oil refining industry

The mineral oil refining industry in the United Kingdom now employs approximately 20,000 persons, and in terms of coal-equivalent[1] its output in 1960 was 75 million tons. The industry is very much a product of the post-war period: manpower is now 6 times and refining capacity 13 times greater than that in 1938 and the United Kingdom is now the fourth largest oil refiner in the world.

TABLE 11

U.K. IMPORTS AND EXPORTS OF MINERAL OIL
1938–60

	Imports				Exports	
	Crude petroleum		Refined petroleum products		Refined petroleum products	
	Quantity '000 tons	Value £mn	Quantity '000 tons	Value £mn	Quantity '000 tons	Value £mn
1938	2,272	5	9,390	41	592	3·7
1946	2,179	10	12,232	78	404	6·5
1948	4,641	31	13,242	126	344	7·2
1951	16,681	159	9,815	145	3,389	32·4
1955	27,854	224	8,537	109	6,281	74·2
1956	28,608	245	9,433	122	7,707	98·5
1957	27,967	281	10,864	157	6,288	88·4
1958	33,747	294	11,135	133	8,398	100·4
1959	39,563	314	12,899	150	8,222	94·5
1960	44,900	334	13,718	145	9,043	99·9

Source: Ministry of Power *Statistical Digest*.

In 1938 Britain imported some 11·6 million tons of oil costing £46·5 million. These supplies were obtained mainly from the United States and the Caribbean area; crude oil accounted for 20% by weight and 11% by value, and refined oil the balance. The position is now quite different, as we see from Table 11. The relative importance of crude oil has increased to such an extent that in 1960 77% by weight and 70% by value of all petroleum imports were

[1] 1 ton of refined petroleum = 1·7 tons of coal.

of this kind. Present U.K. production of refined oil is in excess of domestic consumption and there is now an important export trade in that product. At the same time there have been important changes in the sources of Britain's oil supplies. Owing to her own expanding demands, the United States has ceased to be the world's most important exporter of petroleum products and is now a very large net importer. In consequence the United Kingdom has been forced to seek other markets and the Middle East now supplies 87% of this country's requirements.

The tremendous expansion in oil refining capacity in the United Kingdom is the outcome of a deliberate policy first announced by the British Government in 1948. The underlying motives of the proposed £95 million development programme were (i) the considerable saving of foreign, and particularly dollar, currency which would follow from refining in this country and (ii) the need to establish a petro-chemicals industry. A less important but nevertheless cogent reason was the growing differential between the cost of transport of crude oil and refined petroleum products. It was also felt that the technical personnel for manning refineries would be easier to recruit in this country than in the Middle East.

There are now 9 major and 7 subsidiary refineries in this country with a total annual capacity of 50 million tons of oil. Eight of the 9 major refineries are owned by 3 international concerns, the Shell Group, the British Petroleum Company and the U.S. subsidiary Esso Petroleum, which between them accounted for nearly 94% of the total refining capacity in the United Kingdom in December 1961. The British Government is the most important shareholder in the B.P. group.

The ramifications of the oil industry are extremely complex. For example, the transport of oil in such enormous quantities requires a very large fleet of oil tankers. Some 25% of the gross tonnage of the British merchant fleet consists of tankers, and since 1951 such vessels have accounted for over 50% of the output of British shipyards, one-half of which has been exported. In addition, the United Kingdom is now the second largest supplier of plant and equipment for the petroleum industry: some £101 million worth of orders were placed in 1961 by British oil companies, whereas before the war this country was almost completely reliant on imported equipment. Finally, the oil-refining industry is providing a valuable new source of raw materials used in the manufacture of, for example, plastics, synthetic rubber and chemical solvents. As a result, a petro-chemical industry on a considerable scale has been evolved in this country. Developments in this field are further described in Chapter V.

A feature of the current fuel consumption pattern in the United Kingdom is the growing importance of oil as a source of thermal energy relative to that of coal: in the last 12 years, for example,

TABLE 12

MINERAL OIL CONSUMPTION-PATTERN
1950–60 UNITED KINGDOM

	1950		1955		1960	
	mn tons	%	mn tons	%	mn tons	%
Fuel oil (black oils)	5.34	34·9	9·60	41·3	24·32	57·0
Motor spirit	5·20	34·0	6·24	26·8	7·62	17·8
Aviation spirit	·28	1·8	1·70	7·3	1·76	4·2
'Derv' fuel	1·03	6·8	1·60	6·9	2·58	6·0
Other products	3·33	21·8	4·10	17·6	6·41	15·0
	15·28	100	23·24	100	42·69	100

Source: Petroleum Information Bureau. *U.K. Petroleum Industry. Statistics Relating to Consumption and Refinery Production*, 1950, 1955 and 1960.

oil has more than doubled its share of the total fuel supplies. At the same time the composition of refinery output has also undergone some changes. For instance, as Table 12 indicates, the output of fuel oil (the class of oils most competitive with coal) and motor and aviation fuels has increased relative to that of other petroleum products—particularly bitumen and lubricating oils.

Until comparatively recently a feature of the oil refining industry was that the composition of its output was subject to the limitations of joint supply imposed by the chemical constituents in the crude oil. This, however, is no longer the case: by means of appropriate 'cracking' processes, which may be thermal or catalytic, some of the heavier and more complex hydrocarbons can now be converted into simpler hydrocarbons and, by polymerization processes, built up into more complicated structures as required. Elaborate cracking equipment has been particularly prominent in the new refining installations since the war. The industry has thereby acquired a considerable degree of versatility and is now able to adjust the composition of its output to meet changing demand characteristics much more easily than heretofore. Thirty years ago, crude oil could be made to yield only 18% of gasoline—the constituent from which automobile and aviation spirit is now derived; but today, by various technical processes, this proportion can be doubled. The octane number of the gasoline has also been progressively increased, and this has led to greater economy of consumption in internal combustion engines. The growing demand for petro-chemicals is further contributing to the industry's flexibility.

Atomic energy

Atomic energy as a source of power for peaceful uses is now being developed in this country and it is expected that by the early 1970's electricity will be produced from this source of fuel more cheaply than by conventional methods. A brief description of the principles underlying the generation of energy from the nucleus of the atom is given below.

Though the atomic nuclei of all elements contain energy, it can only be released from one naturally occurring element—the metal uranium. This is an isotopic element which consists of two chemically identical atoms of different atomic weight (isotopes), one fissile and the other non-fissile. The former constitutes only a 140th part of naturally occurring uranium; but, because of the chemical identity of the two forms, tedious and inefficient physical methods have to be used to achieve only a very partial separation. In this way a uranium enriched in the fissile form can be obtained for the more advanced nuclear reactors planned for the future.

The simplest form of nuclear reactor now in operation at Calder Hall uses natural uranium. The fissile component is gradually exhausted as it releases its energy, while some of the non-fissile uranium is converted into an artificial element, plutonium. This latter element is fissile, but does not disintegrate completely in the environment in which it is formed. In time, therefore, the initial charge of natural uranium ceases to generate energy at a suitable rate, partly because of the fall in concentration of fissile uranium and partly because of the 'poisoning' (or inhibiting) effects of the fission products. Even so, weight for weight, natural uranium will release about 30,000 times the combustion energy of coal. The world reserves of the metal are large and extraction methods are continually being improved. And though Britain has to import all her uranium, an atomic energy reactor of the Calder Hall type imposes a balance of payments burden which is about one-third of that which a similar amount of energy in the form of mineral oil would involve. Moreover, this cost is likely to become much less in the future, since it is envisaged that a 'breeder' type of reactor will be developed. These are largely self-generating, and able to run also on the plentiful—but previously unusable—non-fissile uranium and on a very plentiful element thorium.[1]

A source of energy with these characteristics seems destined to play a vital role in Britain's economy even though the supplies of alternative fuels are adequate to meet all demands made of them. Even allowing for the recent re-phasing of plans[2] a programme of moderately rapid development is being pursued and, while the contribution of the nuclear reactors to the energy pool will be comparatively insignificant for some time to come, it is anticipated that within the next decade or so one-quarter of the electricity generated in the United Kingdom will be supplied from this source. The countries of Western Europe who have recently combined to pool their knowledge of this subject in an organization known as 'Euratom' also look to nuclear energy for the ultimate solution of their fuel problems.

In contrast, in the United States, where the need for a new source of energy is less urgent than in Western Europe, a nuclear power station of the Calder Hall type is not such an attractive economic proposition. Because of the potential advantages from enriched fuel and breeder reactors, however, research on a large scale is being undertaken there with the object of designing a reactor which will be economical in the context of the relatively abundant American fuel resources.

[1] The total supply of energy in the reserves of uranium and thorium, when used in breeder reactors, has been estimated to exceed by more than a thousand times that in the reserves of all the fossil fuels. See also, R. L. Meier, *Science and Economic Development*, 1956, p. 96 ff.

[2] See pp. 94–5, 105.

Nuclear energy development in the United Kingdom

Atomic energy as a separate project started in Great Britain in 1945, when the Government decided to produce an atomic weapon. The Ministry of Supply was given responsibility for this work and it set up the Atomic Energy Research Establishment at Harwell and the Directorate of Atomic Energy Production at Risley. Later the Atomic Weapons Research Establishment was created. In 1954 responsibility was transferred to an independent body, the United Kingdom Atomic Energy Authority (A.E.A.), which is now organized in two groups—the research and the industrial—with headquarters at Harwell and Risley respectively. In March 1960 the Authority employed 38,500 people, 18,900 non-industrial and 19,600 industrial employees, and its total assets stood at £450 million.

The first results of the research at Harwell were embodied in the establishment of new factories at Springfields, Windscale and Capenhurst to produce fissile materials for military purposes. By 1950, however, sufficient scientific and engineering information had been gathered to make an atomic power station a feasible proposition. Further research at Harwell and Risley led to the preparation of detailed plans, and the construction of the Calder Hall plant, a dual-purpose station designed to produce plutonium and generate electricity, was started in 1953. While Calder Hall was being built and before any experience of the generation of electricity from atomic energy had been gained, the Central Electricity Authority (C.E.A.), faced with a seemingly permanent shortage of solid fuel, and in conjunction with the newly created U.K. Atomic Energy Authority, drew up a £300 million programme for nuclear power which appeared as a White Paper in 1955.[1] At first 12 stations were envisaged to generate a total of 1,500–2,000 million megawatts by 1965, but by early 1957 sufficient progress had been made to enable the programme to be trebled, i.e. £900 million of capacity with a generating power of 5,000–6,000 million megawatts by 1965.[2] In June 1960, however, as a dual result of the changed supply situation of alternative fuels, and of the remarkable economies that had been achieved in the

[1] *A Programme of Nuclear Power*; 1954–5, Cmd 9389, xiii.
[2] 566 House of Commons Debates, 5th series, 5 March 1957.

construction of conventional power stations, the programme was revised a second time—but on this occasion it was curtailed. It is now expected that only 3,000 million megawatts of nuclear plant will be installed by 1966, and a further 2,000 million by 1968.[1] This means, in effect, that the earlier programme for development in the 1960's had been cut back by half.

The building of the new atomic power stations has been entrusted to private industry under the guidance of the U.K.A.E.A.; and, on a voluntary basis, 5 consortia of engineering and constructional firms (which number 18 in all) with suitable expertise have been formed.[2] At the present time 7 power stations are being constructed at Berkeley, Bradwell, Hunterston, Hinkley Point, Dungeness, Sizewell and Trawsfynydd, all scheduled to be completed by 1965. These Central Electricity Generating Board stations will be of the same basic type as Calder Hall, but the reactors will

TABLE 13

SECONDARY ENERGY PRODUCTION
1925-60 UNITED KINGDOM

(1925 = 100)

	Electricity	Gas
1925	100	100
1930	165	108
1935	265	110
1940	435	115
1945	563	146
1950	825	189
1955	1210	209
1956	1320	212
1957	1370	205
1958	1490	207
1959	1590	205
1960	1798	204

Source: Computed from data in Ministry of Power *Statistical Digest*.

[1] *The Nuclear Power Programme;* 1959–60 Cmnd. 1083, xxvii.
[2] A typical consortium consists of manufacturers of electrical equipment, control gear, structural steel and general fabrication, reactor shells, and civil engineers and builders. For further particulars of this facet of integration by co-operation see Edwards and Townsend, op. cit., pp. 259–63.

have a much higher output and the emphasis will be on operational economy. The plutonium produced as a by-product will be subsequently used in the breeder and near-breeder reactors which are likely to be developed in the future. Each power station is expected to take $3\frac{1}{2}$ years to build, and each of the groups is believed to have the resources to start on the construction of 1 new station every year, a rate adequate to meet the present (revised) target of the U.K.A.E.A.

Secondary energy

The processing of primary fuels into secondary energy is of continually increasing importance. Gas and electricity now account for 25% of the country's consumption of all fuels and 30% of its consumption of coal. The country's geographical location, its climate and the social conditions of its people have greatly influenced the pattern of development. Table 13 shows the growth in output of secondary energy between 1925 and 1960. Though the rate of increase in electricity production is seen to be much more marked than that of gas—for example, electricity was responsible for 90% of the increase in secondary fuel production between 1945 and 1960—both sources of energy have progressed relatively to that of the primary fuel from which they are derived.[1] This expansion is partly due to their technical advantages over coal—flexibility, cleanliness and ease of control—partly to the generally rising standard of living, and partly to the inability of solid fuels to meet the rising energy demands of recent years without steeply rising costs. Resulting from these shifts in demand, large amounts of capital have been invested in the electricity and gas industries. In 1957

---

[1] For comparative purposes we give the average annual rates of increase in electric power production for three major industrial countries since 1920.

	1920–38	1945–51	1952–60
Germany	10·4	18·7	8·6
United States	10·5	11·1	7·2
Great Britain	9·9	8·3	7·7

Source: 1920–51 : E. Shankleman, *Steel Review*, 2, April 1956
1952–60 : *Annual Abstract of Statistics, 1961* ; *Statistical Abstract of the United States, 1955* and *1961*; *The German Economy*. 2nd ed. Deutsches Industrieinstitut 1962.

industrial undertakings purchased 50% of the electricity generated and 29% of the gas, and domestic consumers 30% of the electricity and 54% of the gas. Commercial undertakings, public lighting, public buildings, railways and transport consumed the remainder.

The two secondary fuels are largely complementary to each other in usage. Electricity is pre-eminent in the lighting field and for the production of mechanical energy; gas is used almost entirely for the generation of heat. As a source of thermal energy electricity suffers by comparison with coal and gas, since there is a heavy initial loss in its generation. Nevertheless, because of its greater cleanliness and subsequent saving of labour, electricity is often, on balance, competitive with the other fuels and for certain purposes electric furnaces have marked advantages over their coal-, gas- and oil-fired counterparts. In the production of mechanical energy electricity is both more efficient than either a coal-fired prime mover or a gas-operated engine and more versatile in usage, for electric motors can be constructed in varying sizes and placed in any desired position. Both the secondary fuels are eminently suitable for employment in conjunction with control mechanisms and it is likely that, with the spread of automation, the industrial demand for these fuels will continue to grow.

Structure of the secondary energy industries

These industries are large: electricity supply employs 200,000 people and the gas industry 130,000. Both industries rely almost exclusively on coal as their source of primary energy, but whereas electricity can be processed from a very fine grade of coal, for which there is virtually no other use, gas requires a widely demanded type of coal with a high content of volatile matter. In the manufacture of both fuels there is a loss of energy: in electricity generation because a coal-fired prime mover of low efficiency has to be employed, and in gas manufacture because coal has to be burnt to supply heat for the distillation process. Electricity generation is much more highly capitalized than gas, and with very little more labour it processes $2\frac{1}{2}$ times as much coal as the latter.

Both industries supply products which are subject to marked fluctuations in demand. In consequence, though capacity has to be

D

sufficient to satisfy maximum usage, the load factor (the average proportion of capacity employed at any given moment of time) is only 40 to 45% in the electricity supply industry and 60 to 65% in the gas industry. The domestic consumer who purchases 30% of the electricity and 52% of the gas sold affects the load factor differently in the two industries. In the case of electricity, he helps to stabilize the consumption pattern by making the heaviest demands when the industrial load is at its lowest: in gas, he himself sets the peak load by his domestic cooking requirements on Sunday at midday, while at other times his needs are at an average load factor of only 10 to 15%.

Electricity tariffs are, therefore, designed in favour of the domestic rather than the industrial user, while in gas the reverse is the case. In the United States and Germany, where shift-working is far more prevalent, the load factors of 60 and 50% respectively are higher, with tariffs more strongly in favour of the industrial consumer than in this country.

It is obvious that the higher the load factor, the more fixed charges can be spread. For example, between 1948 and 1960 the load factor for electricity was raised from 42 to 47% and, although operating costs rose by between 60% and 80% in these years, total production costs rose by only 40%. New methods for increasing the load factor are continually being devised. Thus, a cross-Channel electric cable completed in 1961 will enable this country and France, with their peak loads at different times, to exchange electricity in either direction. Likewise, when the most efficient steam and atomic power stations are in operation on a large scale, they will supply electricity in off-peak periods to pump water into storage reservoirs; at the peak this water is used to generate hydro-electricity. At Loch Awe in Argyllshire the largest British hydro-electric project yet undertaken[1]—at a cost of £24·5 million—is to incorporate these features.

Coke, produced jointly with coal gas, has presented the gas industry with marketing problems as the demand for the former has increased more slowly than for the latter. However, the increasing demand for smokeless fuel is easing this disposal problem.[2]

[1] See *The Times*, 18 July 1957.
[2] The demand for coke is likely to grow further as a result of the Clean Air Act of 1956.

At the same time the industry is increasing its output of gas from sources other than coal, e.g. by purchasing coke-oven gas and oil refineries' waste gas, and methods for the complete gasification of coal are being developed. The other coal gas by-products, viz. ammonia liquor and coal tar, are valuable sources of chemicals. The demand for coal-tar chemicals is growing rapidly and is likely to continue to do so as the output of the plastics and man-made fibres industries increases. In the meantime, benzole, the fraction giving benzene and other aromatic hydrocarbons, is used in admixture with petroleum to the extent of 50 million gallons per annum.

Electricity supply: organization and features

The electricity supply industry was nationalized in 1948, and 560 separate undertakings were amalgamated into one comprehensive supply organization. Taking into account the minor changes in administrative structure in 1955, the nationalized industry then consisted of a Central Electricity Authority, 11 semi-autonomous Area Boards and the South of Scotland Electricity Board. The Authority was made responsible for the generation of electricity and its transmission to points of bulk supply, and the Area Boards for its distribution to consumers. The Authority was also given powers of general supervision over the industry. After 6 years of operation a Committee of Enquiry into the industry was set up,[1] and it recommended certain changes which were given effect in the Electricity Act 1957. From 1 January 1958 onwards the industry has comprised the Electricity Council, a Central Electricity Generating Board and 12 Area Boards. The Electricity Council's functions are to promote and assist the efficient operation of the Generating and Area Boards, as part of a co-ordinated system of supply in England and Wales.

On Vesting Day, 1 April 1948, the publicly owned industry had a total generating capacity of 10·36 million kilowatts; by 1 January 1958 it had more than doubled to 21·5 million kilowatts. Fifty-two power stations were brought into commission and many existing

[1] *Electricity Supply Industry* Committee Report, 1955–6, Cmd 9672, xv·

power stations were enlarged or modernized in the same period. Investment is continuing on a large scale.[1]

As we have seen, electricity in Great Britain is generated almost entirely in coal-fired steam-operated plants. Gas turbines running on oil are producing a small proportion of the electricity supply—mainly for peak-load generation—but they are more costly to operate. The new power station on Southampton Water is dual-fired, and the Esso Petroleum Company has undertaken to supply oil from its nearby refinery at Fawley at a price which will make the power station no more costly to operate than one running on coal.

The upward trend in electricity consumption is likely to continue in the foreseeable future. By 1965 it is estimated that the coal equivalent of the electricity generated will rise from its present figure of 47 million tons to 70 million tons.[2] With the supply of coal unlikely to rise at a commensurate rate atomic energy and oil will undoubtedly be increasingly used for operating power stations. In 1965 the distribution of power stations by type of primary fuel used is likely to be as follows:

TABLE 14

ELECTRICITY POWER STATIONS—ANTICIPATED DISTRIBUTION BY TYPE OF PRIMARY FUEL USED IN 1965

Type of primary fuel	Mn tons of coal equivalent	%
Oil	5	7
Atomic energy	9	13
Coal	56	80
Estimated total energy requirements	70	100

The gas supply industry: organization and features

Until the First World War gas was used almost exclusively for

[1] See p. 109–10.
[2] Sir Josiah Eccles, 'The Electricity Council Looks Forward', *Times Review of Industry*, January 1958, p. 11.

UNIVERSITY OF VICTORIA
LIBRARY
Victoria, B C.

domestic heating and lighting. Subsequently, as a result of the increased demand for coal-tar chemicals for the manufacture of munitions, and later for the manufacture of dyestuffs, the by-products became valuable and there was a radical change in the economics of gas manufacture and an appreciable increase in its rate of growth.

Until 1949, when the industry was nationalized, over a thousand undertakings existed, each one operating independently of the other, some two-thirds of which were owned by private companies and the remainder by local authorities. On Vesting Day, 1 May 1949, the industry passed into the ownership of 12 Area Gas Boards directly answerable to the Minister of Fuel and Power. No central authority was set up as in the case of the electricity supply industry, but an advisory and co-ordinating body, the Gas Council,[1] was created to be responsible for capital and finance, labour relations, and research affecting the whole industry.

At the time of take-over the condition and efficiency of the separate undertakings varied enormously; the majority, however, were suffering from a lack of maintenance and some were so obsolete as to warrant closure as soon as alternative supplies could be provided. The greater part of capital expenditure since 1949 has therefore had to be devoted to the replacement of existing plant. By improved methods of working, closing small and unprofitable installations, and concentrating manufacture in larger and more economic units, a progressive increase in productive efficiency has been achieved. By 1958–9 the overall thermal efficiency of production[2] had risen to 77·2%—a 5·2% increase over the corresponding figure for 1948.

The distribution of gas and electricity

To enable the geographical variations in demand to be met, with as little surplus capacity as possible, both the electricity and gas supply industries have evolved grid systems whereby the producing areas are inter-connected. In electricity a network of this kind was already

[1] Composed of a chairman, deputy chairman and the chairmen of the 12 Area Boards.
[2] Measured by the ratio of the thermal output of gas products to the thermal output of coal and oil.

in existence in 1939, but since that date large increases in demand and the scattered location of power stations have imposed such a strain on the existing load that a super-imposed grid (or the super-grid as it is called) is in course of construction. In the gas industry there were very few arrangements for pooling before 1949, but the policy of rationalization pursued by the various gas boards has resulted in some progress in that direction and inter-connections exist over many wide areas. A complete grid coverage, however, is unlikely for some time because of the very high capital cost involved.

Fuel needs and prospects

Assuming that economic progress and rising living standards continue to be closely related to fuel consumption as in the past, the problem of estimating future energy requirements is first and foremost one of estimating the expected rate of increase of the national income.

Between 1948 and 1954 the national income per head of the working population of the United Kingdom rose at an average rate which, if continued for 25 years, would have enabled the British standard of living—allowing for changes in the age-composition and size of the population—to be doubled. Although this would be a higher rate of increase than anything achieved for any similar period in this country in the past, it has been much quoted as being both a feasible and desirable target. Accordingly a number of estimates of Britain's energy requirements to meet such a rate of growth have been made.[1] The most thorough and reliable are probably those of Dr G. H. Daniel of the Ministry of Power. Daniel postulates two possible rates of growth of national income, viz. (i) 3·0% compound

[1] *The Economist*, 27 November 1954, on 3 different bases, gave the estimate as 323, 358, and 473 million tons in 1980. The Esso Petroleum Co. has also projected the country's overall fuel requirements to 1980, and has obtained a value of 500 million tons of coal equivalent, or 85 million tons above the corresponding 'high' estimate value in Table 14. This estimate has been made by analogy: in the American economy real national income per head of the population was thought to be twice as high as in the United Kingdom, so it was estimated that doubling of the British standard of living would involve in 25 years' time the American consumption of fuel per head of population. America, however, is a country with an abundant supply of fossil fuels so that there has been no strong incentive to the promotion of fuel economy.

per annum, which is the rate of increase necessary to fulfil the aim mentioned above, and (ii) 1·7% compound per annum, which was the actual rate of increase achieved in the inter-war period, and is roughly equivalent to that achieved since 1954.

Demand for fuel

In common with most other authors who have produced long-range estimates of fuel requirements, Dr Daniel has been obliged to neglect the price factor. This is an inevitable consequence of the absence of

TABLE 15

ESTIMATED FUTURE TOTAL INLAND FUEL
CONSUMPTION[1]

(*Million tons of coal equivalent per annum*)

United Kingdom

	High	Medium	Low
1954	245	245	245
1960	278	273	261
1965	309	299	277
1970	342	326	291
1975	377	354	305
1980	415	385	320
1985	458	418	336

[1] *Bases of estimates*
   The *high* and *medium* estimates are made on the assumption that the national income will double in 25 years and that every 1% increase in the national output is accompanied by an increase in fuel consumption of 0·7 and 0·6% respectively.
   The *low* estimate is made on the assumption that the national income will grow at the inter-war rate of 2% per annum and fuel consumption increase 0·6 times as fast.
   All figures except 1954 are projections.

Source: Dr G. H. Daniel, 'Britain's Energy Prospects', *Journal of the Institution of Production Engineers*, February 1956, Vol. 35, pp. 76–93.

satisfactory bases for projecting the relative prices of the various fuels. It is not, however, a serious shortcoming, since the demand for energy, as a whole, tends at any given time to be inelastic; and so, provided the supply can respond, the more insistent demands are usually satisfied. In fact Daniel assumes a long-term rate of increase of fuel consumption intermediate between the average for the years 1900–50 when it was 50% of that of the national income, and 1948–54 when it was 75%. He feels that the rate of increase in consumption in the first period was below average because of exceptionally large economies in fuel consumption, while that of the latter was unduly high because of the sudden spurt in demand due to the removal of war-time restrictions on the use of fuel, particularly all kinds of oil. In the absence of such factors, an intermediate value therefore seems probable in the foreseeable future.

The supply position

These estimated demands and the likelihood of their satisfactory realization will depend largely on the pattern of our future fuel supplies. Britain's only indigenous fuel is coal, of which she has a reasonable abundance. A survey carried out in 1945 estimated reserves to be approximately 40,000 million tons, or the equivalent of 200 years' supply at current extraction rates. Abroad there is a plentiful supply of both liquid and solid mineral fuels, and as yet only a fraction of the world has been adequately explored for such reserves. Africa, for example, has vast coal seams awaiting development, while the total known oil reserves of the world have been estimated to be adequate for over 100 years at enormously increased consumption rates.[1] The physical resources are therefore adequate for satisfying the greatest of demands. The advent of atomic energy has, of course, greatly altered the whole energy picture, since the reserves of uranium and thorium when used in breeder reactors are virtually self-generating and likely to be almost inexhaustible. And as the limited successes already achieved at Harwell have shown, there are likely to be developments in the harnessing of thermo-nuclear energy which may well mean that the energy locked up in

[1] In addition, new discoveries are being made all the time. It is now believed, for example, that the oilfields in the Sahara will probably equal or surpass those in the Middle East. Canada also has promising oilfields, and they are believed to be comparable in importance to those in the U.S.A. New oilfields are also being discovered in various parts of South America.

the abundant lighter elements, such as hydrogen and lithium, can be utilized.

The limitations on the satisfaction of our future energy needs, and their likely composition, are thus economic and political rather than technical in character; indeed, perhaps the two main determinants are the relative production costs of the main sources of energy on the one hand and the availability of foreign currency on the other. At the present time, for example, oil is plentiful and cheap, and is displacing coal to such an extent that the National Coal Board is no more than hoping to stabilize output at or around the 1958 level over the next decade. As regards atomic power, the revised programme envisages a contribution of some 9 million tons of coal-equivalent by 1965, 18 million tons by 1970 and 27 million tons by 1975. Thus, apart from a small contribution to the energy pool likely to be made by water power and natural gas, the balance, and an increasingly important part of the total, will have to be met by oil. A hypothetical balance sheet of the future supply position of the major fuels is given in Table 16.[1] This has been based on Dr Daniel's *medium* estimate given earlier in Table 15.[2]

The range of the figures illustrates the difficulties associated with predicting the future role of the oil refining industry in the United Kingdom. It is, of course, true that there are only certain areas in which the various types of fuel compete with each other: thus, while most kinds of fuel oil and coal are largely substitutable, the lighter oils are geared to supplying the needs of road transport and aviation. Since in 1958 the inland consumption for these latter purposes was two-fifths of the output of U.K. refineries, this means that an increase in consumption at the rate envisaged by the *medium* estimate for total fuel would require a minimum of some 40 million

[1] This Table has not been changed since it was first prepared in 1960. It is interesting to note, however, that the actual consumption of fuel in 1960 was 264·1 million tons coal equivalent, made up of 195·7 million tons of coal, 65·6 million tons of oil, 1·7 million tons of water power and 1·0 million tons of nuclear energy. See *Britain, An Official Handbook*, H.M.S.O., 1962, p. 275.

[2] For alternative projections see 'Energy and Expansion', *National Institute Economic Review*, Sept. 1960. The Institute assume rather more fuel economies than Daniel and would appear to pay insufficient attention to the expansion of oil for transportation purposes. In consequence their estimates are usually lower than those given in Table 16 and in our opinion they are unduly low.

tons of coal-equivalent to be produced in 1980. A further 15–20 million tons of coal-equivalent, which is likely to be demanded in the form of feedstock for petro-chemical plants, lubricating oils, refinery fuel etc., must also be regarded as largely non-competitive with coal. The balance of refinery output, estimated to be 55–60 million tons of coal-equivalent in 1980, is, however, of a kind more

TABLE 16

THE DEMAND FOR FUEL

ACTUAL CONSUMPTION IN 1955 AND PROJECTIONS FOR 1960–80 BY TYPE OF FUEL

(millions of tons of coal equivalent)
United Kingdom

	1955	1960	1965	1970	1975	1980
Total inland requirements[1]	250	256	285	310	340	370
Supplies by:						
Coal	214	194	196	200	205	205
Nuclear energy ..	—	—	9	18	27	36
Various[2]	1	2	3	4	4	4
Oil	35	60	77	88	104	125

[1] G. H. Daniel's *medium* estimate based on a slightly revised forecast of national income trends, in the light of 1955–60 developments.

[2] Water power, natural gas etc.

or less directly substitutable for solid fuel. It is this order of magnitude which is perhaps the most difficult to be certain about in that it is implied that by far the greater proportion of the *increase* in energy needs between now and 1980, which either coal or oil could supply, will in fact be met by the latter fuel.

But this need not necessarily be the case. So much depends on the future course of the balance of payments,[1] the relative prices and efficiency parities of coal and oil[2] and the progress of the

[1] To produce the estimated oil output in 1980, assuming constant prices, imports of crude petroleum would need to rise from their present level of £300 million to £800 million.

[2] Given 1954 = 100, oil prices in 1958 were 115 compared with coal prices of 141. Looking ahead, the trend of coal prices will chiefly depend on the relationship between mining productivity and miners' wages, and oil prices on the landed cost of crude petroleum and refinery charges.

nuclear energy programme. As regards this latter, and the estimates contained in Table 16, only the figure of 9 million tons of coal-equivalent for 1965 is a definite forecast at the moment. The other data is very much a speculation by the authors. Here again, uncertainties surrounding constructional and operational costs make the future very difficult to predict.

TABLE 17

GROSS FIXED CAPITAL FORMATION 1948–60 UNITED KINGDOM

(£ million)

Industry	Amount	Percentage
Coal mining	799	2·3
Mineral oil refining	332	0·9
Gas	573	1·6
Electricity	2,796	8·1
Other	30,009	87·1
Total Capital Formation	34,509	100·0

Source: *National Income and Expenditure, 1961*. Table 57; 1961 Non-Parliamentary Central Statistical Office.

The capital cost of expansion of fuel supplies

Any major increase in fuel supplies can only be achieved by large-scale capital investment. During the period 1948–60 total investment in the primary and secondary fuel industries (excluding atomic energy for which no data have yet been published) amounted to £4,500 million or 12·9% of the country's total gross capital formation. The distribution between the four main fuel industries was as shown in Table 17.

Primary fuel industries

(a) Coal-mining

For an industry suffering from the effects of many years of neglected investment, the proportion of the nation's capital expenditure allocated to coal-mining since the war has been surprisingly modest. This is particularly so when it is recalled that only about one-third of the figure quoted in Table 17 has been devoted to an actual expansion of output, the remainder being spent on maintenance and making good depreciation. Hence 0·7% only of the nation's gross capital formation took the form of 'net' investment in coal-mining.[1]

During the 5 years 1960–5 the National Coal Board plans to invest £511 million in the coal-mines[2] which is a reduction of some £175 million over that estimated in 1956. As shown in Table 16, this investment envisages an inland consumption of 196 million tons of coal in 1965; but it also assumes that a further 10 million tons will be exported at that date. The labour force required to produce this coal is thought to be between 585,000 and 626,000. Most of the capital (of which it is expected to finance at least 70% from internal sources) will be spent on reconstruction and mechanization: some 200 collieries will be closed down, leaving 550 to supply the total output, except for 2 million tons which open-cast mining is scheduled to supply.

(b) Mineral oil refining

Since 1948 some £332 million has been invested in the oil refining industry in the United Kingdom, in addition to which there has been a large expenditure on new oil tankers and on oil production facilities abroad, mainly the Middle East. In all it is estimated that an investment of about £40[3] is required to increase capacity by one ton of oil (or some £24 per ton of coal equivalent), and this covers all phases from the oilfield to the consumer. Statistics are not available of the capital investment undertaken by British oil companies in overseas oil wells. The world oil industry, however, is investing at the rate of £3,000 million per annum. Although American capital has

[1] In other words an investment equal to 1·5% of gross national capital formation was necessary in the coal-mining industry simply to maintain a constant output; otherwise output would have declined by 4 million tons p.a.

[2] Of which £71 million is in ancillary undertakings. For further particulars see *Revised Plan for Coal*, National Coal Board, 1959.

[3] Made up of £13·6 on refining and marketing, £8·8 on marine transportation and £17·6 on production at the oil wells, pipelines etc. (See *Esso Magazine*, Winter 1955–6, p. 7.)

the major share in this total, the British proportion must be quite significant. Of the post-war investment expenditure in the United Kingdom a large part has come from U.S. sources with British and other interests contributing the remainder. About 90% of the capital requirements of the world oil industry (U.S.S.R. excluded) are derived from reinvested earnings. To enable the oil industry to expand its output to meet the estimated demands of 1965[1] an investment of £300 million in British refineries, oil tankers, oil pipelines and oilfields may be necessary.

(c) Atomic energy

There has been investment on an extremely large scale in this field. Although the majority of it has been in connection with research for the development of nuclear weapons, there have also been large capital projects connected with the production of fissile material for military use at Calder Hall, Cumberland, and at Windscale. The U.K. Atomic Energy Authority, which took over the development of atomic energy from the Government, has so far built two power stations, one at Calder Hall (1956) and the other at Chapelcross (1959). These are all designed to produce plutonium for nuclear weapons, with the generation of electricity as a secondary object: however, up to the end of 1960 they had produced over 4000 mn. units for the national grid. The other main aspect of atomic energy development, viz. the design and construction of nuclear powered electricity generating stations, is the responsibility of the Central Electricity Generating Board (C.E.G.B.), and progress in this field is dealt with in the following two sections.

Secondary energy

The electricity and gas supply industries between them have accounted for nearly 10% of the country's total post-war capital expenditure, and in the next decade their share of the national net investment is likely to be equally large. As in the past the rate of

---

[1] Assuming the U.K. industry is to remain an important exporter of refined petroleum. In 1960 such exports amounted to 9·0 million tons, some 18% of total U.K. output.

investment in electricity will almost certainly continue to eclipse that in gas: over the period 1960–6 the C.E.G.B. is planning to spend approximately £910 million on new power plants alone— £400 million on nuclear stations and the balance on coal- and oil-fired stations. On the other hand, the Gas Council envisages a capital investment of £424 million between April 1959 and March 1966 of which by far the greater part is to be allocated to the improvement and modernization of existing installations: plant capacity is, in fact, only scheduled to rise by 3.2% in the next six years. At the same time, the composition of the primary energy supplied to the gas industry is likely to undergo some change: for example, while it is planned to raise the daily capacity of its oil gasification plants from a current figure of 0·7 million therms to 1·7 million therms by 1966, the output of coal-gas is likely to decline by an equivalent amount. Together with 'tail' gases bought direct from the oil refineries and processed by the Area Boards, this means that petroleum will form the basis of a third of the total gas made available to U.K. consumers by 1965.[1]

Assuming that the above programmes of the secondary energy industries materialize, the output of electricity—in terms of coal-equivalent—will rise to 70 million tons in 1965 (of which about one-seventh will be from nuclear power stations), and that of gas from 2,839 to 3,084 million therms.

Electricity generation: comparative costs of nuclear and conventional power

Despite improvements in reactor design and constructional techniques, the capital cost of a nuclear power station is still considerably larger than that of a conventional power station. On the basis of experiments at Windscale, the most economical form of nuclear installation, of a size capable of an annual output of 300 megawatts, has been estimated to cost £75 per kw[2] or nearly double that of the most efficient and modern coal-burning power station of a comparable

[1] For further particulars see *Gas Looks Ahead*, The Gas Council, February 1960.
[2] Compared with the lowest tender price so far submitted for the present type of power station of £104 per kilowatt.

size.[1] By contrast, the day-to-day running costs of generating electricity from nuclear power (80% of which consists of fuel costs) are considerably lower than in the case of either coal or oil. For example the uranium charge of a nuclear reactor has a life of four years and even then it contains a plutonium by-product which can either be used in 'breeder' and other advanced reactors of the future or for the manufacture of nuclear weapons. Initially the cost of uranium fuel for the nuclear stations now being constructed is estimated to work out at approximately 0·18d. per kw—about one-third of the comparative fuel costs for a conventional power station.[2] However, if the current downward trend in uranium prices persists until the renewal of Britain's uranium contracts in the mid-60's, the above fuel replacement cost might well be reduced by one-third.

To calculate the total average cost of generating electricity by alternative means, some assumptions must be made concerning depreciation and interest charges on capital and the average proportion of load capacity operated over time. In this country nuclear power stations are amortized over 20 years as against 25 for conventional thermal stations. The interest charge is assumed to be the same—5–6%—in both cases, while average load factors of 70–75% for atomic power and up to 75% for coal are likely to be normal within the next 5 years. On the basis of these assumptions, but discounting the value of the plutonium by-product, the overall cost of electricity from nuclear power stations now being constructed is expected to be between 0·65d. and 0·75d. a kw as against between 0·5d. and 0·55d. a kw from a coal-fired station built on the coal-fields. However, the subsequent generation of nuclear stations, due to be commissioned from 1964 onwards, and incorporating the economies of size and improved technology, are planned to produce electricity at an initial cost of just under 0·6d. a kw falling to between 0·5d. and 0·55d. a kw (the present cost of coal) by 1966. Beyond this date estimates become little more than speculations, though it is thought that with the latest type of reactor now being designed, it may be possible to get nuclear costs down to as low as 0·45d. a kw by 1972. Once again, it must be stressed that these

[1] In both kinds of installations substantial economies of size are to be gained up to a generating capacity of at least 550 megawatts.
[2] Coal prices of £5 per ton assumed.

figures assume that the generating plants, whether nuclear or coal-fired, are working at base load: for example if only 60% of the capacity of a nuclear station should be used, the 'cross-over' point between the cost of nuclear and coal-fired electricity would not be realized until 1970. Similarly, when capital charges account for two-thirds of the cost of atomic power, any change in the period of amortization (and/or rate of interest) can make a substantial difference to the economic merits of this kind of fuel overnight.[1]

Co-ordination of the fuel and power policy

As such a considerable capital expenditure is necessary to produce an expansion of fuel supplies, economy in fuel usage is obviously of the utmost importance; and this involves each type of fuel being used for the purpose for which it is best suited. Efficiency in fuel usage is the combined result of efficiency of production and of utilization. Electrical appliances usually have a high utilization efficiency, but a low generating efficiency. Mechanical power can be produced directly from coal by means of a steam engine or indirectly by the intermediate production of electricity, using the latter to drive an electric motor. In view of the very low thermal efficiency of the reciprocating steam engine and of the much higher efficiency of the steam turbines used in the power stations, it is possible to produce mechanical power electrically with less usage of coal than if a steam engine were used. In addition electricity has the great advantage of flexibility of supply. The thermal efficiency of gas generation is high by comparison with that of electricity, yet because of the very low efficiency of the gas turbine, mechanical energy produced in this way involves greater coal utilization than that produced by means of electricity. The main use of the gas turbine is to generate electricity at peak periods, and for this purpose it is very suitable since it can be easily started up and brought on to load.

[1] In fact, since this chapter was originally written in March 1960, new estimates of the capital costs of nuclear power stations have been published. On the basis of operations at Calder Hall and further technical improvements it now seems likely that the average load factor of nuclear power stations will be 80% (and not 70–75% as at first envisaged) and that their expectation of life will be 30 years (instead of 20 years). This reduces the estimates quoted in the text of the total cost of nuclear electricity by 10–15%. For further particulars see *The Economist*, 2 June 1962, p. 973.

Coal and oil are also competitive with each other in certain fields, and, because of its higher calorific value and combustion efficiency, it seems likely that oil will increasingly replace coal in the years to come. For example, on an average 1 ton of oil can do the work of $1\frac{1}{2}$ tons of coal,[1] but in certain cases the parity is very much more in favour of oil. The following table taken from the report of the Ridley Committee gives the relative coal–oil values for certain modes of using the two fuels:

TABLE 18

ESTIMATED COAL–OIL PARITIES

Iron and steel manufacture

Open hearth furnaces	2·1
Heat treatment furnaces	3·0
Forging furnaces	4·0

Steam raising

Laundries, dairies, etc.	1·8
Electricity stations	1·5
Gas manufacture	1·7
Brick kilns	2·5
Pottery kilns	2·5
Glass manufacture	2·0

Source: P.E.P. *Fuel for 20 Years. Planning*, xxi, no. 377, 1955.

From the above table it can be seen that the greatest potential fuel saving is likely to result from the substitution of oil for coal in the iron and steel industry (the largest user of oil) and in glass, brick and pottery manufacture.[1] In power stations the advantages of substitution are least, but a temporary change-over to oil is inevitable because of the shortage of coal. Moreover, though oil as a fuel is still usually more expensive in price than native coal, it has certain compensatory advantages: it is clean (a most important consideration in 'amenity' uses such as bakeries and hot-air drying processes),

[1] This is the equivalent used by the Ridley Committee, but the Ministry of Power in its *Statistical Digest 1956* gives 1 ton of oil as equivalent to 1·7 tons of coal. (See footnote 1, p. 89).

[2] In cases where 1 ton of oil can compete with nearly 2 tons of coal it has a premium value. Oil has not captured all its premium markets, especially in the steel industry and heat treatment furnaces of the non-ferrous metal and ceramic industries.

it can be readily handled and burned, and it is easily atomized and has a greater radiating power. At Marchwood Power Station on Southampton Water, however, the close proximity of the refinery and power station render the cost of transporting the oil low compared with the high cost of transporting coal to it.

The whole question of fuel utilization is a very complex one. While there appears to be a general consensus of opinion that prices should reflect the true costs of production there is no agreement on whether average or marginal costs should be taken as the criterion. The difficulties are many. In the case of coal, for example, costs of production bear virtually no relationship to the quality of the finished product. This means that the National Coal Board, which is only required to cover overall average costs, is able to sell the coal which has been cheapest to mine at a good margin of profit, while much of the high-cost coal has had to be sold at a loss.[1] In electricity supply, prices and costs are also apt to get out of line for a different reason. As consumers are usually charged prices based on average costs of production, the expensive peak loads are sold at a loss.

Such average-cost pricing, resulting in below-cost sales to some consumers, is frequently stated to be an encouragement to prodigal use. To promote the most efficient allocation of resources between alternative uses it has, therefore, been suggested that the price charged for coal, for example, should be its marginal cost of production, as would be the case in a free market. It is contended that as fuel costs usually constitute but a small proportion of the total cost of production, a considerable rise in the price of fuel would not add greatly to the cost of production, particularly if there were increased

[1] The N.C.B., like other nationalized fuel industries, is required by law to balance its budget taking one year with another, i.e. it must not maximize its profits nor incur losses. The Board's aim is that in the long run the prices of particular coals delivered in market zones should, as far as practicable, cover the cost of producing and delivering these coals. At the same time prices will to some extent be determined by the inherent qualities of the coals and by the strength of consumers' demands and preferences for the different kinds of coal, i.e. of market forces. Thus it has been estimated that the elimination of the pits producing the least profitable 30 million tons in 1953 would have reduced the average cost of coal by nearly 3s. a ton. See A. Beecham, 'The Coal Industry', in a symposium on *The Structure of British Industry*, edited by Duncan Burn, Cambridge University Press, 1958.

efficiency of consumption.[1] However, the counter-argument is that, since the demand for coal is relatively inelastic, there would be no such incentive to greater efficiency, and so the rise in cost of production would be inflationary and add to the difficulty of selling British goods abroad.[2] A rational price policy, which is free from all objections, which promotes the most economical use of coal and the two secondary fuels, which ensures that resources are not used for their production that would be better used elsewhere and which equates supply and demand, has still to be devised. Certainly the imposition of a fuel oil tax in 1961 and the prevention of cheap coal imports from abroad has done little to achieve this object.

[1] This is the argument of that minority section of the Ridley Committee which favoured marginal cost pricing. I. M. D. Little in *The Price of Fuel* (Oxford, 1953) pointed out, for example, that a 25% increase in the price of coal would cause a rise of only 10% in gas and electricity prices. Moreover, apart from the fuel industries themselves and the steel industry, coal costs account for less than 1% of the final cost of the manufactured product in 24 out of 30 industrial groups. In chemicals and miscellaneous manufactures it is 1 to 2%, and it is over 2% only in other mining, china, glass, textile finishing and building materials. And, as the Ridley Committee observed, a 40% increase in the price of coal would cause a rise only of 1 or 2% in the working class cost of living.

[2] This is the argument of the majority section of the Ridley Committee. See G. Polanyi, 'Coal, the Case for a Free Market', *Journal of Industrial Economics,* April 1955, Vol. III, No. 2.

IV

RESEARCH, DEVELOPMENT AND
TRAINED MANPOWER

WITH the acceleration of world economic development and the greater self-sufficiency of the industrializing countries in regard to the simpler manufactured products, the ability of the United Kingdom to adjust her economy freely and quickly to changes in the pattern of international trade is of the first importance. But the fact that this country relies on her manufacturing industry to finance 75 to 80% of her imports of foodstuffs and raw materials means that she must be adequately equipped with the facilities to compete with other industrial exporters in the development of new or improved products, processes and materials at acceptable prices. Already throughout this century Britain has experienced a steady decline in some of her traditional exports, e.g. cotton textiles, as a result of the growing self-sufficiency of her one-time customers. In a dynamic world, therefore, an industrial country must have, in addition to adequate power supplies and a skilled population, ample facilities for innovation.

Scientific discovery and technical innovation have been over-whelmingly responsible for the spectacular industrial developments of the last 200 years which have wrought such profound economic, social and political changes. Until the end of the nineteenth century, however, most inventions were the product of individual research undertaken both by men of formal scientific training, e.g. Faraday, Parsons and Wheatstone, and those without, e.g. Goodyear, Whitney and Bessemer. Organized scientific research in industry, as we know it today, was non-existent. It was in fact Thomas Edison who first fully recognized the need of industry for a regular source of new ideas and in 1876 he set up in the United States a well-equipped and per-manently staffed laboratory to help further this purpose. In the United Kingdom the first steps to co-ordinate research and devel-

116

opment activities in the physical and engineering sciences were taken at the turn of the century with the establishment of the National Physical Laboratory under the control of the Royal Society. This was followed seven years later by the founding of the Imperial College of Technology, and the appointment of a Development Commission by the Government in 1909 to promote research in the fields of agriculture, rural industries and fisheries. A Medical Research Committee was also created as part of the National Health Insurance Scheme in 1913. Despite these developments, however, the Government's annual expenditure on research before the First World War was little more than £600,000, while that of private industry did not exceed £1 million. The proportion of non-operative (including research and development staff) to operative workers employed in manufacturing industry at this time was approximately 1 in 12.

Since 1918, at first slowly and haltingly, but accelerating rapidly in the last twenty years as the value of industrial research in determining economic progress has become better appreciated, the resources devoted to organized invention have increased. By 1958–9 total expenditure on research and development in the United Kingdom had risen to £478 million and the proportion of indirect to direct labour employed in manufacturing industry to more than 2 in 12. In that year this country and the United States devoted 2·3% and 2·4% of their respective national products to research.

Research and innovation are not synonymous. An innovation is an invention which has been successfully developed and made use of by (or in) industry. Not all inventions are innovations, but the real purpose of industrial research is to steer promising inventions to fruition. In so doing it covers 'a spectrum of activities with continuous gradations of utility from the most abstract to the most practical'.[1] Two stages of research are usually distinguished. The first is the search after knowledge for its own sake—*fundamental* or *basic* research. Although long range in character and undertaken regardless of possible practical application, this is the source from which most important industrial innovations originate. The research of the pure scientist into natural processes and phenomena, such as radio-activity, semi-conductance, corrosion, lubrication and the action of chemical substances on living organisms, is principally of this kind. Nevertheless such investigations often result in the discovery

[1] National Academy of Sciences, *Applied Research in the U.S.*, 1952.

of new knowledge of great practical use. Thus the study of radio-activity gave an insight into the structure of the atomic nucleus which in due course led to the discovery of atomic fission; from the investigation of semi-conductance came the discovery of the transistor; and current advances in the chemistry of corrosion are leading to the development of corrosion inhibitors. Fundamental research is undertaken by a wide variety of institutions ranging from the individual inventor, using a minimum of co-operating factors, to the large industrial corporation, with its costly and well-organized research laboratories.[1]

The second stage of research—*applied* research—is that related to the exploitation of new knowledge with a specific object in mind, or to the solving of problems of practical significance. Such research may be of various kinds and designed to meet a multiplicity of ends; it may be short or long term in objective; it may be related to process improvement, product innovation, the discovery of new kinds of materials, waste utilization, or the operation of the company as a whole. Sometimes a third stage of research—*development* research—is also distinguished. This usually incorporates the various adaptations and experiments which have to be made to the innovation before full-scale manufacturing is possible. With the technological complexity of modern production methods, this research is frequently both more expensive and time-consuming than that which precedes it—the development of nylon and penicillin are cases in point—and as such is becoming increasingly the province of moderate- and large-sized firms.

The magnitude of the British research effort

Table 19 summarizes the present-day scope and structure of Britain's research effort. Of the total numbers engaged in research in 1959, some 45,600 were professionally qualified scientists and engineers,[2] and the remainder supporting staff, e.g. managerial and administrative workers, technicians, laboratory assistants etc. About 72% of the total research expenditure was financed by the Government,

[1] See J. Jewkes and others, *The Sources of Invention*, 1958.
[2] Excluding those engaged in school teaching and employed by local authorities.

though only 30% of the actual work was undertaken within the province of its own research establishments. On the other hand, while private industry employed more than one-half of the total manpower engaged on research and was responsible for three-fifths of the total expenditure, it financed only 28% of this latter amount.

TABLE 19

RESEARCH AND DEVELOPMENT IN GREAT BRITAIN 1958–9

Major Sectors	Financial provision for research wherever undertaken		Expenditure incurred on the research undertaken		Scientists and engineers employed on research 1959
	£mn	%	£mn	%	
Government[1]					
(i) Defence Depts.	234·3	49·0	102·9	21·6	3,750
(ii) Civil Depts.	67·9	14·2	42·9	9·0	1,520
(iii) Research councils	17·6	3·7	13·1	2·7	2,703
Industry					
(i) Nationalized	7·8	1·6	6·9	1·4	4,070
(ii) Private	136·0	28·5	266·3	55·8	27,148
(iii) Research assns.	—	—	6·4	1·3	1,537
Universities	1·5	0·3	23·3	4·8	2,088[2]
Other organizations [2, 3]	12·7	2·7	16·0	3·4	2,780
Total	477·8	100·0	477·8	100·0	45,596

[1] Including the Atomic Energy Authority.
[2] Assuming that university and technical college teachers spend 50% of their time on research.
[3] Includes the expenditure of Colleges of Advanced Technology, other technical colleges etc.

Source: *Annual Report of the Advisory Council on Scientific Policy*, 1959–60; Cmnd 1167, xx. *Scientific and Engineering Manpower in Great Britain, 1959*. Tables 7 and 10; 1959–60 Cmnd 902, xx.

Some £243½ million or 51% of the country's total research effort was in the civilian field: of this amount private industry undertook 56%. Some 74% of the Government's outlay was directed to defence commitments, though almost two-thirds of the work was sub-contracted to private industry, the co-operative research associations and universities.[1] In all, some 50% of the total research manpower in Great Britain is employed on defence contracts.[2]

Government-sponsored research

(a) Civil research

The responsibility for the organization and execution of the Government's scientific policy lies in the hands of the Minister for Science. He is advised on all matters relating to civilian research by the Advisory Council on Scientific Policy (formed in 1947), and is in charge of the Department of Scientific and Industrial Research (D.S.I.R.), the Agricultural Research Council (A.R.C.) and the Medical Research Council (M.R.C.). In turn, each of these bodies has a Committee of the Privy Council to supervise and guide its activities. Research is also undertaken within the scientific establishments of Government departments for which the Minister-in-charge is responsible.

The D.S.I.R. was formed in 1916 'to promote and organize scientific research, with a view especially to its application to trade and industry'. A year earlier a Committee of the Privy Council for Scientific and Industrial Research had reported unfavourably on the organization and scale of research by private enterprise and had recommended that closer attention should be paid both to publicizing the results of academic science and to the possibility of establishing co-operative research associations. To this latter end a fund of £1 million was set aside by the D.S.I.R. in 1917 to supplement industrial subscriptions. There was an immediate response from industry and, by 1921, 21 associations had been formed. The subsequent history and present-day scope of these co-operative research associations will be discussed later in this chapter, as will the ways in which the D.S.I.R., through its Intelligence Division, acts as the Government's publicity agent on all research and scientific problems.

---

[1] In 1958 defence absorbed a larger proportion of the total in the U.S. than in the U.K.; civil research and development work was probably $1\frac{1}{4}\%$ of G.N.P. in both countries (Cmnd 1167).

[2] It is true, of course, that defence research often has its wider applications; for example, the invention of radar, jet propulsion and the discovery of atomic fission have each resulted in important non-military developments.

In the year 1917 the first of the D.S.I.R.'s own research establishments—the Food Investigation Organization—was also set up. There are now 15 of these laboratories, each of which is supervised by a director of research who is himself advised by a specialist committee of independent scientists and industrialists.[1] Their function is to undertake research in the national interest and for Government departments: to this end they spent some £15·3 million in 1960–1. The National Physical Laboratory, which before 1918 was under the care of the Royal Society, is the largest of the D.S.I.R.'s establishments. It operates 11 separate divisions (e.g. aerodynamics, engineering, metallurgy etc.) and is particularly concerned with methods of precise measurement and the maintenance of scientific standards. Other specialist research institutions include the Building Research Station, the Chemical Research Laboratory, the Forest Products Research Laboratory, the Road Research Laboratory, the Pest Infestation Laboratory and the Radio Research Organization.

Outside the jurisdiction of the D.S.I.R., but still under that of the Minister for Science, are three other research bodies. First, the Medical Research Council, which was formed in 1920, undertakes and promotes research into the prevention, diagnosis and treatment of disease: its principal research establishment is the National Institute of Medical Research. Secondly, the Agricultural Research Council was established in 1922 and is now responsible for surveying all research work which, directly or indirectly, is likely to lead to an increase in the efficiency of food production. There are now 20 research institutes under the Council's guidance, including the Rothamsted Experimental Station, the Plant Breeding Institute and the National Institute for Research in Dairying.[2] Thirdly, in 1949 the Nature Conservancy was created to provide scientific advice about the conservation and control of the natural flora and fauna of Great Britain. It is also interested in questions of soil conservation, the use of land and the effects of deforestation.

Besides these specialist organizations, a number of Government departments operate research departments of their own. Thus the

[1] Excepting the National Physical Laboratory which is supervised by an executive committee appointed by the Royal Society.

[2] The expenditure of the M.R.C. and A.R.C. in 1958–9 was some £7 million.

Ministry of Power is concerned with research into safety in mines and underground gasification; the Ministry of Aviation maintains scientific departments to study operational techniques, aircraft design, guided weapons and radar; the Post Office undertakes research into a wide range of subjects,[1] e.g. telephone, telegraph and radio systems; the Ministry of Works supervises the whole field of building research and the technical development of the building industry; and the Ministry of Supply is responsible for research into two major civilian fields, viz. industrial gas turbines and civil aviation. Total expenditure on civil research by these departments in 1958–9, including that sub-contracted to outside bodies, was £67·9 million.

Finally, the National Research Development Corporation should be mentioned. This is a public corporation, formed in 1949 under the Development of Inventions Act (1948) to develop and exploit discoveries made in Government research establishments and to assist in the commercialization of new ideas originating either from official sources or from private inventors judged to be in the public interest. It has already accelerated development work on projects of some importance, e.g. the Saunders-Roe 'hovercraft', the electronic digital computer, the flexible barges called dracones, and the stereoscopic motion-picture camera; and by circulating details of the inventions under its care performs a useful service of communication. At the end of June 1961 the Corporation had over 495 licence agreements in force with private firms.

(b) *Defence research*

Policy in this field is co-ordinated by the Minister of Defence with the assistance of a Defence Research Policy Committee. The actual work is undertaken both within Government-owned laboratories and departments, and private industry. A public corporation, the Atomic Energy Authority, is responsible for all atomic research. The Admiralty maintains its own research establishments while the other services are catered for by the Ministry of Supply. It should, however, be remembered that many of the Government's research stations, e.g. the National Gas Turbine Establishment, the Radar Research Establishment and the Royal Aircraft Establishment, in addition to their defence commitments, engage in civil research on

[1] This was the first Government department to undertake research activities on an organized basis; it began these as far back as 1904.

both their own behalf and that of manufacturing firms in their respective fields.

Research in universities and technical colleges

The universities are the home of pure research and the training ground for scientists. Most universities have departments of physics, chemistry, engineering and metallurgy, and some of the newer ones also offer technological courses on, for example, glass, fuel, textiles etc. The State is now mainly responsible for the financing of research at universities and in 1958–9 its contribution (mainly through the University Grants Committee) amounted to £18·7 million of a total expenditure on university research of some £23·3 million; 64·5% was accounted for by scientific and technological research, 28·9% by medical, and 6·6% by agricultural and veterinary research. Sponsored research undertaken for private industry and other organizations amounted to a further £3·1 million, while the universities and colleges found £1·5 million of the cost from their own funds. Academic research is also carried out in the science departments of technical colleges, but on a much smaller scale than that in the universities.

Industrial research

By and large, industrial research work is carried out with practical objectives in view, but some of the larger firms also undertake research of an academic or near-academic character where senior research workers are free to develop their own ideas. However, these are in a minority. In the United States, for example, expenditure on basic research by private industry in 1959 amounted to only 3·6% of the total outlay incurred, and this was usually confined within or closely related to the firm's own field of endeavour. In Britain, the proportion is thought to be higher—probably in the order of 10%.[1]

The research effort of firms varies considerably between industries and within the same industry according to size. Research is expensive; the average annual cost per qualified man in British

[1] *Industrial Research in Manufacturing Industry 1959–60*. Federation of British Industries, 1961, p. 1.

industry has been recently put at £8,750.[1] Such an outlay cannot be freely borne by the smaller firms and 97% of British firms employ 300 persons or less. In the United States in 1953 only 8% of all firms employing less than 100 workers had research budgets, compared with 95% of those companies with a labour force of 5,000 or more. As a whole, only 11·6% of the 135,000 manufacturing firms employing more than 8 workers undertook any research, and 81% of the patents owned by such firms were owned by those employing more than 1,000 people. The situation is much the same in the United Kingdom. In 1959–60, well over 90% of research activity measured in terms of money and employment, was undertaken by firms with a labour force of 2,000 or more. On the other hand, at least 80% of the firms employing less than 300 persons had no qualified research and development personnel. Earlier, the authors of a survey sponsored by the Manchester Research Council found that of the 225 firms in their sample one-third employed five-sixths of the total number of scientists, one-third the remaining one-sixth and one-third none.[2] More specifically, the largest manufacturing firm in Britain—the Imperial Chemical Industries—spent some £15 million in 1961 on research activities; the second largest —Unilever Ltd—employed 2,700 people in its 11 research establishments and factory development units, of whom over 675 were qualified scientists and engineers. At Abingdon in Berkshire the U.K. subsidiary of Esso Research and Engineering Ltd currently undertakes research on behalf of the European and N. African affiliates of the Standard Oil Co. of New Jersey.

The industrial distribution of the research expenditure by private firms in 1959–60 is illustrated in Table 20. We have drawn upon two sources; first the enquiry of the D.S.I.R. carried out in 1958 and second that of the Federation of British Industries, undertaken in 1959–60. Both investigations covered firms thought to account for about 90% of the research and development activity in manufacturing industry. As might be expected there is a considerable variation between the individual trades. The chemical, engineering and shipbuilding, electrical engineering and aircraft industries between them account for 83·8% of the total research expenditure;

[1] *Industrial Research in Manufacturing Industry 1959–60.* Federation of British Industries, 1961.

[2] *Industry and Science*, Manchester University Press, 1954.

the percentage of qualified scientists and engineers engaged on research activities is highest in the aircraft, mineral oil refining and electrical engineering industries, and lowest in the wood, cork, paper and printing, food, drink, tobacco and textiles industries.

Clearly, the amount of research and development undertaken by any particular firm is largely dependent on its estimated importance as a factor influencing economic progress and on the efficiency

TABLE 20

EXPENDITURE AND EMPLOYMENT ON RESEARCH AND DEVELOPMENT IN U.K. MANUFACTURING

	1959–60 F.B.I. Survey		1958 D.S.I.R. Survey[1]	
U.K. Manufacturing Industry	Qualified scientists and engineers	Expenditure £m.	Qualified scientists and engineers	Expenditure £m.
Glass, Refractories and other building material	573	2·1	343	2·4
Chemicals and allied industries	6,597	34·3	6,368	35·4
Iron and steel	693	3·2	640	3·3
Non-ferrous metals	617	3·6	335	2·4
Engineering and shipbuilding	3,289	30·8	3,307	24·2
Electrical engineering ..	8,037	55·2	7,677	48·5
Vehicles	810	10·6	806	14·4
Aircraft	4,290	89·3	3,248	96·7
Instruments	660	4·4	853	11·2
Textiles	1,211	6·8	939	6·4
Food, drink and tobacco	713	3·5	705	3·5
Wood, cork, paper, printing	544	2·2	241	1·5
Other manufacturing ..	561	4·0	763	3·8
Total	28,591	250·2	26,225	253·8

[1] Industrial Research and Development Expenditure, 1958, H.M.S.O., 1960, p. 7.

Source: Derived from Table 1 B, p. 65, Industrial Research in Manufacturing Industry 1959–60, F.B.I., 1961.

and receptivity of management. But there are also a number of other reasons for the pattern of the figures presented in Table 20. For example, in a number of industries, e.g. aircraft and electrical engineering, the Government defrays the major part of the expenditure incurred. In others the proportion of the research personnel to the total labour force is high principally because automation is far advanced in that industry, e.g. as in the case of mineral oil refining. On the other hand, where the industrial group in question covers a wide range of separate trades, some of which undertake virtually no research at all, the employment percentage might underestimate the true importance of science to the industry as a whole, e.g. as in the chemical industry.

It is not surprising that the newer industries would appear to be the most research conscious, since they are faced with the temptation of a vast body of scientific knowledge relevant to their operations, which an increasing supply of scientists from institutions of higher education are anxious to exploit. There is thus a marked contrast between the profitability of industrial research in, say, pharmaceuticals and pottery. In the well-established, traditional and craft-based industries, research is generally less in evidence, although many firms are becoming more conscious of the benefits that it can confer and nowadays often belong to one or more co-operative research associations.

Co-operative research

A co-operative research association may be defined as 'an autonomous body formed to serve the scientific and technical needs of a particular industry'.[1] Co-operative research is the obvious solution for firms which are too small to operate an effective research department of their own. There are now 52 grant-aided research associations and allied bodies which both meet the needs of particular industries, e.g. engineering, fuel, textiles, food etc., and provide services common to a variety of industries, e.g. welding, packaging etc.; their total staff numbers over 4,000 and they represent some 22,000 member firms. As we have already seen, the

[1] C. A. Spencer, *Co-operative Research Associations in the United Kingdom under the D.S.I.R. scheme* (n.d.), D.S.I.R. booklet, p. 3.

first of these associations was established at the end of the First World War and by 1921 there were 21 in existence. Thereafter their numbers remained constant until the outbreak of the Second World War. Since then they have more than doubled under the stimulus of rapid technological progress, a more appreciative recognition of the value of close contacts between science and industry, the need for an integrated war-time research policy and the assurance of permanent financial help from the D.S.I.R. Today the policy for each research association is determined by a council, consisting of leading industrialists appointed by the industry concerned, representatives of the D.S.I.R. and a number of co-opted members such as university scientists and engineers. Their total income in 1959–60 amounted to £7·9 million of which about one-quarter was subscribed by Government grant[1] and the balance by individual firms.

Research associations have two main functions. One is to act as the scientific intelligence unit for the particular industry they represent and provide a consultant, liaison and information service. The other more important function is to undertake research, both fundamental, e.g. that concerned with raw materials and industrial processes, and applied, e.g. that relating to urgent technical problems of general concern to the industry. Qualitative, operational and statistical surveys are also carried out from time to time as is a limited amount of semi-scale or pilot development. Naturally, as the firms contribute towards the upkeep of the associations, they are usually anxious to benefit as much as possible from the co-operative research work. The larger firms, often with research departments of their own, are particularly well placed to make practical use of the activities of the associations, as their own scientists can generally undertake the subsequent development work that is usually necessary. The smaller firms have also gained considerably from the associations' work, but one suspects that closer liaison would have been even more beneficial.

Finally, mention must be made of the research activities of a number of industrial trade associations, e.g. the Lead Development Association, the Cement and Concrete Research Association and the Production Engineering Research Association. These

---

[1] The exact proportion of this aid to their other income varies between research associations according to their size, age and importance.

bodies may both undertake research of their own and sponsor projects in universities and member firms. An estimate contained in Table 19 shows that such organizations account for only a very small proportion of the total research undertaken in the U.K.

Sponsored research

In contrast to the position in the United States, sponsored research, i.e. research undertaken on a contract basis for individual firms, is of only limited importance in this country. The two major institutes are the Fulmer and Sondes Place, the former with a special interest in metallurgy, the latter in applied chemistry and chemical and mechanical engineering. These bodies perform an important dual function. First, they enable smaller firms to benefit from the occasional assistance of a research organization without the expense of operating a full-time research department of their own; secondly, they enable larger companies to extend their overall research programme without any disturbance of internal arrangements.

Sponsored research may, however, become more important in the future. A branch of the U.S. Battelle Institute was recently established in this country, while the Arthur D. Little Research Institute in Inveresk, Scotland, commenced operations in 1958. This institute, formed under the joint auspices of the Arthur D. Little research organization of Cambridge, Mass., U.S.A., and a number of eminent British scientists, is concerned solely with fundamental research, with the emphasis on indicating new and promising fields for the applied scientist. The initial costs of the enterprise have been borne from American sources but projects undertaken will be open to both British and Continental sponsorship. The institute differs from the usual organization of its kind, for while the customer will provide the money and specify the subject, he will not direct the research; moreover the findings will be published freely and not confined to the sponsoring firm. The organization is intended to work in close collaboration with industry and with the universities.

Comparison—the U.K. and U.S.A.

How does the United Kingdom research effort compare with that of the United States?

In 1958–9 the United States spent $10,990 million on all kinds of research and development and employed 277,100 scientists and engineers. Of this sum, expenditure by private industry accounted for $8,220 million, $4,560 million of which represented work contracted for by the Government.[1] In relation to her gross national product the U.S. allocated 2·4% to all kinds of research, 1·0% to civilian research and 0·8% to privately financed research.

On the basis of the above, and data contained in Table 19, and making due allowances for the differences in wage and salary levels and material costs in the two economies,[2] the U.S. is seen to spend 365% more on all kinds of research than the U.K., 307% more on civilian research, and 397% more on privately financed research. Proportionate to her gross national product the respective figures for the U.K. are 2·3%, 1·2%, and 0·8%. Defence research accounts for roughly one-half of the commitments of private industry in both countries. As a proportion of net industrial output, U.S. research expenditure amounted to 5·7% in 1958 compared with 3·1% in the U.K.

It has further been calculated that the real research expenditure per employee in American industry in 1959 was three times that in the United Kingdom, and that in terms of qualified manpower, for every 1,000 workers employed in U.S. manufacturing there were 13 scientists and engineers on research work, whereas for every 1,000 British workers there were only 5.[3] In addition, it has been estimated that the average research expenditure of the 350 largest firms in the U.S. is about five times that of their counterparts in the United Kingdom. Tables 21 to 23 give further particulars of the distribution of research expenditure in the two countries.[4]

[1] Statistical Abstract of the United States, 1961, p. 534.
[2] Following the lead of the National Institute of Economic and Social Research we take the 'research rate of exchange' to be $6·3 to the £.
[3] 'Research and development: a comparison between British and American Industry', *National Institute Economic Review*, No. 20, May 1962, p. 24.
[4] For further details of the numbers of scientists employed in the U.K. and U.S. see p. 134 and p. 142.

E

TABLE 21

RESEARCH AND DEVELOPMENT IN THE UNITED KINGDOM AND THE UNITED STATES (1958–9)

(Percentages of total expenditure)

Major sectors	Cost of research and development work carried out		Source of finance, irrespective of sector in which work was undertaken	
	U.K.	U.S.A.	U.K.	U.S.A.
Government	34·7	15·4	68·5	61·0
Industry	57·1	75·3	28·5	36·4
Colleges and universities	4·8	7·5	0·3	1·8
Other organizations ..	3·4	1·8	2·7	0·8
Total ..	100	100	100	100

Source: *Annual Report of the Advisory Council on Scientific Policy*; 1959–60, Cmnd 1167, xx.

What do these differences mean? It would, of course, be wrong to infer that because the U.S. allocates more resources to research than the United Kingdom the latter's efforts are inadequate by the margin between them. Since there are more firms engaged in similar lines of research in the U.S. there is always the possibility of more duplication of effort, while nothing is implied about the efficiency of the research department or the type of research engaged upon. Neither does it necessarily follow that it is profitable for private industry in this country to assimilate to the U.S. scale of research (because, for example, of the different market structures with which the two economies are faced).

On the other hand, there is little doubt that the absolute superiority enjoyed by the U.S. firms over their U.K. counterparts in research yields important advantages. First, there is a certain minimum size to which any pilot plant must conform so that development costs, whatever the potential market or volume of production, will bulk larger in relation to sales turnover in this country than in the United States; secondly, the economies of large-

TABLE 22

RESEARCH AND DEVELOPMENT EXPENDITURE IN MANUFACTURING INDUSTRY, U.K. AND U.S.

Industry	(1) Research expenditure (1959) US $m.	U.K. $m.	U.S.:U.K.	(2) Qualified scientists and engineers (1959) U.S. (000's)	U.K. (000's)	U.S.:U.K.	(3) Research expenditure as a % of net output (1958) U.S. %	U.K. %	U.S.:U.K.
Capital goods and Chemicals									
Aircraft	3,028	693	4·4	47·2	7·6	6·2	30·9	35·1	0·9
Electronics	1,161	188	6·2	{47·8	{12·4	{3·9	22·4	12·8	1·8
Other electrical	1,079	159	6·8				16·3	5·6	2·9
Chemicals	1,221	245	5·0	42·6	9·4	4·5	6·9	4·5	1·5
Machinery	946	157	6·0	21·3	4·2	5·1	6·3	2·3	2·7
Vehicles	886	74	11·7	13·7	2·4	5·7	10·2	1·4	7·3
Instruments	353	248	7·3	10·1	1·5	6·6	9·9	6·0	1·7
Total Group A	8,654	1,563	5·5	182·7	37·5	4·9	13·0	6·3	2·1
Rubber	111	20	5·5	2·8	0·6	5·0	2·7	2·1	1·3
Ferrous metals	75	20	3·8	{5·6	{1·9	{3·0	0·8	0·5	1·6
Non-ferrous metals	64	23	2·8				2·0	2·3	0·9
Metal products	124	23	5·4	4·1	0·7	5·8	1·3	0·8	1·6
Stone, clay and glass	72	13	5·5	2·4	0·7	3·2	1·2	0·6	2·0
Paper	59	13	4·5	2·3	0·7	3·1	0·9	0·8	1·1
Total Group B	505	112	4·5	17·2	4·6	3·7	1·3	0·9	1·4
Food	89	18	4·9	3·6	1·0	3·5	0·5	0·3	1·7
Textiles and apparel	19	14	1·4	1·3	0·7	1·8	0·2	0·3	0·7
Lumber and furniture	13	1	13·0	—	—	—	0·2	0·04	5·0
Other manufacturing	120	16	7·5	—	—	—	0·9	0·4	2·3
Total Group C	241	49	4·9	—	—	—	0·5	0·3	1·7
Total all industries	9,400	1,725	5·4	219·1	44·3	4·9	5·7	3·1	1·8

Source: *National Institute Economic Review*, May 1962, pp. 22 and 23, Tables I and II.

scale production apply equally to the research laboratory as to the factory; and thirdly, since the larger firm is often in a much better position to develop new ideas from the initial invention to the actual marketing of the product, the average U.S. firm which does research may well have important advantages over its smaller U.K. counterpart. More specifically, in 1951 Professor R. L. Meier estimated that for every dollar expended on basic research in the U.S. $10 of new capital had to be invested before any benefits could accrue,[1] whereas in a report published by the National Academy of Sciences in 1952[2] it was stated that the average annual amount then expended on laboratory facilities and equipment per graduate scientist was $10,000. The invention and commercial exploitation of nylon is said to have cost the Du Pont organization some $45 million,[3] and that of the various broad spectrum antibiotics $100 million spread over 6 companies.[4] It is also reported that it took the Standard Oil Company of New Jersey 5 million technical man hours to develop the fluid catalytic oil cracking process.[5] The desire to reduce the high overhead costs of research, and so strengthen their competitive position overseas, has undoubtedly been a contributory factor to some of the recent mergers in the U.K. aircraft, chemical and electrical engineering industries.

Table 22 summarizes the industrial distribution of research in the two countries. The similarities are clearly more marked than the differences. In both countries the aircraft, electronics, other electrical, chemical and scientific instruments industries are the most research-conscious and the various consumer goods industries and those supplying certain basic materials the least. It is interesting to note that the former industries are also those which have grown the most rapidly in recent years. In relation to its U.K. counterpart, American research activity is most pronounced in the vehicles, machinery, electronics and other electrical industries—all fields in which

---

[1] R. L. Meier, 'The Role of Science in the British Economy', *Research*, May 1951.

[2] National Academy of Sciences—National Research Council, *Applied Research in the U.S.*, 1952.

[3] D. W. Hill, 'Man-made fibres', *Three Banks Review*, December 1953.

[4] R. S. Aries and Associates, *Economic Aspects of the Pharmaceutical Industry*, 1955.

[5] From information provided by the Esso Petroleum Co. Ltd.

TABLE 23

RESEARCH BY LARGE, MEDIUM AND SMALL FIRMS U.S. AND U.K.

Size (employment)	United States, 1958			United Kingdom, 1959[1]		
	large 5,000 or more	*medium* 1,000–4,999	*small* less than 1,000	*large* 2,000 or more	*medium* 300–1,999	*small* less than 1,000
Number of firms	384	1,459	260,000	373	1,061	3,243
Percentage undertaking research	89	50	4	90	58	18
Percentage of total research expenditure	85	8	7	93	6	1

[1] Members of Federation of British Industries only.

Source: *National Institute Economic Review*, May 1962, p.24.

government expenditure accounts for a high proportion of the cost of research—and least pronounced in the chemicals, metal and textile industries. The aircraft industry is an exceptional case in that it attracts a far greater concentration of Government expenditure in the U.K. than in the U.S.

Other comparisons, based on private investigations in this country and official statistics in the United States, reveal some further significant differences. A survey undertaken by the Federation of British Industries in 1950–1 found that the 300 or so of its member firms who did any research employed on an average 100 persons on research activities, 28 of whom had university degrees or other professional qualifications. Comparable figures for the United States (based on a survey of 2,000 firms made by the United States Bureau of Labour Statistics and Department of Defence in 1951) show an employment of 116 persons per firm, 48 of whom were graduate engineers and scientists. On the other hand, the Manchester Research Council enquiry carried out in 1950–3, which confined its scope to manufacturing firms in the Manchester area employing 50 persons and over, showed rather different results. For example, it was found that 225 firms between them employed 684 scientists and 613 technologists, but nearly one-half of these firms employing 16% of the total labour force had no scientists or technologists at all. Such comparisons as these, however, cannot be more than tentative because of the difference in the standard of qualifications in the two countries. In many instances, for example, a British Higher National Certificate is equivalent to an American first degree in science, but while holders of the former are excluded from the 28 persons quoted for Britain as having university degrees or equivalent qualifications, holders of the latter are included in the 48 quoted for the United States.

Research and growth

The determinants of economic growth are varied and complex, and the link between research expenditure and technological progress is by no means a simple one. However, there seems little doubt that a close statistical association exists between research expenditure by industry and growth of output. When the National Institute compared research expenditure as a proportion of net output in 17 industries in 1958 with that of the growth in output of those industries between 1935 and 1958, they found a correlation coefficient of 0·95 for Britain and 0·75 for the U.S.[1] It was also discovered that research activity is most highly concentrated in the rapidly growing industries. Thus the net output of the capital goods and chemical industries (which, as we have seen, account for 90% of the research expenditure in the U.S. and U.K.), as a proportion of the net output of all industries in the U.S., rose from 28% in 1935 to 40% in 1958; in Britain the corresponding increase was from 32% to 45%.[2]

Research efficiency in the United Kingdom

On the basis of the Anglo-American statistics contained in Tables 21 and 22 it is frequently asserted that the United Kingdom should allocate a higher proportion of her resources to research activities. This may well be true, but it by no means follows that, if more research were undertaken by all firms, technical progress would be automatically accelerated. First, if wrongly orientated this would simply result in a duplication or dissipation of research effort; and secondly, there is no guarantee that an inefficient or backward firm is turned into an efficient and progressive concern simply by its setting up a research department. Moreover, because of the speculative nature of research, neither past experience nor the conduct of competitors gives much guidance as to the right research policy for any particular firm to pursue. In some industries, e.g. soft drinks and decorative textiles, research other than 'trouble shooting' (i.e. the investigation of production problems with a view to their solution) appears to be comparatively unimportant, since there is so little latitude for variation in the product. Such firms tend simply to adopt the ideas or developments of their suppliers or research associations. In others, more strongly based on science and technology, the scope for research is greater: indeed the very existence of such industries is testimony to this fact, as is also the constant flow of

[1] 'Research and Development: a comparison between British and American industry', *National Institute Economic Review*, No. 20, May 1962, p.29.
[2] ibid., p. 30.

innovations emanating from existing research programmes. But even if there are less opportunities for scientific research in the traditional industries, this does not exclude the possibility of other kinds of study, such as operational research, the purpose of which is to ascertain the optimum working conditions for existing equipment, and research into management techniques or marketing policy for which firms need to employ statisticians and social scientists.

Yet, however uneconomic it may be for firms to undertake research, there is no reason why all should not attempt to use the results of research: sometimes, in fact, it pays to be deliberately parasitic on others. Even in this respect, however, British firms do not appear to be as enterprising as they might be. For example, the authors of the Manchester Survey classified the firms within their sample into three groups of equal numbers. The top group employed about five-sixths of the total number of scientists and had an obvious need for the aid and stimulus of science. The middle group, which employed the remaining one-sixth of the scientists, appeared to limit its research activities to the competent application of established principles and relied on external sources for new ideas which were 'adopted' if thought likely to be of practical use. The bottom group of firms in the sample employed no scientists and in general were parochial or unprogressive in outlook; in such undertakings there appeared to be a good deal of complacency. The conclusion of this survey, confirmed by Professors Carter and Williams in their researches,[1] was that the degree to which industry makes use of science is determined by the outlook of management. Scientific research is, in fact, a management technique, since it provides the data from which the business executive has to decide whether or not to introduce new products, processes or materials which may sometimes necessitate a complete reorganization of the firm. The need is for research to be properly related to and co-ordinated with the other aspects of a firm's activities; otherwise the repercussions of decisions based on research findings will be imperfectly evaluated. Yet in their study of 150 firms covering a wide range of industries Carter and Williams estimated that such close liaison was achieved in fewer than half the firms conducting research and development.

[1] C. F. Carter and B. R. Williams, *Industry and technical progress*, Oxford University Press, 1957.

Why this is so is difficult to explain. In some instances the preponderance of small firms makes the necessary concentration of effort difficult to achieve. In others long-established traditions or uncertain prospects for enlarged sales may inhibit investment in research and development.[1] Generally speaking, most of the larger firms in the science-based industries are highly research-minded— the limiting factors are external rather than internal by nature. It would seem, however, that more attention ought to be paid to persuading the smaller firms, who are now parochial and self-satisfied in their isolation, to become adoptive and ready to seek and apply new knowledge to benefit their own ends, thereby either raising productivity or accelerating technical change or both.

Balance of research

To lead to improvements in the standard of living, research findings have to be applied successfully. It is frequently claimed that while the quality of the pure research carried out in the United Kingdom is equal to or even surpasses that in many other countries, this country lags behind in applying that research and commercial-izing it successfully. Although evidence for such an assertion is more fragmentary than might be supposed, specific examples can be given: the failure to create an efficient dyestuffs industry before the First World War, when the major technical innovations had originated in this country, is a classic case in point. More recently the feasibility of printing electrical circuits was first demonstrated in Great Britain, but America was the first to develop it commer-cially. The use of resins to de-salt water was the discovery of D.S.I.R. chemists, but the applications for softening water, for recovering gold and uranium from low-grade ores and so on were more quickly exploited in the U.S.A. and Germany than in this country. The electronic computer, the carbon-tetrachloride or 'Pyrene' type fire-extinguisher, penicillin and the transfer-machining of motor-car engines are other examples of products or processes largely pioneered in this country but later commercialized with greater success in the United States. The development of the motor-scooter and rear-engined car, both British innovations, has been

[1] *Advisory Council on Scientific Policy*, 1956–7, Cmnd 278, xix.

largely in Continental hands. This does not mean, of course, that one can argue from the particular to the general. Yet, although proof cannot be adduced, we should in fact expect the United States to take the lead, if only because the overall burden of research is so much lower there. With a considerably larger market potential for the product of a yet undeveloped process, five or six U.S. pilot plants can be set up where only one would be economic in this country; and for the same or even an appreciably higher failure rate among pilot plant investigations, American industry is able to produce a significantly larger number of useful developments.

An American observer, Professor R. L. Meier, believes that American industry benefits more from fundamental research originating in this country than does British industry itself, and he would probably subscribe to the commonly held opinion that applied science in the U.S.A. is largely parasitic on British pure science. Such a view is extremely difficult to substantiate, if only because it is not often possible to trace the direct link between a piece of pure research and its industrial application. For example, between the time when Professor Kipping discovered the class of substances known as silicones and the realization of their practical significance, much additional basic research was necessary. Ideas conceived in one country are in fact often nurtured by scientists undertaking basic research in another, whose work is seldom at an end even when industrial applications have been seen to be possible. Yet cases can also be cited to support the opposite viewpoint: for instance, although the U.S.A. tended to be in the lead in devising a television camera, it was Britain who operated the first fully electronic television service.[1]

In many cases, however, the application of research findings is limited by the financial resources available. Because of this Meier maintains that the marginal returns to expenditure on fundamental research ultimately become negative in Great Britain, since the effort not only produces unusable ideas but, by dissipating the resources potentially available for applied research, causes these latter to be smaller than they would otherwise be. Furthermore, if that fundamental research is developed in a foreign country and this country then wants to apply the process, it will have to pay licence fees.

[1] T. Wilson, 'Science and Industry', *Lloyds Bank Review*, October 1957.

It might be argued that expenditure on fundamental research should be curtailed and resources diverted to the development of existing ideas or even to the purchase of these from other countries. Most certainly both courses would be discouraging to the native scientist—and as scientists have their basic training in fundamental research, irrespective of their later employment, their quality would ultimately be seriously reduced to the eventual detriment of applied research. But more important is the fact that, since the results of basic research, though unpredictable, may also be revolutionary in their effects, the risk of jeopardizing progress by any substantial reduction in its outlay is too serious to be worth while. For example, no one could have predicted that the early fundamental research in atomic physics, to which this country made such important contributions, would have ultimately led to the establishment of an atomic energy industry which is likely to increase the economic potential of the country out of all proportion to the initial research outlay.

The promotion of the application of science in industry

(a) The dissemination of scientific knowledge

Efficient methods of publicizing the results of basic research are essential if scientific advances are to exert their full effect on industrial progress. For the communication of results from scientist to scientist the existing methods are satisfactory so long as they keep pace with the growth in the volume of scientific work and so long as there is adequate abstracting to keep the individual scientists reading within manageable proportions. The real problem is the dissemination of scientific findings to firms where the conditions of receptiveness are not ideal, for example, those employing few scientists, and where the management and other persons strategically placed to apply the findings are themselves non-scientific. Methods of reaching these potential consumers of science are gradually increasing as the need is felt, and such 'scientific middlemen' as technical journalists, technically trained salesmen and manu- facturers' and research associations' advisory and liaison officers are assuming increasingly important roles. The D.S.I.R. itself is active in creating an interest in science by means of films, exhibitions and special courses of instruction, and its Intelligence Division will introduce enquirers to the persons and organizations most likely to help them. Communication within the firm to the managerial level is, of course, facilitated when scientists have a prominent role in management or are directors.

(b) Co-operation in research

Responsibility for the successful application of science and technology to industry is primarily a question of management receptivity and efficiency. The integration of research activities with the production and sales programme and the assurance of good communication facilities between the various departments is essential if potentially valuable ideas are not to be lost. Such ideas do not always or even mainly begin in the research department. Carter and Williams found that 70% of the original ideas from which some 300 innovations in 150 firms sprang emanated from outside the research department. Dr Lodge of British Nylon Spinners gives the figure in his firm as 55%. The actual method by which research is organized may also be important: for example, many firms place special emphasis on the collective efforts of teams of research workers in the belief that cross-fertilization of ideas increases the effectiveness of the research.

Just as there is a need within firms to ensure rapid communication of ideas and co-ordination of research work in production and sales departments, co-operation between firms can produce equally beneficial results. Technologically, modern industry is essentially integrated and inter-related: many important developments in products, materials and processes require united action between related firms within different industries in order to be effective. A parochially minded supplier, by failing to develop his own technology to match that of his purchaser, might seriously impede the introduction of a new product and lose markets which might otherwise have been gained. On the other hand the action of one progressive firm may spark off a chain of reactions which directly helps to advance the technology and efficiency of other related firms. Thus, for example, the development of high-speed aircraft was dependent on the metallurgical industry inventing a suitable metal which would stand up to the vastly increased physical strains, while the introduction of a wide range of petro-chemicals waited on the design of the requisite plant by the constructional engineering industry. In its turn, many an engineering development has been held up in the past because the appropriate machine tools have not been available. In consequence, any serious disparity in the rates of development and innovation between firms at different stages of the production process can hinder the speedy application of scientific knowledge.

Co-operation, however, need not and should not end within a country. Equally beneficial results may follow from international research co-operation. In some fields, for example the pharmaceutical and scientific instruments industries, in which the United States spends well over 10 times as much on research each year as the British industry, a case might be made out that the United Kingdom should rely very considerably on the U.S. for all major developments. Since no American firm has an absolute monopoly of the various instruments or drugs produced, licensing fees should not be exorbitant; and, by providing such firms with a larger market, research expenditure can be widely spread and Britain and the U.S.A. stand to benefit. Applied research in this country would probably be more profitably pursued and extended in those industries which are either faced with a large market of their own or which, in relation to their counterparts overseas, already have an appreciable research lead. This of course is no more than saying that the U.K. should try to expand her research efforts in directions where she already has some relative advantages—that she should keep to the law of comparative costs.

There are ample grounds why an extension of this form of division of labour between the U.S.A. and U.K. should be beneficial. In spite of the higher physical productivity of U.S. industry over that of the U.K., its manufacturing costs tend to be higher, so that, even with payment of licence fees, British industry can still compete with the American industry in overseas markets. Indeed, because of this, and because the changing structure of international trade is leading to the establishment of U.S. manufacturing subsidiaries in the United Kingdom from which non-dollar markets are supplied, it might be agreed that U.K. and U.S. economies are more complementary to than competitive with each other. Research co-operation between the two countries is, therefore, all the more desirable.[1]

(c) The supply of scientists

International statistics of the existing supply of engineers and scientists suggest that Great Britain is lagging behind both the United States and Soviet Russia. For example, in 1954[2] 2,800 engineering and other applied science students graduated in British universities and 8,100 persons obtained Higher National Certificates, i.e. respectively 57 and 221 per million of the population. In the same year the United States produced 22,000 engineering graduates, i.e. 136 per million of the population exclusive of non-graduate engineers, and the U.S.S.R. 60,000 professional engineers and 70,000 lower-grade engineers, i.e. 280 per million and 326 per million respectively, or 606 per million altogether. It has been calculated that, if the 'propensity to enter higher education' were the same in this country as in the United States, the number of university undergraduates would be 7–9 times as great and of post-graduates 6 times as great.[3] Even allowing for differences in international standards and methods of training there is no escaping the fact that Britain lags well behind the United States and even further behind the U.S.S.R. in her provision of graduate instruction in applied science. In particular, observers of the Soviet educational systems have been impressed by the high standards and thoroughness of the advanced education in science, and by the high proportion of women receiving technological training there—three-quarters of the medical doctors and a quarter of the engineers are women. Comparisons made with other countries show that Great Britain is also behind France, Western Germany and Switzerland, but ahead of Italy, in the production of graduates in technology.

Undoubtedly, however, this country's inferiority in scientific manpower and adequate research facilities is accentuated by her failure to pay her scientists salaries which are a true reflection of

[1] For further particulars of this aspect of Anglo-American co-operation, see J. H. Dunning, *American Investment in British Manufacturing Industry*, Allen & Unwin, 1958.
[2] *Technical Education*. App. A; 1955–6, Cmd 9703, xxxvi.
[3] Carter and Williams, op. cit., p. 99.

their scarcity.[1] In consequence many experienced research personnel are now taking up appointments in foreign and Commonwealth countries, e.g. the United States and Canada.[2]

The United States in particular has attracted a steady flow of scientists and engineers from other countries. Between 1953 and 1956, 59,704 professional, technical and kindred workers were admitted as foreign immigrants into the U.S.—14% of all immigrants with an occupational classification on entry. One-third of the engineers and about one-quarter of the natural scientists migrated from Britain. In as much as this export of human capital yields little or no return (save where those migrating later return better trained and equipped), it is to the disadvantage of this country. Indeed, the Government's plans to extend the scale of higher technical education will be of little avail unless the substantial (net) drift of skilled personnel overseas is halted.[3]

Conclusion

Scientific research, at first regarded as a supplementary aid to productivity improvements, is being increasingly recognized as the spearhead of industrial progress and improved living standards. By comparison with that of the United States the British research effort would appear very small, yet any programme of expansion for the latter must be looked at in the light of general economic and social needs and the structure of costs and prices. But of the advantages of research co-operation at all levels and of the efficient utilization and dissemination of knowledge emanating from science and technology there can be no doubt. A closer collaboration between research bodies, an extension of sponsored research and a more appreciative and receptive attitude of management to research is also indicated. One thing is certain; by failing to make the best use of the world's store of scientific knowledge this country will be endangering not only her status as an industrial nation but her high living standards as well.

[1] See, for example, T. Wilson, op. cit., p. 35.
[2] See *Advisory Council on Scientific Policy*. Report, p. 14; 1956–7, Cmnd 278, xix: 'A high proportion, nearly 40% of British scientists who went to North America with fellowships, remained there.'
[3] For further particulars see B. Thomas, *Economic Implications of the International Mobility of Skill*. Paper given at the International Population Union Conference, New York, 1961.

V

NEW MATERIALS AND PROCESSES

THE results of the research and development activities described in the previous chapter show themselves in the marketing of new products and new materials and the introduction of new manufacturing processes. Over the present century technological progress has been so rapid that more than one-quarter of the goods produced in Europe today, and an even higher proportion in the United States, either did not exist 50 years ago, or were only in their experimental stage of development; television, the aeroplane, penicillin are three well-known cases in point. At the same time, existing wants are being satisfied differently and sometimes in a diversity of ways: new materials and new methods of production are making possible improvements in the content, style and performance of products, often at lower cost. Thus, stockings are now made of nylon rather than silk, upholstery of plastic in addition to leather, electric-train coaches of aluminium as well as steel, and so on; the introduction of new production techniques in the motor-car, refined petroleum and metallurgical industries have been no less impressive.

Innovations are sometimes classified as 'spontaneous' or 'induced'. Spontaneous innovations are those which arise as a result of either accident or deliberate research undertaken in the workshops and laboratories of individuals, firms, universities or research associations without any specialized stimuli other than the search after knowledge or achievement for its own sake or the general spur of money profits. Some of the more revolutionary inventions of the present century, e.g. television, D.D.T., insulin, the transistor etc., are possible examples. Induced innovations, on the other hand, are those which arise from a change in extraneous circumstances, outside the innovating institution's control, but which stimulates thinking along certain lines. In practice, of course, it is extremely difficult to trace the origin of a particular invention or to say into which of the above categories it falls. One can, however, examine some of the changing economic and social circumstances of recent years and trace the likely effects which these have had, and are having, on the direction and development of new ideas. For example, it is obvious that since 1939 full employment and the rising cost of labour on the one hand, and the growth of large and standardized markets on the other, have induced business men to increase mechanization wherever possible and to devise means by which productivity might be raised. Again, there is no doubt that the war encouraged research and development along certain lines from which peace-time industry, particularly in the field of plastics, electronics and aircraft, is now benefiting. More recently, the balance of payments situation and the shortage of dollar currency have forced both Government and industry to seek replacements for a variety of imports; an important outcome of this has been the establishment of an oil refining industry in this country. From a longer-term viewpoint, the growing world consumption and increasing prices of certain types of minerals and raw materials have accentuated research into the invention of substitutes. For example, 30 years ago the United States produced a surplus of 15% over her domestic requirements of industrial raw materials: today, she is forced to import an increasing proportion of her needs. Already she has used up 97% of her known resources of mercury, 85% of silver and lead, 70% of bauxite and 60% of copper, zinc and oil. Apart from this, her demands for the materials she is unable to produce herself in any quantity have soared. For example, she now imports 78% of her newsprint requirements, 56% of her wool, 16% of her petroleum, and all her natural rubber, tin, jute and copra; and the impact her demands for these materials can have on world prices was most clearly shown during the Korean war when the terms of trade moved so much against the industrialized nations.

There is no one set of circumstances nor a particular institutional framework which can be said to be the most productive of inventions: sometimes a discovery occurs almost by accident, e.g. penicillin in 1928; sometimes as a by-product of another related piece of research, e.g. nylon; sometimes as an outcome of academic research, e.g. silicones. They may emanate both from within the research organizations of large firms, as in the case of terylene and the transistor, or from the workshop of an individual inventor plugging away at a particular idea with the minimum of material resources, as in the case of the ball-point pen and the zip fastener.

Of the various industries responsible for the innovation of new materials in recent years, the chemical and the metallurgical stand supreme. It is difficult to pick out any one chemical advance in the twentieth century as being the most important; but perhaps the most far reaching in its effects has been that of polymerization, a chemical process whereby small carbon-hydrogen molecules, present in a particular raw material, are linked together to form long chains. Substances so constituted generally have plastic properties; and those materials known simply as plastics, synthetic fibres, silicones and synthetic rubber are all of this kind. Today the necessary raw materials, e.g. ethylene, butadiene and styrene etc., are usually derived from mineral sources, and in this connection the most significant advance of the last 10 years has been in the development of the petro-chemicals industry in the U.K.; its structure is discussed in more detail in the following pages. The fact that such an industry has evolved has also meant that other new materials have been developed, e.g. synthetic detergents, fertilizers and industrial solvents.

In the metallurgical industry progress has been most marked in the sphere of alloys; and the engineering and vehicles industries have been the most affected. Such advances have largely been conditioned by the discoveries of entirely new materials: the high speeds of modern aircraft would not be possible without titanium; aluminium by its light weight has revolutionized fabrication techniques in many spheres; developments in the modern electronics industry have been greatly accelerated by the commercialization of germanium and so on. New techniques of production in these fields, which have affected the quality of the end product, include shell-moulding and the continuous casting of steel. In the following pages some of the economic implications of these advances on 3 chemical and 1 metallurgical product of the twentieth century are outlined.

Chemical products

(*a*) *Petro-chemicals*

As a result of the development of the petroleum refining industry in this country, the production of a new and versatile raw material has been made possible from which a wide range of chemical products can be derived. In the United States 80% of the organic chemicals now being manufactured are made from mineral oil or natural gases; in this country indigenous coal and imported molasses still fulfil the more important role, though in 1957 45% of all the organic chemicals produced were petroleum-based. In recent years there has been a series of significant advances in the techniques of producing petro-chemicals, the exploitation of which has been accelerated by rising coal prices on the one hand and the need to conserve foreign currency on the other. In 1959 710,000 tons of petro-chemicals were manufactured in the U.K. compared with 55,000 tons in 1950 and 10,000 in 1945. The U.K. is now the leading producer in Europe and the second largest in the world; even so the U.S. produces 7 million tons of petro-chemicals a year and is at present supplying 88·5% of the entire world output. Many important products are now obtained from crude petroleum including detergents, synthetic fibres, paints, resins, carbon black, ammonia and agricultural chemicals.

The petro-chemical industry originated in the United States during the 1920's, and throughout the following decade intensive research both in the fundamental chemistry of petroleum and in chemical engineering led to the development of new processes for the manufacture of various industrial chemicals. It was not until 1942, however, that any petro-chemicals were produced outside America. In that year the Shell Company completed a petro-chemicals plant at Stanlow to manufacture a synthetic liquid detergent and the British Celanese Co. (now Courtaulds) built the first catalytic cracking plant in Britain to produce acetone and acetic acid for cellulose acetate rayon. Between 1945 and 1951 both companies enlarged their investment and widened their activities, while at the same time new oil cracking units were erected by I.C.I., British Petroleum Chemicals (now British Hydrocarbon Chemicals) and Petro-Chemicals. The largest growth has, however, occurred since that date and there are now 12 producers of petro-chemicals in this country with a combined capital of more than £120 million.

Petro-chemicals may be derived either from natural gas or from liquid petroleum feedstocks. In this country they are almost all of this latter origin, and the conversion of oil into chemicals is achieved in two main stages. First, the component fractions of the crude oil, i.e. the various carbon-hydrogen molecules, are separated by distillation. Hydrocarbons of suitable chemical structure for direct conversion into the chemical intermediaries desired are often produced. More usually, however, a further process is necessary by which selected fractions (e.g. naphtha) are subjected to a catalytic or steam cracking process by which the molecules are broken up into yet smaller units. These products are then passed through individual recovery and dehydrogenation units which in turn extract a particular olefine, viz. ethylene, butylene, butadiene and propylene. These are finally converted by other production processes, e.g. polymerization, into a wide range of chemical compounds such as polyethylene, liquid detergents, fungicides and synthetic rubber, which form the basis of numerous and varied end products. About 90% of all petro-chemicals are of this kind; the remainder consist of the aromatic compounds, e.g. benzene and toluene, and others which are used in the production of inorganic chemicals such as ammonia, carbon black and sulphur.

The structure of the petro-chemicals industry reflects both its mixed parentage and its complex and highly capitalized production processes. The impetus to development has arisen both from the chemical companies seeking new sources of raw materials and the oil companies seeking additional outlets for surplus gases. Thus, 4 of the 12 producers of petro-chemicals, I.C.I., Courtaulds, Monsanto Chemicals and Union Carbide, are primarily chemical manufacturers. In most cases these firms buy olefines from the petroleum companies for conversion into various chemical derivatives. The first two companies, however, also manufacture petrochemicals direct from selected hydrocarbon oil fractions. On the other hand, each of the main oil refining companies is represented in this field, though the structure of their interests is diverse. The Shell Company, for example, which operates through its subsidiary, Shell Chemicals, is virtually self-sufficient, starting its operations with products of distillation or cracking bought direct from the oil refineries and going right the way through to the manufacture of the end product. This same company also owns Petro-Chemicals Ltd, which not only produces olefines and aromatic solvents but large quantities of specialized chemicals as well. A different policy is adopted by British Petroleum Ltd in that its interests are confined to a financial participation in a number of chemical firms to whom it supplies petroleum raw materials. Thus, with the Distillers Company, it owns British Hydrocarbon Chemicals and, indirectly, Forth Chemicals (a joint subsidiary of British Hydrocarbon Chemicals and Monsanto Chemicals) and Grange Chemicals (a jointly owned concern of British Hydrocarbon Chemicals and the Oronite Chemical Company (U.S.)). The Esso Petroleum Company appears to set a mid-way course: it supplies feedstock to other manufacturers, but in general does not interest itself in the production of chemical end products. In addition to these two main groups of firms there are a number of specialist concerns, often jointly owned by oil and chemical companies, established to convert olefines into intermediary chemicals, e.g. by polymerization or condensation. Of these, the Forth Chemical Company manufactures styrene monomer, Grange Chemicals specializes in detergent alkylate, Associated Ethyl Company in tetra-ethyl lead, and International Synthetic Rubber Company in general purpose synthetic rubber. Sulphur is recovered in pure form at both the Esso and Shell refineries. Seven of the firms mentioned are wholly or partially U.S.-financed and there is little doubt that the technical expertise derived from their transAtlantic associations has enabled the U.K. industry to be developed more speedily than would otherwise have been the case.

Before the growth of the petroleum refinery industry in this country, the location of the petro-chemical industry was mainly influenced by the site of the existing chemical plants; and the largest single petro-chemical scheme is still that of I.C.I. created originally as an extension of its Wilton works. Nowadays, however, due to the advances in refining techniques and the economies of integrated processes thereby made possible, two new areas of concentration are developing, viz. around the Esso refinery at Fawley, which comprises the chemical plants of Monsanto Chemicals, Union Carbide and I.S.R.C. (total net assets £30 million), and in the proximity of the B.P. refinery at Grangemouth, the constituent firms of which are Union Carbide, Forth Chemicals and Grange Chemicals (investment £25 million).

Petro-chemicals are already achieving a significant role in a number of finished goods markets. All the carbon black used as a preservative for rubber tyres is derived from petroleum. Some 40% of the washing and cleaning products bought in the U.K. are synthetic detergents, and these are almost entirely based on petro-chemicals. Some 90% of chemical solvents, which find their outlets in the paints and resin industries, are also derived from petroleum feedstock as are a substantial proportion of the thermo-plastics, e.g. polyethylene, polystyrene, polyvinyl chloride etc., now being produced. General purpose synthetic rubber comes from the olefine butadiene, which is not only used in the production of motor tyres, but is an important constituent of a resin from which shoe soles are being made. In all, products to the value of more than £500 million are derived each year from petro-chemicals.

What are the implications of these developments from the viewpoint of the U.K. economy as a whole? First, a new source of raw materials for manufacturing industry has been discovered, the import-content of which is generally lower than that of their traditional counterparts. Moreover, these materials are enabling new industries to be established and new techniques of production to be utilized. The present output of petro-chemicals is estimated to require only about 2% of the amount of petroleum feedstock converted into fuels and lubricants. Thus the conversion value (i.e. the ratio of the price of the finished product to the cost of raw material imports) is high—much more so than that of the majority of products made from natural raw materials. In addition, there is a direct saving on imported raw materials, e.g. it is believed that by 1960 the general purpose synthetic rubber produced in this country was saving the United Kingdom some $30 million each year.

Secondly, as will be illustrated in more detail from the case studies of the man-made fibre and plastics industries, petro-chemicals are versatile raw materials. They provide the basis for a range of products capable of being put to widely differing uses; they are easy to handle and can be manufactured to a high degree of purity. With advances in industrial chemistry new opportunities are opening up which are both more diverse and extensive than those offered by natural materials.

Thirdly, the attraction of petroleum as a raw material is enhanced by the general stability of its price level and the fact that its elasticity of supply (as a source of petro-chemicals) is at present considerably greater than most natural substitutes. For example, coal-based carbon (the other main source of organic chemicals) is essentially a by-product of coking operations; in consequence, the present rate of growth of this part of the industry has been much slower than that of the chemical industry as a whole in recent years.

Fourthly, the production of petro-chemicals appears to be strongly affected by the economies of large-scale production and it is not perhaps surprising that the five most important U.K. producers are amongst the largest firms in British industry. Moreover, as the other natural raw materials become increasingly inadequate for supplying the intermediates required to satisfy a growing demand for the end products the cost advantages of petro-chemicals become larger. But even so it is worth recalling that the earliest producers of petro-chemicals were concerned with securing an additional source of raw materials. It appears too that, up to a certain volume of usage, it is cheaper to produce ethylene from alcohol, but thereafter it pays to process it from oil. It has been only since the war that the oil companies have begun to take the initiative, partly, as we have seen, in order that their surplus gases might be utilized.

(b) Artificial or man-made fibres

Though the origin of artificial or man-made fibres, as they are now usually called, dates back to the 1880's, it was not until the 1930's that they were manufactured on any scale. In 1900 world production of artificial fibres amounted to 2 million lb., in 1923 it was 35 million lb. and by 1935 it was more than 1,000 million lb. In 1960 it was 6,833 million lb. or 15·8% of total world production of fibres of all kinds. World consumption per head is approximately 11 lb. of natural and $2\frac{1}{2}$ lb. of artificial fibre per annum. The United States is the leading supplier of man-made fibres, its output amounting to 25·0% of the total; Japan (13·8%), Western Germany (8·9%) and the United Kingdom (7·8%) come second, third and fourth respectively.

There are 3 main types of man-made fibres which may be classified according to the raw materials from which they are derived. First, there are the cellulosic—the rayons[1]—which today account for 84·2% of the world and 84·4% of the U.K. output of man-made fibres; they are essentially of the same chemical composition as the vegetable matter—wood pulp and cotton linters—from which they are made. Secondly, and of growing importance, are the synthetics such as nylon, terylene and acrilan which are produced by a succession of chemical processes from organic chemicals; these textiles account for around 15% of both the world and U.K. output. The contribution of the third group, the regenerated or reconstituted protein fibres of animal or vegetable origin, e.g. 'viscara' and 'fibrolane', is as yet relatively unimportant.

It was as rather crude substitutes for silk that the first man-made fibres were used; but over the years advances in manufacturing techniques and the discovery of many new fibres have resulted in the marketing of textiles whose qualities are superior in many respects to their more traditional competitors. Fibre-utility is, of course, a composite of many different properties and no artificial fibre is in every way better than its natural substitute or vice-versa. However, by suitable texturing processes, certain of the more highly desirable properties usually found only in the natural fibres can be incorporated within artificial fibres, e.g. the 'ban-lon' process enables nylon to absorb moisture and insulate the body. Similarly, it is possible to overcome the various deficiencies of the natural fibres by blending them with the appropriate artificial fibres. Nylon and wool and terylene and wool admixtures, for example, are more durable than pure wool.

The first practicable process for the manufacture of an artificial fibre was patented by Count Hilaire de Chardonnet in France in 1884. His method was to convert mulberry fibres (and soon after, cotton) into cellulose nitrate by treatment with nitric acid in the presence of sulphuric acid. The resulting solution was then spun by being forced through the fine holes of a spinnerette, and coagulated by contact with warm air. The process was dangerous, however, as the nitrocellulose fibre produced was both inflammable and explosive, so the product was not very suitable as a textile material.

[1] In the United Kingdom the word 'rayon' is usually used for fibres of cellulosic origin (viscose and cellulose acetate) and the term 'synthetic fibres' for the true synthetics. The rayons and other regenerated fibres are made from some natural fibrous material; the synthetic fibres are not—they are synthesized from simple chemical substances.

The process for making viscose rayon, a regenerated cellulose, from wood pulp was developed soon after (1892) by the British chemists Cross, Bevan and Beadle in their laboratories at Kew. The wood pulp was treated with caustic soda and carbon disulphide which converted the cellulose in the wood into a soluble derivative, leaving behind all other matter. After some time, the solution was extruded into a precipitating bath containing sulphuric acid and sodium sulphate. It took some time for the process to become established and it was only when it was exhibited in Paris in 1900 that Courtaulds, already well established in the textile industry, took an interest and acquired the U.K. patent rights. Even then, because of unanticipated manufacturing difficulties, it was another 6 years before the first samples of viscose rayon yarn appeared on the market. Other firms which became prominent in viscose manufacture were British Enka Ltd,[1] Harbens Ltd, and North British Rayon Ltd, but in 1913 Courtaulds was still producing nearly all the British output of viscose rayon.

The next important development was the discovery of cellulose acetate fibre, or as it is more usually known 'acetate', in the years following the First World War. In 1917 the brothers Henri and Camille Dreyfus were invited by the British Government to establish a factory in this country to manufacture cellulose acetate dope for waterproofing fabric aeroplane wings. When the war ended this market completely disappeared, so the Dreyfus brothers had to seek new uses for their product. After a period of intensive research they discovered a method of converting it into artificial silk and in 1921 began marketing their fibre under the name of 'Celanese'. Subsequently other competitors, including some foreign firms, sold the same product under different trade names.

Unlike viscose, which is a regenerated cellulose, acetate is a derivative. It is made by treating cotton linters with acetic anhydride to produce cellulose acetate which is then dissolved in acetone, extruded through a spinnerette and dry spun. The elegance and simplicity of the dry-spinning process (as compared with the wet-spinning process used in the manufacture of viscose) quickly led to the widespread development of acetate fibres and by 1939, despite

[1] A subsidiary of Algemene Kinstzijde Urie, the Dutch holding company which controls 11% of world output of viscose and cuprammonium rayon.

severe competition from its cheaper and more durable substitute, acetate output amounted to one-third of that of viscose.

The first truly synthetic fibre to be invented was nylon. In 1927 the U.S. firm of E. I. Du Pont de Nemours began a programme of fundamental research in inorganic chemistry under the direction of Dr W. H. Carothers of Harvard University. Carothers chose as his basic project the study of polymerization, but it was not long before the possibilities of producing a new textile fibre became apparent. This was eventually achieved in February 1935 and three years later patents were published covering the production of the '66' polymer—nylon. After a short period of experimental production, a large-scale plant was set up at Seaford (Delaware) in 1939, and in the following year I.C.I. were granted the sole British manufacturing rights. Later, in association with Courtaulds, I.C.I. formed the British Nylon Spinners Ltd to produce and sell nylon yarn. In 1942 one of Courtaulds factories was converted to spin the yarn for parachutes and tow-ropes. Immediately after the war a site of 112 acres at Pontypool in Monmouthshire was chosen for a new and specialized factory, and by 1950 it was producing 10 million lb. of yarn each year. The present figure is more than three times this amount.

The basic raw material for the manufacture of nylon is benzene, a by-product of the distillation of coal (and latterly of oil as well). After undergoing various chemical treatments nylon in a molten condition is obtained; this is then allowed to solidify and crushed into small chips. These processes are carried out by I.C.I.; the chips are melted at British Nylon Spinners and are then extruded through a spinnerette and the filaments follow a similar process to that of the rayons.

The success of nylon encouraged the efforts of other countries to produce new fibres from synthetic substances. Fibres similar to nylon were subsequently discovered in Germany and the United States, but the next major development was the invention of the polyester fibre, terylene, by the British chemists Whinfield and Dixon in 1941 in the laboratories of the Calico Printing Association. Unfortunately, the war delayed the commercialization of this new textile and it was not until 1955 that I.C.I. (who had earlier acquired the world rights outside the U.S.A.) began full-scale production at Wilton. The initial annual capacity of the plant was 11 million lb., but this has quickly expanded to 30 million lb. In this country the main raw material of terylene is ethylene—a petro-chemical; the basic production process is similar to that of nylon.

Finally, a third class of synthetic fibres must be mentioned—the polyacrylics such as 'orlon', 'acrilan', 'winyon' and 'dynel'. Manufacture of these has only recently (1957) started in the United Kingdom, but in the United States they already account for one-sixth of the output of synthetic fibres. Courtaulds were first in the field in this country with their 'Courtelle', but they are now facing competition from two U.S. companies, Chemstrand and Du Pont de Nemours, who have recently completed acrylic fibres plants in Northern Ireland.

Space forbids any further historical treatment of the various man-made fibres. An idea of the rapid growth of the production of synthetic fibres in relation to their main competitors is given in Table 24.

Since 1945 there have also been a number of important technical advances both within the rayon industry, e.g. the development of high-tenacity rayon and tri-acetate yarns, and in the field of textiles derived from regenerated animal or vegetable proteins. Courtaulds, for example, started producing 'fibrolane' from casein as far back as 1937, while at one time, in their Dumfries plant, I.C.I. had an annual capacity of 22 million lb. of 'ardil' (made from groundnuts); unfortunately, however, this latter fibre failed to achieve popularity and in September 1957 the plant was closed down.

The production of fibre material is essentially a chemical operation. As in the chemical industry, the manufacturers concerned tend to be highly capitalized enterprises undertaking a group of related operations involving certain basic raw materials, with joint-supply, vertical integration and diversity of product the usual pattern. Integration is both backwards to the raw material stage, e.g. British Celanese operates an oil cracking plant to produce its own raw material for the manufacture of nylon, and forwards into the weaving, knitting, bleaching, dyeing, finishing sections and in some cases the manufacture of garments as well. In the main, however, since the scale of production at which mechanical processes can be carried on efficiently is considerably smaller than that of the chemical processes, the production of continuous filament yarn and the subsequent operations are usually performed separately. Many small firms can undertake the textile activities of extrusion; the production of polymer is largely in the hands of the chemical firms. For example, I.C.I. is the most important producer of both nylon polymer and terylene, while Monsanto Chemicals, Union Carbide and British Hydrocarbons have all

TABLE 24

ESTIMATED WORLD FIBRE PRODUCTION

Million lb.

	1934–5 to 1938–9 (*average*)	1946–7 to 1950–1 (*average*)	1955–6	1959–60
Natural				
Wool　　.. 　..	2,024	2,186	2,784	3,221
Cotton　.. 　..	14,549	12,981	21,188	23,566
Other[1]　.. 　..	7,362	6,067	8,448	9,471
	23,935	21,234	32,420	36,258
Man-made				
Rayon　.. 　..	1,444	2,505	5,020	5,563
Non-cellulosic　..	1	86	594	1,270
	1,445	2,591	5,614	6,833
Man-made fibres as per cent of total .. 　..	5·7	10·9	14·8	15·8

[1] viz. silk, flax, hemp and jute.

Source: Commonwealth Economic Committee, *Industrial Fibres*, H.M.S.O., 1961.

established plants to produce polythene, a material with promising fibre applications. Our concern here is mainly with the latter section of the industry. Indeed it is convenient to regard the textile industry proper, viz. the spinners and weavers, the producers of hosiery, knitted warp goods, woven cloth, lace goods etc., as the main market for the fibre material produced; the cotton industry, for example, draws one-sixth of its raw material for spinning and one-third of its yarn for weaving from man-made sources.

The dominant firm in fibre manufacture is Courtaulds, which has also integrated forwards into the production of fabrics, including warp knitting, and of textile machinery. With net assets of £186 million this company is the main producer of viscose, and together with British Celanese, a firm which it acquired in 1957, controls 90% of all U.K. rayon output, including all acetate staple and most acetate filament production. It also produces a range of synthetic and regenerated protein fibres and, in equal partnership with I.C.I., owns British Nylon Spinners. This latter firm specializes in the spinning of nylon polymer, purchasing its raw materials from I.C.I., and its products vary widely in denier from silk-stocking filament to tyre cord.

I.C.I. is also a multi-product fibre manufacturer. Excluding Courtaulds and I.C.I. there are some 9 other producers, but these are mainly specialized.[1] In all, 6 firms produce viscose rayon, 3 acetate, 2 nylon, 2 other types of synthetic fibres and 2 protein fibre. Six of the 11 firms manufacture other products including textile machinery, plastics, chemicals and transparent films. The total number of employees is 40,000 and there are 22 establishments. The industry is exceptionally highly capitalized with a capital per employee of £3,250. Four establishments employ less than 300, eight between 300 and 2,999 and ten 3,000 or more. Apart from the B.N.S. plant at Pontypool, all the factories are located in the Midlands or North of England, 9 within Lancashire—the traditional home of the textile industry. Because of the large capital and research costs[2] involved the optimum size of each firm tends to be large in relation to that of the industry as a whole; and, with oligopoly being the prevailing market characteristic, the danger of collusion and monopolistic pricing is a very real one. In general, however, it would appear that this power has not been used against the public interest and one writer has gone so far as to say that in the rayon industry the optimum balance between competitive

[1] Since this chapter was written, one of those firms, Harbens Ltd, has been acquired by Courtaulds.

[2] In 1960 the U.K. industry was estimated to be spending £3·4 million annually on research.

conditions and monopolistic forces now prevails.[1] Price stability has allowed sufficient profits for expensive research to be undertaken, but at the same time competition (both from within the industry and from without) has been sufficient to ensure the attainment of a high degree of technical and economic efficiency.

The uses of man-made fibres are manifold. Two-fifths of the output of viscose rayon is bought by the rubber tyre industry.[2] Acetate finds its market mainly in the dress and underwear fields where softness is desirable and where there are opportunities for blending. It has also been widely used as an electrical insulator. Nylon has over 100 separate industrial functions. Of the finished output of continuous filament yarn and staple fibre produced by the man-made fibres industry in 1956, 34·3% was bought by weaving manufacturers, 12% became warp knit, 10·1% went to the hosiery industry and 16·5% was exported. Industrial uses accounted for one-third of the total output. Synthetic fibres are now responsible for 22% of the household and clothing markets, 11% of the industrial fibre and 85% of the tyre fabric.

Concerning the wider economic significance of the man-made fibres industry, it is interesting to compare the conversion value of its products in relation to those of the natural fibres. For example, on an average, £100 of imported materials makes possible £300–£350 worth of cotton products, £175–£300 worth of wool products, £225–£325 worth of silk products, and £950–£1,250 worth of rayon and acetate products.

It is further estimated that the utilization of man-made fibres

[1] D. C. Hague, *The Economics of Man-made Fibres*, Duckworth, 1957, p. 296.
[2] Fibres are used in tyre manufacture to increase strength. The comparative costs of various tyre yarns are given in the following table:

Comparative cost of cotton, rayon, nylon and steel tyre yarns, March 1957

	Cost per lb. (cents)	Tenacity Grams per denier	Cost per unit of strength (cents)
Cotton	72	2·26	32
Rayon	69·5	3·32	21
Nylon	175	6·99	22
Steel	140	3·20	44

Source: G. D. Mallory, Textile Research Institute, August 1957. Quoted by R. Robson, *The Man-made Fibres Industry*, p. 93.

for the production of cloth enables the following savings to be effected:

TABLE 25

UTILIZATION OF MAN-MADE FIBRES FOR THE PRODUCTION OF CLOTH

Saving pence per lb. of fibre used in place of:

	Cotton	Wool	Silk	Flax
Rayon and acetate ..	23	80	252	15
Synthetics	33	90	262	25

Source: *Man-made Fibres.* Man-made Fibres Producers' Committee (n.d.)

It is obviously too early to judge the true economic significance of man-made fibres. At the least, however, they perform an important function in supplementing the output of natural fibres and helping to maintain the import bill of raw materials for fibre production at a reasonable level. Thus, to produce a poundage of cotton or wool equal to the consumption of man-made fibres for 1956–8 would have cost an extra £26 million per annum in imports. Moreover, the expansion of world population and the fact that the natural fibres are produced in climatic regions suitable for the growing of foodstuffs, while the raw materials for the man-made fibres make fewer demands in this respect, suggests that prices will move more in favour of the latter. Indeed since the man-made fibres industry relies for its prosperity on the skill of labour rather than on the quantity of material resources, the industry may well be ideally suitable for the U.K. economy in its present situation.

(c) Plastics

There is no simple comprehensive definition of plastics; nor is it at all easy to delineate the boundaries of the plastics industry as we know it today. For our purposes, however, we shall take plastics to mean 'a group of chemically modified substances, usually of synthetic origin, which are capable, at some stage of their production, of being shaped (i.e. plasticized) into any desired form', and the plastics industry as comprising those firms which either manufacture such substances or convert them (e.g. by moulding, extrusion or calendering operations) into mouldings, sheets, rods, tubes etc. from which finished articles or components may be produced. On the basis of these definitions, some 575,000 tons of plastic materials were produced in 1960 compared with 158,000 tons in 1950 and 28,000 tons in 1938. Weight figures, however, belie the true significance of such materials to the British economy; when specific gravity is taken into account, for example, their present volume exceeds that of all the non-ferrous metals, and is equal to two-fifths of the hardwood and one-seventh of the steel. There are indeed few industries which do not use plastics in appreciable quantities and few consumer markets in which plastic articles are not represented. Largely owing to the nature of their chemical composition, plastics are the most versatile of all materials and the plastics industry is in a position to meet specific requirements in finite terms. Thus, by suitable modification, the finished product may be soft and pliable as for packaging materials and clothing, hard and rigid as for electrical fitting and floor tiles, or even liquid as for paints. From the viewpoint of fabrication techniques, plastics are of two main classes, thermosetting and thermoplastic. The former undergo a chemical reaction when heated and become permanently hard and inflexible, the latter soften on heating and harden again on cooling and can be made to do so indefinitely.

The origins of the plastics industry date back to 1846, when the German scientist Schonbein discovered nitrocellulose. Moulded articles made from this substance were exhibited in this country by Alexander Parkes in 1862, but it was not until 1868 that, in response to a $10,000 prize offered for the invention of a substitute to elephant ivory, an American, Hyatt, developed a new composition by treating cotton cellulose with nitric acid: this he called celluloid. This same material was subsequently marketed in this country by the British Xylonite Company, and helped not only to supplement supplies of ivory for such uses as billiard balls, piano keys, knife handles, shoe horns etc., but to form the basis for the new photographic and cinematograph industries. In spite of its unsuitability as an insulating material, celluloid remained for many years the only plastic substance in widespread use.[1] At the beginning,

[1] In 1884, however, artificial leather was produced by the application of nitrocellulose coatings and castor-oil to a fabric backing, while six years later came the discovery of casein, a plastic material derived from skimmed milk, from which such articles as knitting needles and buttons are still produced today.

the demand for this former product was met by the vulcanized rubber industry, but for technical reasons the quantities available were strictly limited. It was thus timely that a suitable new plastic resin, formed from the reaction between phenol and formaldehyde, was discovered in 1907 by Leo Baekland. This was called 'bakelite', the first truly synthetic plastic, and also, when compounded with a fibrous filler, the first which could be moulded or compressed. Moreover, unlike its earlier counterparts, bakelite was hard and infusible and did not soften when heated.

The early development of bakelite is very much associated with that of the electrical industry; and, without the availability of phenolic moulding powders at that time, it is doubtful whether the growth of the radio industry during the 1920's would have been so rapid. Later, the use of thermosetting plastics was extended by the discovery of a ureaformaldehyde polymer powder which made possible a fuller colour range of moulding materials. At the same time the material manufacturers were seeking to improve their production methods and during the 1920's the injection moulding technique was first utilized on a new cellulose acetate material. This not only improved the quality of existing plastics components but paved the way for the important discoveries of the next decade.

The year 1933 is generally regarded as marking the beginning of a new era in the development of the plastics industry. About this time, the first of a whole new range of thermoplastic materials began to appear on the market; these were unique in that they were derived from organic chemicals especially produced for that purpose. These in turn were the result of research into the characteristics of synthetic organic polymers and the way in which they might be broken up and reassembled to suit specific requirements. For example, the basic chemical constituents of polymethyl methacrylate ('perspex') and polyvinyl chloride were already known before the First World War, but commercial application was hampered by the difficulties associated with the actual conversion techniques in the former case, and by the lethargic state of the market in the latter. In 1932, however, J. W. Crawford of I.C.I. discovered an economic process of synthesizing methacrylic acid, the result of which was the marketing of a tough, light, transparent plastic called 'perspex', which is now being extensively used as a substitute for glass. Most aircraft screens are made of this material. In the case of

F

polyvinyl chloride (p.v.c.), a plastic especially resistant to abrasion and chemical attack, British chemical interest remained unaroused until 1939, by which time articles made from it were being sold in both Germany and the U.S.A. It was in fact as a possible substitute for rubber that the future possibilities of this plastic were first foreseen, and in 1944 bulk production of p.v.c. began from a Government-owned plant. This plastic is now used for the production of raincoats, floor covering, leather cloth and cable covering. The other new thermoplastic of this era was that of polyethylene, a material first synthesized by I.C.I. in 1933 as an indirect result of the studies of the chemical effects of high pressures. In this instance, the translation of laboratory results to full-scale commercial production was both time-consuming and expensive, but by 1939 the erection of a full-scale plant had begun. Polyethylene is flexible and strong and its excellent insulating properties make it a very suitable material for electrical purposes. Its other uses range from domestic ware to toys, cable insulation and water pipes; film of it is used for food packaging.

Since the wider use of plastic materials has been encouraged by the post-war shortage of competitive substances, the output of the plastics industry has rapidly increased in recent years. In 1932, before the new materials had come into prominence, the annual production of plastics materials was only 20,000 tons: by 1950 this output had expanded eightfold and by 1958 twentyfold. Of this latter amount, the newer plastics accounted for 245,000 tons and those which had been in commercial production before 1930 the balance. In the case of two thermosetting plastics—the phenolics and aminoplastics—and two thermoplastics (p.v.c. and polyethylene) output exceeded 45,000 tons.[1] In addition, brief mention must be made of two other groups of plastics, viz. the polyamides (the development of which dates from the work of Carothers on nylon in the United States during the 1930's) and the polyesters (commonly used in conjunction with glass fibre), which are a by-product of the discovery of terylene first patented in this country in 1941.

The United Kingdom is now the third largest producer of plastics materials in the world, exceeded only by the United States and Western Germany. Britain, however, exports a slightly higher

[1] viz. in 000's of tons: phenolics and cresylics 65, aminoplastics 50, polyvinyl chloride 73, polythene 55.

proportion of her output (25%) than either of these two countries: imports are less than one-tenth in all three cases. On the other hand production figures are not necessarily a good guide to a country's consumption of plastic materials. For example, in 1959, Sweden and Holland, both relatively small producers of plastics, consumed 21·5 lb. and 15·8 lb. per head respectively compared with the U.K.'s 16·5 lb.

The present structure of the plastics industry is interesting. There are two main groups of firms: first, the suppliers of plastics materials, e.g. moulding powders, resins and rennet casein; and second, the converting manufacturers who process these plastics materials into various shapes and forms for sale either to user-industries or to the general public. Essentially the first group has evolved as an off-shoot of the chemical industry on the one hand and the petroleum industry on the other. To appreciate why this is so, a word must be said about the three main types of raw materials from which plastics are derived: (i) naturally occurring raw materials, e.g. bitumen, shellac etc.; (ii) chemically modified naturally occurring materials, e.g. nitrocellulose, casein etc.; (iii) minerals, e.g. coal and petroleum. Of these, the third group is by far the most important and is the basis for 90% of all plastics materials: coal is the primary source of the intermediate chemicals —phenol, urea, naphthalene, acetylene—while benzene, ethylene, acetic acid and butadiene are derived from petroleum. This latter mineral in particular is rapidly assuming a pre-eminent position as a raw material. At present it is the source for 45% of all plastics, and this proportion may well rise to two-thirds in the course of the next decade. Since the production of these intermediate chemicals (like the second group of plastics) is essentially a chemical (or petro-chemical) operation, it is not surprising that a number of the more important plastics materials suppliers originated as producers in these or related fields. Thus I.C.I., Shell Petroleum, Distillers, Courtaulds and Monsanto Chemicals have each embarked on the production of plastic materials as a logical extension of their existing activities. These probably account for the major part of the output of plastic materials. There are also a number of specialist companies, such as Bakelite, British Xylonite and British Industrial Plastics, some of which originated as plastics moulders. Production is highly capitalized and most firms make only a limited range of substances. The manufacturing process is continuous by nature and highly automated; in consequence, a high proportion of the labour force (which is small in relation to other industries of the same sales turnover) is made up of skilled technicians or research chemists. Research is undertaken by all the main chemical companies as part and parcel of their wider activities and most of the important new developments have emanated from outside the plastics industry as such. Some of the larger plastics specialists also have their own laboratories while a number of companies have close financial or technical associations with foreign concerns, particularly German and American.

The other main branch of the plastics industry comprises those firms which convert the materials into a variety of forms, e.g. moulding and extruding mixtures, sheet, rod, tube, film, foil and resins, which are either bought by appropriate user-industries or incorporated internally into subsequent production processes. These firms are the true 'plasticizers' and are of four main kinds, engaged respectively in moulding, extruding, laminating and calendering operations. Of these the moulding group is perhaps the most important. It comprises some 400 enterprises (some of whom are also producers of plastics materials), who manufacture plastic articles of various forms either by compression moulding (in the case of thermosetting plastics) or injection moulding (in the case of thermoplastics). Firms may be either general purpose—supplying by specification to industry at large—or specialists. Of this latter group some tend to limit their interests to the production of particular types of plastics, some serve particular industries and quite a number produce mouldings as components for assembly either within their own company or associate companies. Much the same structure applies to the other branches of the industry. There are, for example, some 100 extruders[1] which are of two distinct types—electrical and general extruders. The cable makers and wire coverers comprise the former; the numerous jobbing shops, which extrude rods, tubes and sections to customer's order, and the various well-established concerns who have branched out into the plastics trade make up the rest. There are also a number of specialist firms engaged in laminating and calendering

[1] Extruding is a process by which the material in question is forced under heat and pressure through a shaping orifice or die and then cooled.

processes, both of which are used for the production of plastic sheet and film. Each of the main converting operations is highly automated and the labour content is comparatively low. The types of machinery are as many and varied as the products made and thus it is possible for firms of differing size and financial strength to compete with each other.

Broadly speaking the converters comprise three main categories of firms. First, a number of the chemical concerns mentioned above have integrated forwards, and regard conversion and the production of plastics materials as part and parcel of their organizaton. Thus, I.C.I. manufactures not only polythene and methacrylic acid but such products as artificial leather and perspex as well, while Monsanto Chemicals supplies a wide range of plastic articles based on its own products. These firms may be almost self-sufficient, selling direct to the final consumer. Secondly, there are those enterprises whose main interests lie outside the plastics industry as such, but for one reason or another have found it profitable to manufacture their own moulds, dies, extruders etc. First within this group are those firms manufacturing competitive materials, e.g. non-ferrous metal tubes, which have in recent years entered the field of polythene water piping, and the suppliers of rubber cables, who have added plastic materials to their existing interests. Second, there are those consumers of plastics materials who have integrated their activities backwards. For example, E. K. Cole, producers of radio and television sets, used to buy their wooden cabinets from specialists; now they not only make their own mouldings, but are themselves important suppliers of plastic articles in their own right. The third group of firms (the greatest numerically but not in importance) are the specialist companies.

The plastics industry is thus shown to be of hybrid origins and composed of firms of diverse interests and experience—a factor which has probably aided its technological progress. Competition is a mixture between monopoly and oligopoly, with easy entry from established producers in related fields. Most plastics are, in any case, replaceable one by another, in part if not in whole, and though one producer may have a monopoly or near monopoly of one kind of material, there is no producer who has a dominant hold over all markets. With the present rapid developments, competition is on the basis of technical qualities rather than price. Moreover, the impetus to research and development is multifold. It originates both from suppliers of the basic raw materials seeking ways in which to enlarge their markets and also from user-firms, particularly in competitive industries, looking for new or improved materials in order to ensure continuity of production and increase manufacturing efficiency.

The markets for plastics are as wide as industry itself. In spite of the unique characteristics which individual plastics possess, most materials have the common properties of lightness, strength, non-absorption, chemical resistance and electrical insulation. Classification is difficult because of the very nature of the materials themselves; any one of them can compete with any other substance and even one material can have a multitude of end uses. For example, according to its final characteristics, p.v.c. can be substituted for leather, steel, wood or paper; polyethylene competes with paper, tin, aluminium, glass and earthenware; polystyrene replaces ceramics, glass, wood and various metals, and so on. Industrial uses are prolific and now include conveyor belting for mines, packaging materials, cable coverings and aircraft wind-screens, to mention but a few. Domestically the ubiquity of plastics extends to kitchen ware, upholstery, toys, gramophone records, paints and adhesive tape.

Even so plastics are not, in general, cheap materials. For example, when viewed in relation to volume, the cost of moulding powders at £250 a ton is not usually less than the equivalent in steel, timber or earthenware. But the special advantages of plastics, e.g. their lower processing and fabrication costs and the special properties which the finished article possesses, often outweigh the differences in costs.

Metallurgical products

Metallurgical advances have both conditioned and been conditioned by progress in other spheres of industry. In particular the exacting needs of the aircraft and atomic power industries for constructional materials with special properties have resulted in the development of new alloys which, either by enabling the introduction of better-quality products or the use of more efficient manufacturing methods, have subsequently benefited other branches of industry. For example, important technical advances in the field of alloy steels have made possible greatly improved corrosion- and heat-resisting products, while the growth of the chemical, oil and atomic energy industries has stimulated the production of a number of the rarer metals, the most important of which are zirconium, niobium, vanadium, tantalum, molybdenum and beryllium. In other cases, shortages of existing materials have resulted in the development of substitutes; thus, in place of nickel used in the subplate of chromium-plated objects, a plain anti-corrosive steel requiring no plating has been developed. Improved tungsten steels are enabling more accurate machine tools capable of higher speeds to be produced, thereby contributing to the efficiency and development of automation methods. One metal—aluminium—deserves especial attention.

Aluminium and aluminium alloys

Next to steel, British industry uses a larger tonnage of aluminium than any other metal; in 1960 some 350,000 tons of fabricated or semi-fabricated aluminium products were manufactured in this country—a fivefold expansion over the corresponding output for 1938. Moreover, owing to its relative cheapness and highly desirable properties of low density, strong corrosion resistance and high thermal and electrical conductivity, aluminium is not only supplying an increasing proportion of the world's metal requirements, but in some applications is replacing non-metallic materials as well. For example, because of the increasing price of tin and paper and the extension of pre-packing and self-service in the distributive trades, aluminium foil is being increasingly used as a packaging material. In building and structural engineering and bridge construction, for example, the high corrosion resistance of this metal is an enormous asset as it enables maintenance costs to be drastically reduced, while its lightness of weight makes it an invaluable material in the manufacture of airframes and aircraft components. For this reason the use of aluminium in the construction of ships makes possible an enlarged carrying capacity and, by the lowering of the centre of gravity, increases stability and enhances navigational safety. The bodies of public service and goods vehicles are also being built in aluminium, the underframe and the coachwork being economically fabricated as one single integrated structure. By the adoption of this metal for low-tension distribution lines the various Area Electricity Boards are saving up to 30% in capital costs, while it is also beginning to be used in the field of insulated power cables for electricity supply. Other important consumers of aluminium include the building, atomic power, chemical and motor-car industries.[1]

Aluminium is abundant in the combined state in nature, coming next to oxygen and silicon. Yet it was not until the electrolytic method of extraction was discovered in 1888 by U.S. and French scientists that large-scale production became possible. Moreover, capital costs are high, varying between £600 and £1,000 a ton of annual capacity of plant. A limiting factor to the metal's development in this country has been the shortage of cheap electric power: it takes some 25,000 kwh. of electrical energy to produce 1 ton of aluminium, or the equivalent of 20 times the coal consumed in producing 1 ton of iron. World production increased from 100,000 tons in 1921 to 750,000 tons in 1946 and 5 million tons in 1961. On a weight basis, world output is almost 30% of the total production of non-ferrous metals and on a volume basis it exceeds the total of all the other non-ferrous metals. The consumption per head of population in a number of countries is shown in the following table.

TABLE 26

CONSUMPTION OF ALUMINIUM IN SELECTED COUNTRIES

(*lbs per capita*)

	1951	1961		1951	1961
United States	16·5	25·2	France	4·8	8·9
Switzerland	10·5	18·3	Australia	4·6	8·1
United Kingdom	12·3	16·0	Italy	2·6	6·0
Canada	10·5	15·5	Japan	1·2	3·9
West Germany	5·2	14·7	India	0·05	0·2

Source: E. G. West, 'Aluminium in Britain 1960–1970'. Paper read to the Royal Society of Arts, November, 1962.

[1] About 10% of U.K. aluminium consumption is accounted for by building and constructional work (compared with nearly one-quarter in the U.S.) while an average passenger car embodies some 36 lb.

In the United Kingdom aluminium is produced from bauxite —virgin aluminium as it is called. The sole supplier is the British Aluminium Company which first started production in Scotland in 1896, the electricity being obtained from a hydro-electric plant. The initial production of 200 tons per annum did not find a ready market and the company was twice forced to close down before 1910. Subsequent growth has been steady and the company has integrated both vertically and laterally. Nevertheless, production of virgin aluminium at 30,000 tons a year is still only one-tenth of the country's total requirements and the smelting of non-virgin aluminium and aluminium alloys accounts for the main activities of the U.K. producers. The structure of the industry is a mixed one. Thus while 2 firms—British Aluminium, a subsidiary of Tube Investments Ltd and Reynolds Metal (U.S.), and Northern Aluminium, a subsidiary of the U.S. company Aluminium Ltd—at present account for two-thirds of the total output of aluminium fabricated products, the remaining one-third is produced by more than 150 enterprises of various sizes.[1] For the most part, however, these are specialist suppliers, limiting their interests to a particular range of products such as rolled aluminium, castings, foil, extruded and drawn products, and wire and electrical conductors etc.

These establishments also consume home-produced secondary aluminium. The output of the metal from scrap—secondary aluminium—is about 40% of that of virgin aluminium. In 1961, for example, over 100,000 tons of the former were produced compared with 250,000 tons of the latter. Much of the secondary aluminium is produced in the processing and fabricating establishments.

---

[1] During the past three years there have been a number of structural changes in the aluminium industry. In September 1959 the Aluminium Company of America (ALCOA) joined with Imperial Chemical Industries in the formation of the Imperial Aluminium Company with the aim of increasing I.C.I.'s share of the domestic wrought aluminium market. Then, more recently, the Aluminium Company of Canada and Enfield Rolling Mills have set up a new company—Alcan Enfield Alloys —to produce a range of foundry alloys from scrap and primary aluminium. Together with a 50% interest held in James Booth Aluminium by the U.S. Kaiser Aluminium and Chemicals Corporation, this means that all the major North American aluminium concerns now have a direct stake in the U.K. market.

F*

New methods and techniques

In addition to pioneering new materials, industry has, in recent years, both greatly improved its existing techniques of production and introduced entirely new methods, with self-regulating or automatic features, generally known as automation. These advances have taken many forms.

In the past the mechanization of production methods has not proceeded as an integrated whole. Thus, while machines have been devised to perform a number of unit processes, the movement of materials from one machine to another has, in the main, remained unmechanized. Even in those plants which are otherwise highly capitalized there is often scope for further mechanization of the materials handling processes.[1] As human (physical) energy costs about 500 times as much as electrical energy,[2] there is obviously considerable incentive for the development of labour-saving devices in materials handling, an incentive which in recent years has been further stimulated by the growth of large and standardized markets on the one hand and more widespread adoption of continuous or flow method of production on the other.

Since 1939 several new types of materials handling equipment have come into widespread use in this country. These include fork-lift trucks, conveyors, and weight-lifting and transporting devices, each of which, when used in conjunction with the appropriately designed containers and platforms, has enabled substantial savings in labour and floor space to be achieved without necessitating any major reorganization of existing factory lay-out. In contrast, the incorporation of other materials handling methods entails a complete replanning of factory lay-out and labour deployment to attain maximum efficiency. These, however, are better thought of as automation devices, the scope and implication of which are sufficiently important to warrant a separate discussion in the concluding sections of this chapter.

[1] S. Melman in his *Dynamic Factors in Industrial Productivity*, 1956, estimates that 30% of all production costs in the U.S.A. are traceable to materials handling operations.

[2] See L. Landon Goodman, *Man and Automation*, Penguin Books, p. 20.

Automation

Automation is a term which originated in the United States in 1936 and usually means either the 'automatic handling of parts between progressive production processes',[1] or 'the use of machines to control machines'.[2] Neither of these definitions, however, nor a combination of both, is entirely satisfactory. The difficulty arises from the double meaning which the word has gradually acquired: it is now used to describe a production process as a whole when essentially the word only conveys information about the relationship between the successive operations in a complete process. When the basic production operations are integrated to achieve as full a mechanization of mental processes and physical effort as possible, e.g. by such means as transfer processing, automatic assembly, control engineering and instrumentation, either singly or in combination, the whole sequence frequently becomes 'automation'. The machinery used for integrating the separate stages is, in fact, a particular kind of automation technique, the applicability of which is dependent on the nature of the basic production process.

The difference between mechanization and automation is largely one of degree, and is mainly a reflection of the different rate at which the two processes can be introduced and their implication on labour deployment. The mechanization of a factory is a continuous process which can evolve gradually as isolated operations along a chain of production are changed piece-meal. Automation methods are, in the main, indivisible and have to be adopted to a certain minimum degree or not at all. Increased mechanization usually only results in a displacement of labour at the point where the machine is introduced, leaving the rest of productive operations unaffected. The implementation of automation almost invariably involves elaborate changes in factory lay-out and managerial responsibility, with a simultaneous effect on many sections. Thus,

[1] It was first used by Mr D. S. Harder, now a Vice-President of the Ford Motor Company of America, when he was with the General Motors Corporation.
[2] Ascribed to Mr Peter Drucker.

when the Standard Motor Co. recently automated some production lines by introducing a number of transfer machines, a wholesale reorganization of the factory became necessary, for 2,000 people could produce the output that previously involved the employment of 6,000.

In addition, automation often causes the limit on the ultimate growth of an enterprise to recede. It is generally accepted that, in most manufacturing industries, an enlargement in the scale of output first decreases average costs and later increases them. One of the reasons traditionally cited for the emergence of this second phase is the inability of top management effectively to cope with the increased responsibility and administrative burden which a large business imposes: in particular the co-ordination of decision-taking and policy-making is after a point likely to be less effective. With the introduction of automation, however, devices ensuring the proper functioning of operations, previously done manually and thus dependent on the co-operative efforts of the labour force, may in fact require less by way of managerial intervention. In consequence, the onset of diminishing returns may be delayed and the increased returns to management are the result of automation. The rapid increase observed in recent years in the ratio of administrative personnel, i.e. those primarily concerned with management decisions, to production personnel as the degree of mechanization increases[1] in no way invalidates the argument: such a change is to be expected simply because the number of plant operatives is falling in relation to production. Another measure—the ratio of administrative personnel to the volume of production—might show a markedly different trend.

The automation techniques

There are four main forms of automation, some of which may be used in conjunction with one another, but more usually each is a self-contained process in its own right and applicable to a different set of circumstances.

[1] S. Melman, *Dynamic Factors in Industrial Productivity*, 1956.

(a) Transfer processing

This automation technique is used in 'assembling' industries and involves the linking of fabrication operations normally performed individually by mechanical handling devices.

The first-ever transfer machines were installed in 1923 in the Morris Motors factory at Oxford, but it was only after the Second World War in the American motor industry that they were really successfully developed. The larger British motor manufacturers have since introduced transfer machines and their use has spread to some other industries, mainly the metalworking trades engaged in the mass production of such durable consumer goods as refrigerators, sewing machines and typewriters.

The exact function of the transfer machine may best be illustrated from the manufacture of motor-car engines and other components, where lathe turning and hole drilling are especially important operations. Before automation each operation in the production process was performed by a special purpose tool, which was controlled by an operator who stopped and started the machine and who positioned and removed the work. Next, automatic machines were developed which operated continuously, the raw material being stored in a feeding unit and the finished work ejected into a hopper. One operator could then look after several machines while transferring the material from the ejection hopper of one machine into the input unit of the next machine in readiness for the next operation. In practice, however, it was found that the handling and loading of components into and out of the hoppers was a no less time-consuming and arduous operation. It is the function of transfer machines to reduce this work element: man-handling of the component is only necessary after 20 to 30 unit operations have been performed.

In the Austin Longbridge works, where the peak pre-war output was 1,800 vehicles per week, output in 1947, shortly after the introduction of automatic machine tools (but not transfer machines), was 2,700 and by 1950 it had further increased to over 3,000 per week.

The subsequent installation of transfer machines in the period 1952–7 raised the output yet again—to 5,000 vehicles and a further 3,000 engines for incorporation in other British Motor

Corporation[1] vehicles. This latter increase was accomplished by only a small addition to the labour force, and no enlargement in floor space.

Transfer machines can be designed either to perform a given number of predetermined operations only (in which case a change in the design of the product necessitates the installation of an entirely new machine) or to be general purpose in character. In America where production runs are usually so much larger than in this country the machines are generally of the first kind, but British manufacturers prefer the unit (or 'Meccano') method involving interchangeable machines fitted with interchangeable attachments. A change in product design then involves only rearrangement and retooling with little scrapping of existing plant. This greater flexibility results in fewer operations being grouped together in one transfer sequence. A transfer machine for the manufacture of Ford V8 engines installed in America in 1954 can automatically perform 555 separate machine operations. Equally impressive series of operations are performed by transfer machines in the Renault motor-car factory in France, where automation is reputed to have progressed further than in any other country in the world.

Not strictly 'transfer processing' but not properly included under the other headings, the *assembly line* is a production technique which has recently been acquiring many new characteristics. Assembly itself has in general not been automated, but in 'Detroit automation' (as it is sometimes called) the main assembly line is connected to the various separate component production units by complex conveyor systems which eliminate the handling and storage of components. In the Austin Longbridge factory, a Hollerith installation marshalls the whole production operation in the correct sequence from the raw material stage onwards. A few hours' stock of raw materials and components only is carried, so that replenishments have to arrive at the factory in accordance with a strict schedule; and they are brought in specially designed containers which integrate with the factory's conveyor system.

(b) Automatic assembly

The automatic assembly of components is still largely in its infancy and is mainly confined to the electronics industry where recently a

[1] The Austin and Morris Motors Companies merged to form the British Motor Corporation (1952).

number of firms have fully automated their assembly of radio and television receivers. The process in its first stage involves the machine-printing on a plastic board of the large numbers of interconnections in a receiver. The base board then travels past a succession of 'stations' at each of which a component is positioned and attached by machine, just as sheets of paper are stapled together. Finally the whole assembly is lowered into a dip-soldering bath, where all the connections are simultaneously soldered.

This method of assembly eliminates the need for an expensive process of inspection at the sub-assembly stage. One American company (the Stromberg-Carlson division of the General Dynamics Corporation) reports a saving of $37\frac{1}{2}\%$ in the labour costs of production of one of its radio receivers. Likewise the 'Autofab', a piece of equipment recently devised by the engineering division of the American firm, General Mills, is said to assemble in one minute as many part electronic units as a human operator in several hours. The estimated net saving is 40 operators on the production of 400 radio receivers a day.[1] Methods of printing circuits in 3 dimensions are now being developed and if they are successful will add greatly to the potentialities of the method.

The advantages accruing from this isolated example of an automatic assembly technique are so great that (in the United States[2] in particular) much research is being devoted to the development of techniques for other industries. For example, in the motor industry experiments in the automatic assembly of car engines are now being carried out. Components are also being redesigned to facilitate the change to automatic assembly methods.

(c) Control engineering

Just as the scope of the previous two automation techniques is mainly confined to the 'assembly' industries, so control engineering is primarily the province of the 'continuous processing' industries. This kind of automation is by no means new: the first continuous processing flour mill began operating in Philadelphia in 1782, and

---

[1] See *Financial Times*, 15 February 1956.
[2] It is interesting to note that although the American electronics industry has developed circuit printing more extensively than its British counterpart, the technique itself was pioneered in this country during the Second World War.

by the First World War the manufacture of such products as electric light bulbs, tin cans, bottles and cigarettes was fully mechanized. Control devices usually rely on sensing equipment of various kinds. This equipment virtually 'sees', and what it observes it 'feeds back' to the control device, which takes the appropriate corrective action to maintain a given set of conditions within the production process. The sensing unit itself usually contains measuring and regulating instruments responsive to various physical stimuli such as temperature, pressure, rate of flow, liquid levels and composition of mixtures. Processes can thus be kept in adjustment within smaller tolerances than are possible by human operation. Automation of this kind usually requires the use of much fewer co-operating factors than those previously described. In the Esso Oil Refinery at Fawley, for example, 6 men on a shift, working on a 3-shift basis, are able to operate a complex distillation plant with a throughput of 8 million gallons of oil a day.

As might be supposed, control engineering techniques have so far found their greatest applicability in the chemical and related industries (e.g. oil refining, brewing, food processing etc.). The chemical industry is the largest purchaser of industrial instruments which now account for up to 8% of the cost of a modern chemical plant. Steel strip mills and electricity power plants are also capable of being mechanized in this way: in the latter case, for example, powdered coal is fed in at one end and emerges at the other as ash; water is converted into steam, passed to the turbines and the condensate flows back to the starting point.

(d) Computerization

Electronic digital computers are a development of the last decade. When applied to clerical and accounting operations in commerce they have been responsible for great savings in manpower, and latterly they have enabled 'information engineering' to develop into an important production technique with great potentialities.

Computers have provided management with a powerful new tool, since the programming of the detailed operation of complicated physical and chemical processes involving lengthy calculations can be reduced to a routine operation. One of the best-known electronic machines used primarily for commercial purposes is the 'Leo' machine installed by J. Lyons & Co., the large catering firm, in 1953. This machine will produce the pay-slips of 10,000 employees at the rate of approximately 40 a minute, whereas the work previously occupied 30 clerks a whole week. The computer is also used by the company for other purposes and its services are hired out to outside firms on a contract basis.

Probably the most revolutionary form of automation is the computer control of machine tools. The essence of this operational technique is the translation of drawing-board details of the article to be manufactured into mathematical terms by means of an electronic computer, which produces a programme on magnetic tape. The latter is then fed into the control unit of the machine tool and, by means of servo-mechanisms, a suitably designed machine tool can reproduce all the operations necessary for the execution of the work.

Computer control eliminates the need for manual skill, because, apart from the operator in charge, the machining proceeds unaided at an exceedingly fast rate, while sensing equipment 'observing' the results and relaying impressions to the control unit automatically corrects for slight deviations.

The capital cost of these high-precision machine tools, even without the electronic control mechanisms, is substantial; but the latter, although an expensive addition, in many cases quickly pay for themselves by the high rate of utilization which they make possible. Furthermore, different programmes can be fed into the same control unit without any adjustments to the machine tool being necessary, and a variety of different components can be made on the one machine.

This system of production is especially valuable for producing prototypes, for example in the aircraft industry which has a high ratio of development work to production. It is also valuable for manufacturing small numbers of different components of compli- cated shape for which the installation of transfer machines and automatic or semi-automatic machine tools would be too expensive, as retooling would be necessary every time the product was changed. In the American economy, where large-scale production is the rule, it has been estimated that the bulk of production consists of runs of less that 25 items of the same kind at one time,[1] so in the U.S., and

[1] S. Moos, 'The Scope of Automation', *Economic Journal*, March 1957, p. 31.

still more in the U.K. where production is on a smaller scale, there is considerable scope for this kind of automation.

The possible scope for automation in British industry

Although, as we have seen, suitable automation techniques have been devised for application both in continuous processing and fabricating industries, the scope for such techniques in British industry is at present limited by both technical and economic considerations.

In terms of manpower, the industries in which automated production methods are now thought to be technically possible employ about 40% of the country's manufacturing labour, or 15% of the total labour force.[1] However, when the operations within those industries unsuitable to automation are discounted, this proportion is very much reduced. For example, only 7% of the hourly paid workers in the Ford Motor Co. (U.S.) are employed in plants where automated lines are used, and it has been recently estimated that the potential maximum of productive operations capable of being automated in the motor industry is 25 to 30%.

Industries producing capital goods, such as the electrical and general engineering, are virtually untouched by automation since the markets served are neither sufficiently large nor standardized to justify the installation of the equipment in question. Computer controlled automation methods may in due course permeate such industries, but progress in this direction would seem likely to be slow. In addition, most automation schemes require a large initial capital investment. Since depreciation allowances set against existing equipment assume a given capital intensity, it may well be that, in the last resort, the main limitation on the rate of automation is a financial one. In any event progress in this field is bound to be gradual, not only for this reason but on account of the inelasticity of supply of manpower to produce the complex machines and to

[1] These include biscuits and bread, beverages, cigarette manufacture, confectionery, canned food, natural and man-made fibres, paper and paper products, printing, chemicals, plastic articles, glass and glass products, various types of machinery and equipment, communications, electricity and gas production and distribution. (List compiled from Goodman, op. cit., p. 224.)

operate them. This is not to argue that automation will be prevented by economic factors: simply that its *speed* of application may well be rather more controlled than is commonly supposed.

Effect of automation on labour

There are wide divergencies of opinion as to the likely effects of automation on the demand for the co-operating factors of production. On the one hand, there are those who fear that it will inevitably lead to severe and prolonged unemployment: on the other, those who believe only a limited amount of short-term frictional unemployment will result. Whatever the truth of the matter may be, it is important to view the subject of automation in its proper perspective. First, from experience of the past 150 years, there is no evidence that, in the long run, increasing mechanization brings anything but rising living standards and shorter hours of work. Secondly, one must not forget that the successful deployment of automation techniques is itself dependent on a high and stable market for the goods produced: if industry thought that automation would result in a large amount of unemployment, it would in effect be courting its own bankruptcy.

Apart from its installation either in an entirely new plant, e.g. the Esso Oil Refinery, or by firms in a very rapidly expanding industry, e.g. electronics, automation will undoubtedly cause an initial displacement of labour in that part of the factory where it is introduced. That is, after all, one of its purposes, but it by no means follows that this will lead to unemployment of the labour displaced. To begin with automation makes possible lower costs and prices, and if demand is sufficiently responsive a larger rather than a smaller labour force might be needed. This was the case when, as a result of automation, the Corning Glass Company of the U.S. was able to reduce the price of its television tube blanks from $75 to $8.50: demand increased to such an extent that jobs for more than 2,000 people were created. Secondly, if automation is introduced gradually to affect only a limited part of a firm's labour force, then it may be possible to absorb the displaced labour elsewhere in the organization. This is particularly likely where the programme of mechanization has been carefully pre-planned and where advantage can be taken of the normal wastage of labour through retirement and voluntary turnover. This view would seem to be shared by the D.S.I.R., who in its report on automation some years ago concluded that 'automation has rarely caused workers to be dismissed though it very often leads to substantial savings in labour'; and in a recent study concluded by the U.S. Department of Commerce it was revealed that the complete automation of the assembly process in a major American electronics firm was carried out without any redundancy, although some transference of labour was needed as a result of the creation of 6 new job categories.

Thus even where the displacement ratio in individual sections of a manufacturing plant can be quite high as a result of automation (since 1 man after the change may be able to do the work previously done by 10), over the whole factory the ratio may be very small. For example, the adoption of transfer processing techniques by the Ford Motor Company in 1954 resulted in a *net* labour saving of only 900 persons out of 146,000 hourly employees. Moreover, in this case, not only were 1,850 persons switched over to other jobs within the Ford organization, but an additional 980 skilled men had to be recruited for machine-maintenance work. On the other hand, when the Standard Motor Company automated its tractor assembly plant at Coventry in 1956 more than 2,000 employees were laid off,[1] while recently it was estimated that, at the present rate of progress in U.S. telephonic automation, some 100,000 workers will be displaced within the next 10 years.

But, even assuming that particular firms will lay off workers, it is by no means inevitable that this situation will spread to other parts of the economy. Whether or not it does will depend on the general level of employment and the ease with which labour can move between different occupations, industries and areas. Regarding the first variable, it would seem reasonable to suppose that, initially at least, automation will create as many employment opportunities as it supplants. For automation in most cases is net investment and in consequence the demand for labour in the capital goods industries is likely to increase. Moreover, in as much as the rate of replacement demand (and possibly that of obsolescence) may also be greater, part of this demand will be a permanent one. From a wider

[1] Though this figure might have been less had there not been a slump in car sales at the same time.

viewpoint, any reduction in the length of the working week (which has been generally assumed to be one of the benefits of automation) would mean an increase in demand for services such as transport, distribution, entertainment etc. and hence a shift in the distribution of the labour force.

On the other hand, there is the very real problem of labour immobility to be tackled and, until this is resolved, opposition by employees' representatives to labour-saving devices is bound to continue. This, in turn, is bound up with a number of complex socio-economic questions such as those relating to compensation allowances and retraining, but if automation is to be introduced with the minimum of hardship, a flexible labour force is the first prerequisite. It may be argued that to avoid labour frictions it would be better not to automate too quickly and too widely. The economic effects, however, of *not* automating at all are likely to be far more deleterious than those of automating, for Britain's overseas competitors will mechanize their factories whatever this country does or does not do, and the benefits which they will reap in the form of lower manufacturing costs and/or an improved end product will be our loss in the form of reduced export earnings.

Changed skills

The smaller labour force employed after the change-over by a particular firm to automation will need a different distribution of skills. In view of the more complicated nature of the capital equipment used in automation, an increased number of persons will be employed on maintenance work. There will be fewer plant operatives, but an increased proportion of these will hold more responsible jobs than heretofore. The supervisor of a large automatic chemical process or of a battery of transfer machines has little to do so long as the plant is functioning properly, but immediately something goes wrong he has the responsibility for securing a quick return to normal working, thus avoiding expensive breakdowns. Established firms will have their cadres of such personnel—high-grade technicians of perceptive skill who have come to the notice of the managements and have been nurtured by them. Subsequent recruitment, however, will bring problems of selection and training.

Electricians and maintenance engineers will also be required in greater numbers and a larger proportion of them will require more advanced technical training. A practice enabling less skilled technicians to be used for such work is the scheduled maintenance shutdown during which wearing parts are replaced by new ones at set intervals.

Yet, if automation exacts a new pattern of work and decreases the demand for certain types of skilled labour, in other directions jobs are simplified. The proportion of jobs made easier to those made more complex is difficult to estimate, but it is at least feasible that more workers may be downgraded than upgraded as a result of more mechanization.

More generally automation is bound to affect the occupational structure of industry as a whole. In the United States, for example, while manufacturing employment fell by 5% between 1953 and 1960 (in spite of an increase in output of 17%), employment in commerce rose by 11%, the service industries 20% and the government 27%. Moreover, while professional and technical employment increased by 55% in the 1950's, the number of 'blue collar' workers rose by only 5%.[1]

Managers and technologists

At the same time, with the increasing complexity of processes, managerial control becomes more exacting and involves a larger ratio of managers, supervisors and technicians.[2] For example, in the Ford engine plant at Cleveland, Ohio, where the degree of automation is extensive, there is 1 foreman to 18 operatives, but at the Detroit plant, which is less advanced technologically, the ratio is 1 to 31. In a British steel-making firm, the change-over to a continuous strip mill process resulted in almost a 50% increase in the proportion of managers, supervisors, clerical workers and technicians.

---

[1] *American Economic Report*, May 1961, p. 11.
[2] This is a feature of mechanization processes in general. See S. Melman, *Dynamic Factors in Industrial Productivity*, 1956.

Capital formation

The extension of mechanization in general and automation in particular results in a more intensive usage of capital. The industrial situation favourable to these trends is moreover one in which better equipment is being continually developed and produced so that the rate of obsolescence is high, with automation equipment being scrapped long before reaching the end of its useful life. In the words of D. J. Davis of the Ford Motor Company of America: 'If a machine tool manufacturer comes out with something better than he did last year, and it saves us money, your competitor is going to buy it if you don't.'[1]

Little is known regarding the cost of adopting automation methods of production, though some rough estimates have been made for the United States. The cost for each worker displaced by automation has been put at $35,000, while in 1960 annual installations of automation equipment were valued at $6 billion, an increase of 75% in six years.[2] The net additional cost of automation is more difficult to calculate mainly because the new techniques made possible may be capital saving as well as labour saving, and frequently floor and storage space is economized. The Austin Motor Co., for example, installed a 13-station transfer machine for £25,903, while the estimated cost of the 13 separate machines was £30,950 or 15% more. The hourly cost of machine operation (excluding labour) was £3 13s. 3d. for the transfer machine, but £4 8s. 9d. for the separate machines, with the labour cost of the former 11s. per hour compared with £2 17s. 2d. on the standard machines. The output of the transfer machines was, furthermore, 20% greater.[3]

In relation to output, the capital cost of automation per machine operating hour is found to be smaller than that of the non-automatic equipment which could be currently installed, although of course the actual cost of the former might exceed that of the latter. The efficient marshalling of raw material and component stocks, usually

[1] Quoted by Paul Einzig in *The Economic Consequences of Automation*, 1956, p. 96.
[2] *American Economic Report*, May 1961, p. 11.
[3] See F. T. Hunter, 'Cost of Automation', *Institution of Production Engineers Journal*, 1957, pp. 416–22.

made possible when automation methods are used, makes considerably less working capital necessary. If the American estimate of cost is at all accurate, then in the British economy, so far as increase in national output is concerned, considerable progress towards full automation of the comparable group of industries might well be possible during the next decade.

Effect on the location of industry

Automation is labour saving so that the automating of a factory causes its employment and its output to move in opposite directions. In terms of numbers employed and of floor space, factories may well become smaller and located where site values are relatively low, and away from the congested urban areas. In the U.S.A. some decentralization of industry has already taken place with the larger firms constructing relatively small plants. The American General Electric Company, for example, has an old plant employing 20,000 persons, but its newer plants are in the range of 50–1,500.[1] Sylvania Electric Products, Inc., which has become highly automated, has spread its 26,000 employees over 43 plants, averaging 600–700 persons per plant. With increased demand for decentralized sites and a fall in the demand for sites in towns and other urban areas, the factors determining the location of industry are likely to undergo some change.

Conclusion

In the main, the effects of automation are not unlike those accompanying any intensive mechanization programme, but their initial impact is greater, with marked effects on labour and labour productivity. As hitherto developed, mechanization had mainly been a substitute for human muscular effort: automation has an altogether wider significance extending to mental processes as well. As in the field of new materials, the impact of science and technology on the rate of development is once again very apparent. Thus while processing and automatic assembly were mainly the outcome of an

[1] S. Moos, op. cit., p. 30.

accumulation of practical and empirical knowledge, more recently academic and Government research laboratories have been principally responsible for the major advances in control engineering and computing techniques. In this latter respect, defence research, particularly in the field of guided missiles, has played a major part. With its considerable economic advantages, it seems inevitable that there will be an extension of automation in fields where its suitability has been proved, and advancing technology will undoubtedly render possible its extension into entirely new fields.

VI

THE STATE AND INDUSTRY

The emergence of State control

The increasing participation of the State in industrial affairs over the past half-century has its origins in three concurrent and related trends: first, the pronounced change in informed public opinion with regard to the concept and composition of national economic welfare, and the State's role in promoting this change; secondly, the inadequacy of the competitive system evolved in the nineteenth century to deal effectively with the various problems associated with twentieth-century industrial expansion and technological change; and thirdly, the growing tendency for economic power to be concentrated within the hands of a limited number of individuals, or groups of individuals, thereby increasing the likelihood of decisions being taken which are detrimental to the rest of the community. As a result of these developments, not only has the size of the public sector of the economy expanded out of all recognition and the influence of the State, acting as a primary, secondary or third party over industrial activity, much widened, but a new attitude of mind has arisen, as signified by a transition from the intense individualism of the liberal state to the group consciousness of the welfare state.[1]

Modern State intervention in industrial affairs dates back to the decade immediately preceding the outbreak of the First World War. The legislation introduced by the Liberal Governments between 1905 and 1914, though principally social rather than economic in content, illustrated most clearly the State's acceptance of its responsibility for ensuring at least a minimum degree of social security and welfare for its citizens. During this period measures were introduced to

[1] U. K. Hicks, *British Public Finance, 1880–1952*, 1953, p. 1.

control the exploitation of labour by fixing minimum wages in 'sweated' industries, to regulate hours of work and to provide for workman's compensation in the case of accident or illness. The Old Age Pensions Act of 1908 replaced the provisions of the old Poor Law and granted non-contributory pensions for the first time to persons of 70 years and over. The principle of progressive taxation gained acceptance, and in Mr Lloyd George's controversial budget of 1909 death duties and the rate of income tax were increased and super (now sur-) tax was introduced. Expenditure on the social services quadrupled between 1900 and 1910. In this latter year the first labour exchanges also began operating and two years later a national insurance scheme against sickness and unemployment was started.

The impact of the First World War completely transformed the pattern and organization of industry and its relations with the State. By 1918 direct controls had replaced the pricing mechanism in almost every branch of the domestic economy, while the substitution for free trade and the gold standard of import quotas and exchange control gave the State virtually complete command over shipping space and the balance of payments. In the finance of war commitments, budgetary policy played an important role: the standard rate of income tax rose from 1s. 2d. to 6s. in the £ between 1913 and 1916 and the proportion of the national income collected in taxes by the Central Government increased from 9% to more than 50% over the same period. In addition to the specific measures implemented in respect of materials allocation, direction of labour, rationing of consumer goods and control of production, the State acquired a closer insight into the operation and organization of private industry. This was mainly achieved by means of a series of meetings with representatives from all branches of industry, and the relationships established between Government and private industry in these years did much to set the pattern for the consultative machinery of the future. At the same time, a number of official and semi-official national organizations were set up, such as the Department of Scientific and Industrial Research (the origins and subsequent history of which have already been described in a previous chapter) in 1917, the British Manufacturers' Association in 1915[1] and the Federation of British Industries in 1916.

[1] Later the National Union of Manufacturers.

The war also produced one of the earliest examples of direct State assistance to a particular industry. In 1914 Britain was importing 90% of her annual consumption of dyestuffs from Germany, and it was not long before the textile trades were faced with an acute shortage of dyes. The Government was thus forced to take immediate action in co-operation with the various interests concerned. This resulted in the formation of a new company, British Dyes Ltd, which was intended to be a combination of dye-users for the manufacture of dyes. Though the share capital of this venture was privately owned, the Government undertook to lend a sum not exceeding £1·7 million at a low rate of interest and also to help finance research into the production of dyestuffs. Together with a private concern, Levinstein Ltd, with which it amalgamated in 1918 to form the British Dyestuffs Corporation, British Dyes Ltd supplied almost the entire output of dyestuffs during the war. Outside manufacturing industry as such, the State also lent its support to agriculture in the form of the Corn Production Act of 1917, which not only fixed minimum prices for corn and a minimum wage for farm labourers, but instituted controls over the acreage of land to be devoted to arable farming and the efficiency with which it was to be farmed.

After the emergency, industrial control speedily reverted to private hands[1] and most of the war-time consultative machinery was abandoned. Yet the pre-1914 policy of *laissez-faire* in economic affairs was never again resurrected in its entirety, for the war years had both illustrated certain advantages of centralized planning and had created many precedents of varying kinds of State intervention. Indeed the very creation of a Ministry of Reconstruction in 1917 and its subsequent investigations into a number of U.K. industries lent support to this view. In other fields, too, certain measures of State paternalism first taken in the war were not only retained but extended in scope. For example, apart from a year's lapse in 1924, the McKenna duties, initially imposed in 1915 on the import of motorcars, motor-bicycles and their accessories, musical instruments, clocks and watches and cinema films, as a war-time measure to maintain the foreign exchanges and to discourage expenditure on luxury articles, remained in force right up to the Imperial Preference

[1] e.g. food rationing and most price controls had ended by 1920 and the Ministries of Food, Munitions and Shipping were abolished in March 1921.

Tariff of 1932. In addition, on the recommendation of a war-time committee which had been appointed to consider industrial and commercial policy in Britain after the war, the Safeguarding of Industries Act (1921) levied a $33\frac{1}{3}\%$ *ad valorem* import duty on the products of certain key industries, which it was thought desirable, for strategic reasons, to supply from home sources. The initial period of coverage was 5 years, though in 1926 the scope of the duties was further extended and in one or two cases the rate of duty was raised to 50%. Another part of the 1921 Act also attempted to control the dumping by overseas countries of goods below their fair market value; such imports were now to be subject to a $33\frac{1}{3}\%$ *ad valorem* duty.

Protective legislation was also enacted to aid the development of a number of other industries in these years. First, the Dyestuffs (Import Regulation) Act, 1920, prohibited the importation of synthetic organic dyestuffs, colouring matters and their intermediaries for a period of 10 years; secondly, the U.K. rayon industry was stimulated by the Finance Act, 1925, which levied customs duties of varying severity on imports of natural and artificial silk and articles made thereof; and thirdly, the Cinematograph Films Act, 1927, which required the Board of Trade to keep a register of films shown in the United Kingdom, according to their country of origin, and stipulated that the imports of foreign films were to be governed by a statutory quota of British films which must be exhibited. The effect of this latter legislation was to give a considerable boost to the U.K. cinematograph industry, and the proportion of British films exhibited in this country rose from under 5% in 1927 to 24·3% in 1934. In addition, financial assistance was granted to the sugar, flax and coal industries, while under the Trade Facilities Acts 1921–6 guarantees for loan repayments were given by the State to a large number of firms borrowing money in the iron and steel, engineering, electrical and building industries.

As regards direct State participation in industry, the scope of the public corporation was also extended. Thus, in 1926 the generation of electricity passed out of private hands into national ownership with the establishment of the Central Electricity Board. A year later the British Broadcasting Corporation was created by Royal Charter, initially for a period of 10 years. In 1933 most of the passenger transport services of Greater London were integrated and placed under the control of a specially appointed body, the London Passenger Transport Board. While these enterprises were subject neither to political control nor to day-to-day interference by the State, ultimate responsibility rested in the hands of one or more Government departments. Thus, the members of the boards of the C.E.B. and B.B.C. were appointed, respectively, by the Minister of Transport and Postmaster General, while the former was also closely concerned with the overall policy of the L.P.T.B.

Except for these cases, however, the Government continued to exercise little direct influence over the course and direction of internal economic activity during the 1920's. Instead, policy was almost exclusively directed towards the general problem of restoring Britain's position as a great financial centre (of which the return to the gold standard in 1925 at pre-war parity was regarded as an integral part) and, up to 1927 at any rate, of adjusting wages and prices to meet this new parity. At the same time, this was a period when the factors underlying the desirability of State intervention were changing. As Chapter II has already described, the traditional economic mechanism was proving inadequate in making the adjustments necessitated by shifts in world consumption patterns and the introduction of new production techniques. By themselves, industrial undertakings in the basic trades had neither the resources nor the incentive to introduce the drastic measures of reform which were necessary. Only as a last resort was individual sovereignty surrendered and superseded by centralized industrial control, though eventually almost every staple industry was granted assistance, directly or indirectly, by the State.

The beginning of the 1930's witnessed the introduction of a profound change in British economic policy. In 1931 the United Kingdom abandoned the gold standard and in its place substituted a managed currency. As a result of the Ottawa Agreements of the same year she reverted from a policy of free and multilateral trade to one of protection, exchange control and bilateral agreements. At home, a period of cheap money was inaugurated, with the bank rate remaining unchanged at 2% between 1932 and 1951.[1] In an effort to stimulate industrial recovery the State deliberately fostered collective agreements to restrain competition, and guaranteed the interest

[1] Except for a period of 2 months at the outbreak of the Second World War.

on loans for a number of important projects, e.g. the construction of the *Queen Mary*, and supported the creation of artificial marketing controls and price and output agreements in agriculture. At the same time, various efforts were made to promote recovery in those geographical areas suffering from above-average unemployment, while a specialist committee, under the chairmanship of Lord Macmillan, was appointed to examine the structure of the U.K. monetary and financial system and to recommend any improvements which might accelerate the recovery of industry. Encouragement was given to schemes of self-government in various industries and to the reduction of surplus capacity. More specific financial aid was also made available by official or semi-official sources, e.g. the Bank of England loaned £10 million to Richard Thomas Ltd for the erection of new steelworks and strip mills at Ebbw Vale in 1935, and several new finance companies, e.g. the Charterhouse Investment Trust and Agricultural Mortgage Corporation, were formed.

Thus, during the years before the Second World War, the State's role in industrial affairs both widened and deepened; it evolved, in fact, from being purely that of a 'policeman' or 'monitor' to that more akin to a 'Father Christmas'.[1] Yet the measures adopted were, for the most part, *ad hoc* by nature and were directed to a specific problem. By and large, the overall control and planning of industrial activity remained in private hands; where the State intervened it did so selectively and with some hesitancy. The justification for an integrated economic policy was still not fully appreciated; the rationale of compensatory finance was only just beginning to be understood; J. M. Keynes and Lord Beveridge had yet to produce their theories of employment and money which were to have such a profound effect on the post-war relationships between State and industry.

With the Second World War, industrial activity once again became completely State controlled. As in the 1914–18 period, there was a vast growth in the number and scope of all kinds of institutional associations. Direction of labour, price control, materials allocation and rationing of consumer goods were extensively invoked; and, to pay for the war, not only was income tax raised to 10s. in the £ in 1941, but in 1940 a selective purchase tax was introduced with the dual purpose of redirecting resources away from

[1] *The Economist*, 18 March 1939, p. 551; quoted in P.E.P., *Government and Industry*, 1952, p. 9.

consumer goods industries to armament production and of reducing inflationary pressure. But, from the viewpoint of subsequent economic planning, the most important event of these years was the publication of the White Paper on *Employment Policy* by the Coalition Government in 1944. For the contents of this paper clearly showed the fundamental changes destined to take place after the war in the relationships between Government and industry, irrespective of the political party returned to power. Reflecting the principles propounded by Keynes and Beveridge, the State now accepted responsibility for the fulfilment of certain basic economic aims, the nature of which would inevitably involve a measure of centralized control over both the volume and direction of private spending and thus over industrial output.

The State has found it necessary to intervene in the industrial sphere in recent years for three main reasons. Obviously, the very fact that intervention is thought necessary presupposes a divergence between private and social interests, and between the way in which scarce resources are allocated under private enterprise and the way in which it is considered they should be allocated for maximum social welfare. It is, however, possible to be a little more specific than this. First, the State is concerned with seeing that the level of industrial production is sufficient to ensure the full employment of the nation's resources and that the resulting flow of goods and services is distributed in the community in a way which maximizes social welfare (as conceived by the State). Secondly, it is concerned that the pattern of industrial output, e.g. as between the production of consumption and investment goods, should be compatible not merely with maintaining existing living standards but with achieving a steadily rising national product. Finally, it is concerned to prevent the achievement of the above two aims from conflicting with that of a third—the maintenance of external stability—by ensuring that the volume of exports is sufficient to cover the cost of imports and any long-term overseas investment judged desirable. With these broad economic aims may be considered a number of subsidiary ones, e.g. the prevention of the abuse of monopoly power against the public interest, the minimization of the wastes of competition, the encouragement of research and technological development and various non-economic objectives, such as the strategic and social, which necessarily affect or are affected by the allocation of scarce resources.

The State attempts to achieve these objects in various ways, which, for the purposes of this chapter, may be conveniently discussed under 5 main headings:

(i)   Direct participation in industry, e.g. nationalization, municipal trading etc.

(ii)   The operation of selective physical controls, e.g. in location of industry, materials allocation, capital issues and the granting of building licences.

(iii)   The provision of certain services for industry and the publishing of information about industry.

(iv)   Legislation against undesirable business practices and the exploitation of the weaker party to an exchange, e.g. the Monopolies and Restrictive Practices Act, 1956.

(v)   The operation of monetary and/or fiscal measures to fulfil a particular economic aim.

Sometimes the State intervenes to protect producers' interests, sometimes those of the consumers. Professor P. Sargant Florence, in his book *Industry and the State*,[1] distinguishes between the State's role as a primary, secondary or third party in industry. His analysis, however, is more detailed and of wider coverage than it is possible for ours to be, and includes such questions as public health, town planning, wage arbitration and factory legislation.

Direct participation

The State is a participator in industry in its own right through the operation of public corporations and municipal trading ventures.[2] As has already been shown, the concept of the State as a producer is by no means new; the Port of London Authority was created in 1908 and the Metropolitan Water Board and the Mersey Docks and Harbour Board shortly afterwards. In the inter-war years, the setting up of the Forestry Commission, the Central Electricity

[1] Hutchinson University Library, 1957.
[2] In addition the State operates as a productive enterprise in its own right, e.g. H.M. Stationery Office, and is an important shareholder in several others, e.g. British Petroleum and Short Bros. & Harland Ltd, but, owing to lack of space, these aspects will not be further discussed.

G

Board, the British Broadcasting Corporation, the London Passenger
Transport Board and the British Overseas Airways Corporation
were all indications of the extending scope of the public corporation.
Technological advances, changing social values and the failure of
private enterprise to deal adequately with the depressed economic
conditions of the inter-war years all led to the extension of State
ownership. Usually, where the State has intervened, competition has
been replaced by a public nation-wide monopoly, though not invariably so (e.g. in the transport field). Moreover, though in each case
the appointed governing body is financially and administratively
independent of Parliamentary control, the actual form and characteristics of management vary considerably. The medium of ownership adopted since the war and effected principally through the
Nationalisation Acts 1946-9 has been that of the public corporation. In this instance, control is vested in a mainly autonomous
board appointed by the appropriate Minister (except in the case of
the Bank of England where appointment is made by the Crown),
from whom it seeks guidance on matters of policy, the spending of
large amounts of capital and its training, education and research
programmes. The actual extent to which administration is centralized
or regionalized naturally varies according to the technical characteristics of the industry. For example, since electricity is more easily
transmitted over distances than gas, the Regional Gas Boards have
a greater amount of autonomy than their counterparts in the electricity industry: the problems of the coal industry are not the same
as those of civil aviation and so on. As a whole, over the years,
management decisions have tended to become more and more
delegated, though many problems of centralized planning co-ordination still remain; and in certain circumstances efficiency has been
lessened as a result. At present just over 2 million people or 1 in 12
of the total working population are directly employed in the
nationalized industries.[1]

Apart from the well-known political arguments in favour of
State operation of industries, there is the economic case which rests
on the threefold belief that public ownership is: (i) a means of

[1] The distribution of the labour force is as follows: coal-mining 763,000,
electricity supply 212,000, gas supply 136,000, railways 476,000, road
transport 467,000 and civil aviation 38,000. The figure quoted in the text
excludes those in the Bank of England, Post Office, National Health
Service and Government departments. (1959 figures.)

ensuring that private monopolies do not exploit the public, (ii) the most effective way of achieving the economies of rationalization and ensuring the maximum technical efficiency, and (iii) a means of operating the basic industries and services on which the economic life and welfare of the community depend and which cannot be left in the hands of a group of private owners not answerable to the community. And, in fact, most of the industries now in public ownership possess one or more characteristics relevant to the above arguments. For example, the coal-mining and public utility industries supply products which are both essential to the proper functioning of an industrial economy and are bought by the great majority of consumers. In addition, these latter industries are of a kind which require large and costly plants for their efficient operation, and so competition would be largely wasteful. The danger of (private) monopoly power is claimed to be present in other industries which the Labour Party has scheduled for nationalization, e.g. cement, sugar and basic chemicals, while in the case of coal-mining and gas the organization before nationalization was claimed to be inefficient and costly.

The problems of the nationalized industries are many and varied and cannot be dealt with at length here.[1] For example, those relating to pricing policy (e.g. should marginal or average costs be taken as one's criterion of price fixing?), the raising of new capital (e.g. should the nationalized industries be given any preferential treatment in this respect?), the achievement and maintenance of efficiency and enterprise without the profit incentive, the possible clash between consumer and national interests, accountability to Parliament, managerial structure (e.g. how much autonomy in decision-taking should be allowed regional boards?), compensation terms and so on, are common to all industries. They have been particularly emphasized by the coal industry's recent history where the creation of a price structure, which satisfies both economic efficiency and social equity, has yet to be determined and where investment plans have frequently had to be revised in the light of subsequent events. The nationalized industries are constantly under public review, and they are obliged to present to Parliament an annual report giving far

[1] See P. Sargant Florence, *Industry and the State*, pp. 132 ff. R. Edwards and H. Townsend, *Business Enterprise*, pp. 495 ff. W. A. Robson, *Nationalized Industry and Public Ownership*, 2nd ed., Allen & Unwin, 1962.

G*

fuller details of the past year's trading activities and financial conditions than a public joint-stock company. In addition, a Select Committee, originally appointed in 1953, but whose composition and investigating machinery has subsequently changed, is periodically charged with examining the aims, activities and problems of the nationalized industries and with reporting to Parliament not only on matters of productive efficiency, but also on their relationships with the consumers, workers and the public as a whole.

In spite of a low priority given to railways and coal-mining, the share of total manufacturing investment undertaken by the nationalized industries in recent years has been on an average double that for private industry. And while the rate of technical progress and productive efficiency do not yet compare favourably with that in some of the newer U.K. industries,[1] and the problems associated with administering an industry-wide organization were probably underestimated, particularly in regard to labour relations, there is little doubt that many of the original fears expressed by the opponents of nationalization have not (as yet at any rate) materialized. In all, however, in spite of the increased incursion of centralized control, it would be wrong to regard nationalization as a complete substitute for *laissez-faire*. As in private enterprise, a State-operated concern has to compete for its labour, materials and capital in the open market, while in the last resort its output and price policies are not determined by any dictatorial decision, but rather by the pressure of organized labour on the one hand and the reactions of consumers to changes in market conditions on the other. It is a mistake to assume that nationalization necessarily involves a greater abrogation of consumers' sovereignty than a private monopoly.

Apart from the nationalization of certain industries previously privately owned, the State maintains general supervision over the iron and steel industry through the medium of the Iron and Steel Board. Initially appointed in 1946, the Board's present function is to promote full productive efficiency under competitive conditions, and subject to Ministerial approval, it can fix prices, control capacity,

[1] By the end of 1959 the nationalized industries had, on balance, a cumulative deficit of £250 million. Five of the nine boards made profits in 1959 and four recorded losses. Of the latter the most serious deficits were incurred by the British Transport Commission (£73·8 million) and the National Coal Board (£24 million). See *Financial and Economic Obligations of the Nationalized Industries*; 1960–1, Cmnd 1337.

restrict imports and grant loans for research, training and education in pursuit of this aim. In addition, its approval must be sought for any major capital projects within the industry. The members of the Board are appointed by the Minister of Power from people experienced in the various aspects of iron and steel production; and, as in the case of most nationalized industries, an annual report on the Board's proceedings has to be presented to Parliament. Up to 1962 8 such reports have been issued and 2 special reports which discuss the probable future of the iron and steel industry up to 1965.

Outside the basic industries, the State has also been directly responsible for the progress of the atomic power industry since 1945 (see Chapter III) and indirectly, as chief buyer of its products and as financier of its research and development work, for that of the aircraft industry as well. Such participation is but another reflection of the economics of modern technology; for, even assuming the absence of the threat of war, it is highly doubtful whether private enterprise by itself could possibly have financed the vast capital outlay necessary for the design and construction of, say, the Calder Hall power station, and much of the research which has been the means of developing new aircraft and aero-engines in recent years. The need to establish a precision engineering industry in Britain on strategic grounds also led the State to encourage the development of a watch-making industry in this country after the last world war.[1] Finally, mention must be made of the fact that the Government, in the form of the National Health Service, is the main buyer of pharmaceutical products in this country and that both the Post Office and Service departments purchase large quantities of electronic and telecommunication equipment. Official influence in these spheres extends both to the type of products produced and to the prices charged.

Physical controls

By selectively imposed physical controls, the State is often able to achieve its economic objectives without directly participating in

[1] See Edwards and Townsend, op. cit., p. 40 et seq.

industrial affairs. Such measures as these, however, are usually viewed with distaste by democratic society, as they invariably restrict the individual's freedom of choice by some prohibitive action or other. The pricing system is replaced by quantitative rationing of goods and services, with or without price control, as determined by the appropriate planning authority in the light of its own assessment of the country's needs. Choice and initiative are thus stifled and economic freedom curtailed.

Generally, this type of Government intervention does not play an important role in a private enterprise economy except in war and its aftermath. Thus, since 1945, there has been a gradual relaxation of most types of physical controls: for the consumer, clothes were derationed in 1948, petrol in 1950 and food in 1952. Direction of labour, through Registration for Employment Orders, Control of Engagement Orders and Essential Works Orders, was finally abolished in 1950. Materials allocation schemes and licensing controls remained in force rather longer and, though these are now at their post-war minimum, in other respects the scope of the State has widened. The utility schemes were also introduced during the war to ensure a minimum supply of certain classes of essential goods of serviceable quality and at controlled prices: at one time these schemes covered 75% of all the clothing produced and 50% of all the furniture. These were also continued for some time after the war and undoubtedly aided the trend towards more standardized production of certain goods.

But perhaps the most far reaching of all quantitative controls, until they were recently lifted, have been those relating to the direction and flow of investment capital. Until February 1959, for example, the Capital Issues Committee, first set up before the war, still regulated the borrowing and raising of money by the issue of shares (of £10,000 and over in any one year)[1] while, in the field of short-term finance, the joint-stock banks remained subject to Treasury guidance in the granting of overdrafts up to the autumn of 1958. In both cases, from time to time, directives from the Treasury listed the type of industries to which loans might be granted and for what purposes. The borrowing powers of the nationalized industries are still, of course, subject to Parliamentary approval.

[1] It was raised to £50,000 in 1958. In the 5 years up to 30th June 1958 the C.I.C. dealt with some 6,626 applications.

Until 1948 the State's most powerful control over the character and location of new industrial building was that of the building licence, the granting of which had to have the approval of at least 4 Government departments. Since that date legislation incorporated in the various Town and Country Planning Acts has required that application for industrial buildings in excess of 5,000 square feet[1] must be accompanied by an Industrial Development Certificate stating that the development in question is consistent with a proper distribution of industry. In addition, of course, the local authority has to be satisfied that the proposed siting of any new factory is in conformity with its planning programme. The ways in which the State has exerted considerable influence on the location of industry have been described in a previous chapter.

On external account, the State's main weapons of control over the volume of goods and services imported and exported are import and export licensing, centralized purchasing, import duties and exchange control. In general it is the first and last of these regulating methods which are the most commonly used at the present time.[2]

Services and indirect aid to industry

Hand in hand with the State's increasing interest in economic affairs has gone its need for more information from industry about such activities as sales, output per period of time, consumption of fuel and raw materials, capital investment undertaken, labour turnover etc., which might be used as the basis for framing policy. Such facts, after being assembled and sifted by the appropriate Government department, are usually published in aggregate form to give the individual firm or plant a wider viewpoint of the situation. The Census of Production, first taken in 1907 and subsequently at intervals of roughly five years until 1935, is now an annual procedure and the scope of questions asked (which include those relating to value of output, numbers employed, wages and salaries, shift-working, consumption of materials and fuels etc.) has widened considerably over the years. A full census is taken every three years and a partial one

[1] Since April 1960, 3,000 square feet.
[2] For further details see P.E.P., *Government and Industry*, 1952.

in the remaining two. Even though it appears that the average British business man makes little use of such information—the common complaint being that it is out of date before it is published —the Census is undoubtedly proving useful in helping to frame national investment policy and is likely to be even more important when work now being carried out by the Department of Applied Economics at Cambridge on the input-output relationships between the different branches of the economy is completed. In the same way, statistical data on trends in industrial production, raw materials, wholesale and retail prices, imports and exports, wages and salaries, stocks of finished products etc., originating from both official and non-official sources, considerably aid industrial planning and, indirectly at least, enable resources to be more efficiently employed. Since 1947 an Economic Survey, which gives the Government's assessment of the present and likely future economic position of the U.K., has been published annually: together with the National Income Blue Book and the Balance of Payments White Papers this document provides detailed statistical information concerning the state of the British economy.

The State, through its Departments, also offers various facilities for the benefit of industry. The Ministry of Labour, for example, operates the employment services and makes provision for the training and resettlement of disabled persons. The work of the employment exchanges is currently responsible for settling over 2 million placings each year, while the Youth Employment Service found jobs for nearly 425,000 boys and girls in 1960. Special mention should also be made of the 90 Remploy factories operating throughout the country which now give employment to more than 6,000 disabled workers. The first of these establishments was set up in 1945: since that date growth has been rapid, and in the financial year ending 31 March 1960 some £5·1 million worth of brushes and light engineering products were produced.

More generally, the Central Office of Information and Her Majesty's Stationery Office are responsible for publicity in all its forms on behalf of the Government. Information both about, and of interest to, industry is periodically put out in the form of reports, booklets, films, posters etc. State services helping in the supply of capital and credit are confined to the provision of insurance to U.K. exporters against the commercial risks of overseas trading by the

Exports Credits Guarantee Department,[1] and to subsidies paid to help finance either particular industries or small and medium type firms generally. For example, there is the National Film Finance Corporation to which the Board of Trade has already made substantial advances, while a grant equal to two-thirds of the cost of removing redundant capacity and up to one-quarter of the cost of re-equipment for approved schemes is now being offered to firms in the cotton industry, under the provisions of the Cotton Industry Act, 1959.[2] The Government also sponsored the rationalization scheme in the aircraft industry in 1960, by which the major firms were consolidated into five main groups and is currently subsidizing much of the industry's research and development. State help to individual firms includes Bank of England participation in the Finance Corporation for Industry and the Industrial Commercial Finance Corporation. In addition, under the Borrowing (Control and Guarantees) Act of 1946, a National Investment Council was established by which loans of up to £50 million in any one year can be made available to industry.

Other services at one time assisted by the Government in one way or another, e.g. the British Export Trades Research Association and the Dollar Export Board, have now become private responsibilities, though the British Standards Institution remains an officially supported body. But perhaps the most vital State service from which industry benefits is that provided by the Department of Scientific and Industrial Research and Government research departments, a

[1] Such risks include insolvency or default of buyer after acceptance and political risks, e.g. exchange transfer and import licensing changes. Between 1947 and 1958 the guarantees assured by the E.C.G.D. amounted to some 13·5% of all exports. Over 95% of this business covered 2 main types of guarantees, viz. short term credit of up to 6 months on consumer goods and medium term credit up to 3 years for 'quasi-capital' goods, e.g. agricultural tractors etc., and up to 5 years for 'major capital' goods. For further particulars see Report of the Committee on the Working of the Monetary System; Cmnd 827.

[2] By the end of 1960 schemes worth more than £20 million for the elimination of surplus capacity in the spinning, doubling and weaving sections of the industry had been put into operation. So far about one-half of the spindles and 40% of the looms in Lancashire have been scrapped and capacity in the finishing sections has been reduced one-quarter. Compensation is paid to displaced persons by means of levies subscribed by firms which are still operating. In all, during the last decade some 550 mills have been closed. Fortunately, however, due to the increased diversification of Lancashire industry in recent years, unemployment has been kept down to the national average (and in some towns below it).

detailed account of which has already been given in a previous chapter. Other Government-sponsored bodies include the Council of Industrial Design set up in 1944 to encourage improvements in the standards of design of British products, and the British Institute of Management whose function is to suggest ways and means by which the quality of managerial practice in private industries may be raised. Normally these services are financed from national taxation though often loans or grants are given for a temporary period or while the industry or firms concerned are learning to stand on their own feet.

Mention must also be made at this stage of the work of the Development Councils. These were the outcome of the Working Parties set up by the President of the Board of Trade shortly after the end of the war to enquire into the structure and efficiency of some 17 British industries and to suggest what steps might be taken in the national interest to strengthen their economic position in both the home and export markets. Each report, in its turn, advocated the setting up of some kind of centralized tripartite body which should undertake certain functions on behalf of the individual industries in question, and machinery for this was substantially provided by the Industrial Organization and Development Act of 1947. By this legislation and through any one of its eight Ministries, the Government was empowered to create a Development Council in a particular industry or group of industries, wherever there was substantial support by the interested parties. Membership of the Council consisted of representatives drawn from both sides of industry and a smaller number of independent members, one of whom was to be appointed chairman. They might be called upon to deal with up to 20 functions, including the promotion of scientific and industrial research, measures for the improvement of design, the certification of products, labour utilization, home and export trades, the improvement of accounting and costing procedure and so on.

In actual fact, only four Development Councils (viz. in the cotton, jewellery, furniture and clothing industries) were ever formed and these were only partially successful in fulfilling their objects.[1]

[1] Two of these still exist—the Cotton and Furniture Development Councils. The former operates departments in connection with market research, the collection of statistics, productivity, industrial relations etc.; the latter carries out research into the methods of testing the durability of furniture and also promotes work study of one kind or another.

The main reason for lack of enthusiasm was the objection of the employers, first to the independent members and union officials sitting on the Council, and secondly, to the payment of a compulsory levy by all firms. The fear that these tripartite bodies might in some way give the Government a greater measure of control over industrial affairs also intensified the opposition.

Latterly a watered-down type of Development Council has emerged in the form of a Joint Advisory Committee or Council which provides a channel of service and communication between Government and industry: such bodies exist in branches of the engineering and shipbuilding industries. The Government's responsibility is confined to the setting up of the Committee and sometimes the appointment of individual members. Mention must also be made of the Anglo-American Council on Productivity (now the British Productivity Council) which was formed in 1948 to arrange for the exchange of information on such matters as production techniques, industrial organization, managerial efficiency etc., with particular reference to conditions in U.K. and U.S. industry. This body, though privately sponsored, gained the support of the State after its inception and has subsequently been responsible for sending out some 66 teams, representing management, technicians and operatives in a wide range of U.K. industries, to America between 1949 and 1953 to study the experience of the U.S. in raising productivity and to see which of the methods adopted there could be applied to the needs of British industry.

Finally, since 1947 the National Production Advisory Council for Industry, which consists of representatives of senior civil servants, industrialists and the Trades Union Congress, has operated under Treasury auspices. Its terms of reference include advising the Government on industrial and general production questions, and on any other subject that may arise from the proceedings of the Regional Boards for Industry. The function of these latter bodies is to report upon local industrial conditions and upon the steps that may be necessary to make full use of marginal resources in capacity and labour. Both organizations form a liaison between Government and industry and an essential channel for the exchange of ideas. Matters discussed by them include shortages of labour and raw materials, licensing policy for industrial building, advice on town and country planning, suggestions for overcoming localized unemployment and difficulties associated with farming marginal land.

Control of monopoly and restrictive practices

So far this chapter has been primarily concerned with describing the ways in which the State has intervened in the workings of private industry so that the level and direction of economic activity should best satisfy the community's interests. But is is also the function of the State to ensure that the waste of scarce resources through productive inefficiency is minimized, that there is no exploitation of the weaker party by the stronger in an exchange transaction, and that smaller competing interests are not destroyed by the more powerful in order to secure a monopolistic stranglehold.[1] Direct intervention —through nationalization or municipal trading ventures, the setting up of liaison bodies, Working Parties and Development Councils, support of the work of the Anglo-American Council on Productivity, the establishment of a Committee of Industrial Productivity, the extension of research organizations and so on, have all helped in the achievement of the first aim. The changing structure of industry, the stronger power of the seller in an inflationary period and the growth of trade associations—which *The Economist* had earlier described as 'the central stronghold of monopoly and the most insidious danger'—have all accelerated the trend towards monopoly, and hence the necessity of solving the second increasingly difficult problem. In the 1944 White Paper on Employment Policy the Government recognized its responsibility in this respect and pledged itself to 'take appropriate action to check practices which may bring advantages to sectional producing interests but work to the detriment of the community as a whole'. This action was partly at least the outcome of Government support for the International Trade Organization, an important section of whose charter was concerned with ways of curtailing the power of international monopolies and cartels. Thus, any member state could lodge a complaint against another, if it was felt that the practices of such bodies were deliber-

---

[1] The State also controls the sale of certain types of consumer goods, e.g. dangerous drugs, alcohol etc., and lays down certain standards of quality in other cases, e.g. foodstuffs and medicinal products.

ately against its own interests, and the I.T.O. would then investigate the claim and, if necessary, remedy the situation.

As already mentioned in Chapter II, the Government itself encouraged the formation of trade associations during the war for administrative convenience, and recent years have seen a vast growth in their numbers. This trend towards the cartelization of industry has inevitably increased the possibility of monopolistic prices being charged, output being restricted and insufficient attention being paid to research, development and technological progress. Concentration had been accelerated during the war to avoid unnecessary excess capacity and waste of resources. When the time for decentralization eventually came, not all firms wished to revert to the pre-war competitive struggle, particularly as technical advances then being made favoured the larger-scale production units. Meanwhile a number of *ad hoc* enquiries were instituted into the extent and implications of monopolistic practices. The various Board of Trade Working Parties, the fforde Committee on cement costs, the Simon Committee on the distribution of building materials and their components, the Lloyd Jacob Committee on resale price maintenance, all served to confirm the belief that restraints on competition were becoming increasingly prevalent in private industry, and each recommended that some sort of concerted action should be taken. Thus we see, in little over a decade, policy being switched from controlling the wastes of competition, or depression economics, to controlling the power of monopolies created in its stead. Attention has thus been focused on securing the technological benefits of large-scale production, while minimizing the danger of exploitation which such advantages may make possible.

The Monopolies and Restrictive Practices (Enquiry and Control) Act was passed in 1948 to provide machinery for the investigation of monopolies and restrictive arrangements in industry and trade, and to give the Government special powers for dealing with those found to work against the public interest. A permanent investigating body, the Monopolies and Restrictive Practices Commission, was established. It consisted initially of not less than 4 and not more than 10 members, the chairman being appointed from the members. To this Commission the Board of Trade could refer an enquiry wherever, in the words of the Act, 'at least one-third of the goods of the industry in question were supplied to or by any one person, or two or more persons being in connected bodies corporate, or if any agreements or arrangements (whether enforceable or not) were in operation, the result of which was that in the United Kingdom, or any substantial part of it, the goods in question were not supplied at all'.[1] Included in its terms of reference were 'the supply of, or the application of any process to, goods, buildings or structures', which thus included all branches of industry (with the notable exception of the nationalized undertakings), but excluded transport, distribution and professional services; neither was it concerned with the activities of trade unions.

Its task was threefold: (i) to assess whether the conditions appertaining to the Act did in fact apply, and to what extent; (ii) to examine the things done by the parties in question for the purpose of preserving these conditions; and (iii) to assess whether these conditions and the things done for their preservation might be expected to operate against the public interest. The precise interpretation of the term *public interest* was left to the Monopolies Commission to decide in each individual instance, but in general terms it was laid down that attention should be directed to the following criteria: the production, treatment and distribution of goods by the most efficient and economic means, in such volume and at such prices as will best meet the requirements of home and overseas markets; the organization of industry and trade in such a way that their efficiency is progressively increased and new enterprise is encouraged; the fullest use and best distribution of men, materials and industrial capacity in the United Kingdom; and the development of technical improvements and the expansion of existing markets and the opening up of new ones. The findings of the Commission were to be published, if the terms of reference included an investigation of whether or not the public interest was being upheld; if they were purely factual in content, then they need not be.

Between 1949 and 1956, when the Commission was reorganized, 21 industries were investigated. Up to December 1953 only 7 reports had been issued; but, after a report by the Select Committee on Estimates on the work of the Monopolies Commission and the subsequent amending Act of 1953, the maximum number of members was raised to 25. In addition, the Act also permitted the functions

[1] Monopolies and Restrictive Practices (Enquiry and Control) Act, 1948.

of the Commission to be exercised by separate panels composed of not less than 5 members, which, in theory at least, meant that 5 investigations might be undertaken concurrently. Thereafter, with its growing experience, the Commission's reports became more frequent and, between January 1954 and December 1956, 14 were published. Apart from 1 general report on collective discrimination and boycott practices, the investigations were all *ad hoc* in character, relating to specific industries.

Lack of space forbids a detailed examination of the findings of the Commission. It is sufficient to say that while several practices, e.g. exclusive dealing, the collective boycott, control over raw materials or machinery, etc., which aimed deliberately at precluding competition by making it difficult for a newcomer to enter into the industry or others, e.g., quota schemes and the fixing of common prices, which were likely to be to the detriment of the consumer, were condemned by the Commission, others were justified either because there was sufficient counteracting power on the part of the buyers of the goods in question or because as a whole they were operating in the public interest. Thus, in its report on metal windows the Commission found that Crittalls had not abused its monopoly position: '. . . (we) do not criticize either its prices or its profits and find it a fact that its methods of pricing and exchange of costs and technical information have reduced its member costs', while in the electric lamp industry price agreements were considered reasonable, if they were linked with the cross-licensing of patents and the exchange of research and development information.

Yet notwithstanding the good work done by the Commission, this method of dealing with monopolies was open to criticism on several grounds. Of these, slowness of operation, timidity of approach, inadequacy of legal powers, width of scope, insufficient distinction between the fact-finding and judgment functions of the Commission etc. were frequently cited. The Select Committee earlier mentioned argued that it might be better if the Commission were to concentrate on certain aspects of a particular industry's mono-polistic position, and that the Board of Trade should satisfy itself that any action taken voluntarily by firms to comply with any recommendation of the Commission was of the kind required. More-over, each case had to be considered on its own merits; there was little guidance given as to the interpretation of 'the public interest' and the final decision as to whether or not the Commission's recommendations were accepted rested with Parliament.[1]

In 1956 the Restrictive Trade Practices Act was passed, which put an end to *ad hoc* legislation and attempted to deal with the monopoly problem as a whole. In Part I of the Act it was laid down that a Registrar of Restrictive Practices should be appointed and made responsible both for preparing, compiling and maintaining a register of restrictive agreements and also for taking proceedings on such agreements before a special court. Particulars of these proceedings are from time to time entered and filed in the register. Every agreement subject to the Act has to be registered; the onus of showing that the agreements are in the public interest now rests on those who wish to continue the practices. This concept is more clearly defined than heretofore and the occasions on which a practice, normally considered restrictive and contrary to the Act, might be allowed are clearly stated. These include occasions where its removal might result in serious industrial unemployment or price instability, cause loss of earnings in the export trade, discourage research, re-equipment and innovation, or deprive consumers of specific and substantial benefits, and also where the restriction is necessary either to enable the parties to negotiate on fair terms with a strong buyer or seller, or to maintain an agreement which the Court considers compatible with the public interest. The Court itself consists of 5 judges and not more than 10 lay members who have experience in industry, commerce or public affairs. The old Monopolies and Restrictive Practices Commission has been re-named the Monopolies Commission and its functions are now confined to the investigation of single firm restrictive practices or monopolies. The maximum number of its members is now 10. It is the Court which now decides whether or not the restrictions are contrary to the public interest and has the power to declare them void. Part II of the Act deals with resale price maintenance, legislating against collective boycotting while supporting individual dealer/manufacturer agreements.

Faced with the need to register all agreements and the growth of

---

[1] The only direct order issued to cease a particular restrictive practice was in the case of dental goods. However, there are several instances of trade associations giving undertakings to the Board of Trade not to participate in certain agreements.

public hostility to restrictions, many firms abolished or curtailed doubtful trade practices within the first few months of the new legislation. Of those which were originally registered under the Act, 1,090—or more than one-third—had been terminated, or removed from the register as no longer appropriate, by the end of 1960. Of the first 380 scheduled by the Registrar for court proceedings, 250 have since been abandoned. The fate of many more is thought to depend upon the outcome of cases already started. A single judgment by the Court might well affect as many as 100 of these agreements and could often settle a dozen or more. The fact that, win or lose, the defendant firm or trade association has to meet its legal costs of at least £5,000 is an additional reason for the high rate of abandonment.

At the end of 1960, there were some 2,340 restrictive trading agreements on the register of the Registrar. Though the form of restriction varies the vast majority of agreements relate to exclusive dealing arrangements, by which the entry of new competitors is impeded, or to the charging of common prices by which the consumer is often forced to pay more for his products than under competitive conditions. According to the Registrar, however, most of the agreements on the register arise as protective measures against the severities of competition rather than as instruments of exploitation.[1]

The Board of Trade may tell the Registrar the order in which the cases are to be taken and, if he learns of agreements which have not been registered, he can take the parties to the agreements to the High Court. Up to the end of 1960 the Court had heard 14 cases, and in all but two of these judgment was given in favour of the Registrar, in spite of some formidable arguments put forward by the defence. For example, the first case concerned the efforts of the Chemists' Federation to restrict the sale of proprietary medicines to chemists on the grounds that such a system of distribution protected the public from injury: the Court, however, was not convinced this was so. The claims put forward by the Yarn Spinners' Association in defence of its minimum price agreements, e.g. that they were necessary to ensure quality, guarantee employment, maintain capacity and aid research and development, were also found to be

[1] See *Not Enough Competition*, by J. B. Heath, Hobart Paper 11, 1961, p. 11.

insufficient to support the agreement. Similar judgments were subsequently given against the Blanket Manufacturers' Association in respect of its minimum price agreement and regulations dealing and the British Constructional Steelwork Association in respect of a quota equalization arrangement.

In all of the above proceedings, the Court either rejected the claims of the respondents out of hand or felt that they had failed to prove that the public interest was served more than it was injured. Thus, the plea that a particular restrictive practice was necessary to maintain price stability was turned down unless it could be shown that such stability was not at the expense of a free market. On the other hand, in the case of the Water Tube Boilermakers' Association, the Court ruled that the ending of the agreement in question (which consisted of an elaborate scheme of price consultation) would be so harmful to the industry's export performance that on balance the public interest would be harmed. The Court also upheld the plea of the Black Bolt and Nut Association that a 'specific and substantial benefit' was conferred upon the intermediate purchases of black nuts and bolts by a common price policy which saved them shopping around. Nevertheless, the overall effect of the judgments so far made has been to create a climate of opinion in which trade agreements are no longer respectable; and to this extent at least the present legislation is a marked improvement on that which it superseded.[1]

Other means of State intervention in industrial activity

By a variety of other means the State is able to affect the pattern and direction of industrial activity. In 1961, for example, the central authority's tax revenue accounted for 29% of the national income, while the gross capital formation of the public sector of industry was 80% of that of the private sector. Through the budget, and particularly by varying the level, scope and intensity of indirect taxation, the structure of production can be adjusted to suit the needs of the moment. Purchase tax and customs and excise duties on the one hand and subsidies and grants on the other have been important weapons in recent years for promoting the Government's investment

[1] For further particulars see J. B. Heath, op. cit., p. 31 ff.

policy and export programmes. Indirect taxes are, of course, an important source of Government revenue, yielding at present some 40% of total budgetary income. Yet the non-revenue purpose of the tax has often been of equal or even greater significance. Thus, in 1947, at a time of acute fuel shortage, the raising of the purchase tax on gas and electrical appliances did much to restrict the demand for coal; the imposition of the tax on commercial vehicles in 1951 was intended to redirect sales from the home to the export market; a year later, at the beginning of the rearmament programme, the tax was again raised on many engineering and electrical products so that productive capacity could be released for Government contract work; and the budget of 1955 included some alterations in the structure and incidence of indirect taxation to encourage production of quality goods.

In the same way subsidies have aided the post-war development of agriculture—the cost of which rose to £515 million in 1948, but has since fallen—and that of civilian airlines, housing and various manufacturing industries, while the investment programme of the nationalized industries (other than coal-mining) has been partially financed out of taxation.

Generally speaking, fiscal policy, though administratively somewhat less flexible, is more selective and predictable in its results than most monetary controls. It is, for example, less possible to assess how an increase or decrease in the price of credit will react on industrial activity than a change in the rates of income or expenditure taxes. However, in recent years, it has become increasingly recognized that the two types of control, the one affecting the flow and price of money as such, and the other that of the level and distribution of money incomes, are complementary rather than competitive. They are, thus, now being jointly used to further economic policy as a whole.

VII

INTERNATIONAL TRADE AND INDUSTRIAL
PROGRESS

FROM early times, the United Kingdom has derived great advantages from overseas trade. The division of labour with the rest of the world, which first became pronounced during the industrial revolution, still persists today to such an extent that this country is now more dependent on trade than any of her major industrial competitors. Clearly it is only in this way that the United Kingdom can obtain those things which she is unable to produce for herself, such as metallic ores, crude oil, tea, coffee, cocoa, natural rubber, tobacco and cotton—goods which at present account for approximately one-half of the import bill of the United Kingdom. In addition, however, it is to the advantage of the United Kingdom to engage in further trade wherever her comparative costs of production differ from those of other countries. Thus, for more than a century, she has been a net importer of wheat, since by exchanging the products of manufacturing industry for wheat she can obtain a greater net return from her resources than if they were utilized on British farms. Today about one-third of Britain's imports consist of foodstuffs and agricultural products which could be produced at home were it an economic proposition to do so.

Moreover, as other countries have become industrialized, so the pattern of international trade has increased in complexity, with the result that the United Kingdom today both imports and exports manufactured products. Thus, a third of Britain's imports in 1960 were made up of manufactured products, usually of a special kind not produced domestically—for example, certain essential chemicals, coarse unworked metals and highly specialized machinery, especially machine tools, and even some special textile products.

Apart from food, however, by far the larger part of British

imports consists of raw materials vital to the United Kingdom's economy. In fact, without these, Great Britain could not engage in world trade at all: in 1950, for example, 18% of the value of her exports was contributed by the imported goods used in their manufacture. The balance of overseas earnings helped to purchase the very much larger volume of raw materials used in the production of goods for home consumption. Skilled labour rather than the contribution of British natural resources (other than coal and iron and steel) is thus the main constituent of British exports.

In the past there has been a close association between the volume of overseas trade and the domestic standard of living. This is because the consumption of imported raw materials and semi-manufactured goods is directly related to the level of domestic industrial

TABLE 27

GROSS NATIONAL PRODUCT, EXPORTS AND IMPORTS 1938 AND 1947–61 UNITED KINGDOM (1954 = 100)

	Volume of gross national product	Volume of exports of goods and services	Volume of imports of goods and services
1938	79	76	96
1947	81	61	82
1948	83	76	82
1949	86	83	87
1950	90	100	89
1951	93	98	100
1952	91	92	92
1953	95	95	99
1954	100	100	100
1955	104	105	112
1956	105	112	111
1957	106	113	115
1958	106	110	114
1959	111	114	123
1960	116	121	138
1961	119	123	135

Sources: *Statistics of National Product and Expenditure, No. 2,* 1938 and 1947 to 1955. O.E.E.C., 1957. *National Institute Economic Review* (N.I.E.S.R.), May 1962. Change of base has been made by the authors to render series comparable.

H

activity, which in turn, through its effects on the size and distribution of the national income, influences the demand for foodstuffs and consumer goods which make up the remaining imports. Table 27 shows how the trends of these items and those of exports as well have varied since 1938.

World trade

As manufacturing countries are so reliant on imported raw materials, it is only to be expected that there should be a close connection between movements in world manufacturing production and world trade in manufactured products. As shown by Table 28, between 1950 and 1958 the latter has grown more rapidly than the former, while the following Table (29) illustrates the changing importance of trade between industrial and non-industrial countries during these same years. Thus, whereas the value of exports between industrial areas increased by 95%, those from manufacturing countries to primary producers rose by 86%, and those between non-industrial and industrial areas by 31%, and between non-industrial areas by 46%.

Naturally such changes have been accompanied by some redistribution of trade among the different countries. Table 30 illustrates the share of the major industrial nations in the world trade in manufacturers between 1937 and 1961. The United States is seen to have increased her stake in total manufacturing exports from 19·9 to

TABLE 28

VOLUME OF INTERNATIONAL TRADE AND OF WORLD MANUFACTURING PRODUCTION 1951–8
(1950 = 100)

	1951	1952	1953	1954	1955	1956	1957	1958
World trade in manufactures[1]	116	114	116	129	145	158	170	168
World manufacturing production	108	111	119	119	132	138	143	139

Source: Data derived from *National Institute Economic Review*, March 1960.

[1] Of the industrial nations.

TABLE 29

TRADE WITHIN AND BETWEEN INDUSTRIAL AND NON-INDUSTRIAL AREAS 1950, 1956 AND 1958

(Values in $1,000 million and percentages of world exports)

EXPORTS *Destination* →		Industrial areas		Non-industrial areas		All areas	
Origin ↓		*Value*	%	*Value*	%	*Value*	%
Industrial Areas	1950	19·5	34·3	13·7	24·1	33·2	58·4
	1956	37·3	40·3	23·4	25·2	60·7	65·5
	1958	38·0	39·7	25·6	26·8	63·7	66·5
Non-Industrial Areas	1950	16·5	28·9	7·2	12·7	23·7	41·6
	1956	22·2	24·0	9·8	10·5	32·0	34·5
	1958	21·7	22·6	10·5	10·9	32·2	33.5
All Areas	1950	36·0	63·2	20·9	36·8	56·9	100·0
	1956	59·5	64·3	33·1	35·7	92·6	100·0
	1958	59·7	62·3	36·1	37·7	95·9	100.0

Source: G.A.T.T., *International Trade 1956*, Geneva, 1957. *International Trade 1957–8*, 1959.

20·5%, while that of the United Kingdom has dwindled from 21·9 to 15·8%. Both Western Germany and Japan have now largely regained their pre-war positions and the former country is now, with the U.S., the joint largest exporter of manufactured goods in the world.

As industry develops and new products are created, the commodity composition of trade also changes. Thus, although since the turn of the century a hard core of one-third of the trade of the 11 most highly industrialized countries (excluding the Communist bloc) has consisted of chemicals, non-ferrous metals, agricultural equipment and other items, important changes have occurred in the constituent items of the remaining two-thirds. Trade in beverages and tobacco, railway equipment, ships, clothing and textiles, for example, has declined from over one-half of all trade in 1899 to about one-quarter in 1950, while there has been a compensatory increase from about one-eighth to three-eighths in the trade in motor vehicles, industrial machinery, electrical equipment and other iron and steel manufactures.

215

TABLE 30

WORLD[1] MANUFACTURING PRODUCTION, WORLD TRADE IN MANUFACTURES AND INDUSTRIAL COUNTRIES' SHARE OF THE TOTAL TRADE 1937 AND 1950–61

| | World manufacturing production Volume 1953=100 | World trade in manufactures Value $000 mn | World trade in manufactures Volume 1953=100 | Shares (% of total value) | | | | | |
				United Kingdom	Western Germany	Japan	U.S.A.	France	Others
1937	—	—	—	21·9	22·8	7·3	19·9	—	28·1
1950	83	20·0	86	25·5	7·3	3·4	27·3	9·9	26·6
1951	92	27·8	100	21·9	10·0	4·3	26·6	10·0	27·2
1952	94	27·8	98	21·5	12·0	3·8	26·2	9·2	27·3
1953	100	27·6	100	21·2	13·3	3·8	25·9	9·0	26·8
1954	100	29·8	111	20·3	14·8	4·7	25·2	9·0	26·0
1955	111	33·8	125	19·6	15·4	5·1	24·5	9·3	26·1
1956	116	38·4	136	19·0	16·4	5·7	25·3	7·8	25·8
1957	119	42·8	146	18·0	17·5	6·0	25·4	8·0	25·1
1958	117	42·0	145	17·8	18·6	6·0	23·3	8·6	25·9
1959	127	45·2	158	17·3	19·1	6·7	21·3	9·2	26·4
1960	135	—	179	15·9	19·4	6·9	21·7	9·7	26·4
1961	140	—	187	15·8	20·4	6·9	20·5	9·6	26·9

[1] Excluding the Communist countries.

Sources: *Board of Trade Journal*, 28 July 1956, Appendix I, Table I; *National Institute Economic Review* (N.I.E.S.R.), May 1962.

The more recent changes of this kind are summarized in the following table with respect to the main world exporters of manufactured goods:

TABLE 31

EXPORTS OF MANUFACTURED COMMODITIES BY SPECIAL CATEGORIES 1937 AND 1956

Classification of commodity groups[1]
(% share of total exports)

		Expanding	Stable	Declining	Not classified	Total
U.K.	1937	35·9	13·7	50·2	0·2	100·0
	1956	58·1	14·3	25·7	1·9	100·0
	Change	+22·2	+0·6	—24·5	+1·7	0
U.S.A.	1937	61·9	18·9	18·9	0·3	100·0
	1956	73·3	11·0	14·0	1·7	100·0
	Change	+11·4	—7·9	—4·9	+1·4	0
Germany	1937	48·3	15·0	36·6	0·1	100·0
	1956[2]	63·5	16·6	19·8	0·1	100·0
	Change	+15·2	+1·6	—16·8	0	0
Japan	1937	20·0	7·3	72·4	0·3	100·0
	1956	34·6	17·8	47·6	0	100·0
	Change	+14·6	+10·5	—24·8	—0·3	0
France	1937	33·9	17·7	48·1	0·3	100·0
	1956	41·0	25·3	33·6	0·1	100·0
	Change	+7·1	+7·6	—14·5	—0·2	0
World	1937	41·2	18·1	40·5	0·2	100·0
	1956	56·6	18·0	24·3	1·1	100·0
	Change	+15·4	—0·1	—16·2	+0·9	0

[1] Broadly speaking, those commodities which have increased their share of world manufacturing exports between 1937 and 1956 are regarded as expanding and those which have decreased their share as declining. Stable commodity groups cover those products for which there has been a less than 0·02 trend either way.
[2] Western Germany only.

Source: S. Spiegelglas, 'World Exports of Manufactures 1956 vs 1937', *Manchester School of Economic and Social Studies*, May 1959.

It is interesting to note that in contrast to the situation during the inter-war years, the U.K. has increased the share of the expanding trade group[1] by more than that of any of her major competitors and, apart from Japan, decreased the share of the declining group[2] most rapidly. This is, in part, a reflection of the marked decline in the relative importance of textiles, which has affected the U.K. more than any other industrial country, but, more significantly, of the way in which the U.K. has adjusted her economic structure to the demands made on it.

The United Kingdom's reliance on imports

The extent to which British industry is dependent on raw material supplies and semi-manufactured goods from abroad is not always appreciated. In fact this class of imports, of which raw cotton, wool, wood pulp, mineral fuels and non-ferrous metals are the most important items, accounted for nearly 60% of the U.K.'s purchases from abroad in 1950. The proportion, expressed in value terms, of the import content of non-food manufactured goods in relation to their gross selling value has been put at 20 to 25%; but, as Table 32 shows,

TABLE 32

IMPORTED PRODUCTS USED IN CURRENT
PRODUCTION AS A PERCENTAGE OF THE VALUE
OF FINAL OUTPUT IN SELECTED INDUSTRIAL
GROUPS
(1950)

	%
Agriculture	11
Mining and quarrying	8
Chemicals and allied trades	54
Metals, engineering and vehicles	10
Textiles, leather and clothing	37
Food, drink and tobacco	17
Other manufacturing	37
Building and contracting	4

Source: Derived from data in *National Income and Expenditure Blue Book*, 1956.

[1] Items in this group include industrial equipment, vehicles, electrical goods, chemicals and agricultural machinery.
[2] Items in this group include textiles, tobacco, beverages, clothing and metal manufactures.

industries differ greatly in the extent to which they are dependent on imported products.

Agriculture, mining and quarrying, and building and contracting are mainly self-sufficient: the metal industries appear to be similarly placed but, in this case, the low import content belies the true importance of the raw material concerned, e.g. copper, aluminium, nickel ores, without which many of our most widely demanded products could not be manufactured at all. The food, drink and tobacco and the textile industries are respectively moderately and highly dependent on overseas countries for most of their essential raw materials. The group with the highest import content of all is the chemical, but this is largely because of the prominence within it of mineral oil refining, an industry which, by its very nature, has a net output that is low in relation to the cost of the raw material.

Since the import content of the final output of various industries differs greatly, changes in both the structure of industrial output and in the prices of imports naturally affect the composition of the latter. As Table 33 shows, there were in fact some marked changes in the pattern of imports between 1938 and 1954. Movements in the

TABLE 33

VALUE OF RETAINED IMPORTS BY BROAD
COMMODITY GROUPS AS A PERCENTAGE OF
TOTAL IMPORTS 1938, 1954 AND 1960

		1938	1954	1960
Food, beverages and tobacco	..	48·8	39	33
Basic materials	..	24·6	31	25
Mineral fuels and lubricants	..	5·5	10	10
Manufactured goods	..	21·0	20	32
		100	100	100

Source: *Annual Abstract of Statistics.*

relative prices of imports must be held partly responsible for this, but the change in volume composition was the more important influence. It was as a result of these changes that a 50% increase over 1938 in the volume of industrial production was achieved in 1955, although there was a considerably smaller increase in the volume of imports. Again, partly as a result of the expansion of home agricultural production by 60%, the proportion of foodstuffs, including beverages and tobacco, to total imports fell between 1938 and 1960 from 49 to 33%. The relative importance of mineral oils has nearly doubled, but even this increase underestimates the growth in U.K. consumption, as current imports are comprised almost entirely of crude oil instead of the more costly refined products. 'Basic materials' in 1960 consisted almost entirely of commodities which were essential for production and which could not be produced at home—cotton and other textile fibres accounted for £267 million, metallic ores £167 million and timber products £187 million of the total of £1,063 million.

Imports of manufactured goods have risen particularly rapidly in the last six years due to the relaxation of import controls. By 1960 they were worth some £1,449 million, although a high proportion were semi-manufactures used as raw materials for industry. Over one-quarter of the value of manufactured imports consisted of various metals, for example iron and steel (£101 million) and non-ferrous base metals (£279 million), while included amongst the finished manufactures were machinery and other products which, because of demand limitations or of the highly specialized manufacturing techniques involved, it was uneconomical to produce in this country.

Exports

The United Kingdom's exports provide the main earnings of foreign currency to pay for imports. In 1960, for example, some $3\frac{1}{2}$ million to 4 million persons, nearly double the number pre-war, were employed in the production of goods for export. These latter resulted in an income of £3,536 million to offset an expenditure of £4,557 million on commodity imports. Of the former, 85% consisted of manufactured goods which represented 37% of the net product of manufacturing industry. Since 1945 a considerable increase in the volume of exports has been necessary to compensate for the diminution in invisible receipts—a task made all the more difficult by the unfavourable terms of trade (at least in the early years) which have been aggravated by the large expansion of exports.

The composition of the country's exports has also changed during the twentieth century. The contribution of the textile industries has continued to decline, and reliance on these manufactures is now less than at any time in the last 150 years. On the other hand, the export contribution of the metal and engineering industries has become increasingly prominent. For example, the value of motor vehicles exported in 1960 was equal to one-seventh of the total exports of U.K. manufacturing industry, and this industry is now the U.K.'s chief earner of foreign currency. Table 34 shows the main changes which have taken place since before the war.

TABLE 34

U.K. EXPORTS OF MANUFACTURED GOODS BY BROAD INDUSTRIAL GROUPS 1935–60

	Average 1935–38 £mn.	%	1950 £mn.	%	1960 £mn.	%
Chemicals	29·4	8·5	141·2	7·7	316·6	10·5
Iron and steel	29·9	8·6	104·4	5·7	215·5	7·2
Manufactures of metals	21·1	6·1	106·2	5·8	157·9	5·2
Non-electrical machinery	42·0	12·1	299·3	16·4	711·8	23·7
Electrical machinery, apparatus etc. ..	17·1	4·9	136·8	7·5	233·8	7·8
Vehicles and aircraft ..	26·8	7·7	300·3	16·4	525·7	17·5
Textiles and clothing ..	119·7	34·4	308·6	16·9	308·8	10·3
Wood, cork and paper manufactures ..	7·7	2·2	26·5	1·5	44·1	1·5
Other manufactures ..	54·0	15·5	404·1	22·1	486·9	16·3
	347·7	100·0	1,827·4	100·0	3,001·1	100·0

Source: *Annual Abstract of Statistics*

For various reasons, e.g. the problem of product comparability, volume comparisons over a long period of time are of doubtful validity. However, with a view to showing which industries have progressed most and least in the export field in the last decade, Table 35 classifies a group of 15 selected products according to their volume changes, expressed in relation to the average for all manufactures of 176, on the basis 1947 = 100.

For 1948, an Input-Output Table constructed by Mr I. G. Stewart[1] enables an assessment to be made of the value of exports in relation to the output of various industrial groups. Summarizing his conclusions we see that the metal, engineering and vehicle groups of

[1] *Times Review of Industry*, December 1958, L.C.E.S. Supplement.

industries exported over 19% of their output, textiles and clothing 15%, the other metal industries 14% and chemicals 13%. Very low in the scale come food, drink and tobacco, and farming and mining. The picture would be rather different today, since (as we saw in Table 34) all industries have not expanded exports to the same degree. Moreover, *within* these broad groups there were wide divergences. In 1948, for example, 32% of the output of the motor vehicle industries was exported while in 1959 the figure was nearly 50%;

TABLE 35

EXPORTS OF PRODUCE AND MANUFACTURES
OF THE UNITED KINGDOM

Index Numbers of Volume 1960 (1947=100)

	Selected Products	Index No. 1947=100
ABOVE THE AVERAGE	Petroleum and petroleum products	1001
	Chemicals	317
	Road vehicles and aircraft	300
AROUND THE AVERAGE	Iron and steel	245
	Food, drink and tobacco manufactures	213
	Basic materials	206
	Machinery other than electrical	202
BELOW THE AVERAGE	Electrical machinery and apparatus	190
	Non-ferrous base metals	185
	Paper and paperboard manufactures	185
	Woollen and worsted yarns	135
	Synthetic yarns and fabrics	119
	Metal manufactures	113
	Miscellaneous textile manufactures	104
	Cotton yarns and woven fabrics	67

Source: Data derived from *Annual Abstract of Statistics, 1961*

the corresponding proportion of iron and steel exports in this latter year was 14%, of non-ferrous metals 16%, of mechanical engineering products 28%. Among the textile groups 28 to 29% of the output of both cotton and silk and of woollen and worsted products was sent overseas.

In contrast to the situation in the inter-war period, an especially welcome development since the war has been the increasingly important contribution made by the new, or virtually new, industrial products to the export drive. These newer exports are not confined to the engineering industries but are also to be found among many of the other science-based industries, the products of which are primarily the fruits of recent research. Those developed exclusively since the war, such as electronic apparatus, combine harvesters, fork-lift trucks, diesel locomotives, synthetic detergents, antibiotics, sulphonamides and nylon clothing, provided exports valued at £73 million or 3% of all manufacturing exports in 1955. Virtually new exports—i.e. those which were of negligible importance before the war, including diesel engines, track-laying tractors, oil drilling and refining equipment, cash registers, alarm clocks, fluorescent lamps, foam rubber articles and soluble coffee powder—were worth £70 million in 1955. Finally must be mentioned the 'greatly expanded' exports, i.e. those which have increased 25–150 fold since 1938. The most important of these are commercial vehicles and chassis, agricultural tractors, earth-moving equipment, domestic refrigerators, washing machines, office machinery, refined petroleum, plastic and cellulose materials and refined precious metals. Altogether these greatly expanded exports amounted to £263 million in 1955, or 9% of all manufacturing exports.[1]

British overseas trade and economic welfare

After noting the salient features of both British and world import and export trade, it is pertinent to ask whether the United Kingdom's trade is developing along the right lines. Is the best use being made of the nation's productive resources so that welfare is maximized? This question involves a discussion both of the direction of British trade—a subject inseparable from the terms of trade—and of the composition and volume of exports and imports.

The direction of trade

About two-thirds of the United Kingdom's export trade is with the poorer and less highly industrialized countries whose people have comparatively simple tastes. In consequence, the urge to emulate

[1] For further particulars see 'Progress in New Exports of U.K. Products, *Board of Trade Journal*, 13 October 1956.

western and especially American standards of consumption—a most potent factor stimulating the demand for the more sophisticated industrial products—hardly exists. Moreover, as such countries try to improve their standards of living by industrialization, the first domestic industries they usually establish are those that produce consumer goods, such as textiles, soap and edible fat which, more likely than not, they previously bought from the United Kingdom. Sometimes, in fact, these countries even become competitors of the United Kingdom in the remaining overseas markets for the products concerned. It is not surprising, therefore, that Britain's share of world trade has been falling.

Apart from a tendency for its volume to diminish relatively, the trade between a highly industrialized country like the United Kingdom and the primary producing countries tends to be less stable than trade between industrial countries. With 75% of imports consisting of foodstuffs and raw materials and 85% of exports consisting of manufactured goods, the British terms of trade are largely an indication of the rate at which manufactured goods exchange for primary products. Over recent years, the terms of trade between the primary producing and the industrial countries, as determined by the relative strength of supply and demand for the relevant products, have fluctuated around a trend which from the viewpoint of the industrial countries has been slightly, yet progressively, deteriorating. For, on the one hand, the industrialization of primary producing countries, as we have just observed, has reduced the dependence of these countries on certain classes of manufactured imports, thus depressing their prices. On the other hand, a simultaneous and consequent increase in demand by these same countries, both for raw materials to supply their new domestic industries and also for foodstuffs to satisfy the needs of a higher living standard consequent on industrialization, forces up prices in the commodity markets of the world. The terms of trade then move against the industrial country and it has to export a growing quantity of its products to gain a given volume of imports. The United Kingdom, being so highly dependent on the trade with the less developed countries, has therefore found it especially difficult to earn enough foreign currency to pay for her imports.

However, there are factors which will halt a tendency to a continual decline in the terms of trade of industrial countries. An enlargement of primary countries' productive capacity, as a result of increased investment by industrial countries, is one such factor, while the discovery of new and unexpected sources of supply of raw materials and the development of synthetic substitutes for other raw materials also have the same effect. These factors have been at work in the post-war period, but it was only after the intense buying of raw materials during the Korean War in 1951 had stopped, followed by a reduced amount of strategic stock-piling, that there was any marked fall in the prices of primary materials. The terms of trade then began to move in favour of the United Kingdom, and by the end of 1958 they were more favourable than they had been for the greater part of 20 years.

As recent experience has shown, however, an improvement in the United Kingdom's terms of trade has unfavourable reactions on primary producers—their income falls and they find it more difficult to purchase manufactured products. The volume of British exports would as a result, be expected to fall, reacting on the balance of payme,nts position. If, however, the experience of the inter-war years—when Britain's terms of trade were relatively very favourable —is a guide, the net effect seems likely to be to this country's advantage. But low prices for primary materials will not last indefinitely, for their long-run supply is rather inelastic and the trend in prices, particularly as the best sources are exploited before the more difficult and less productive, will tend to be upwards.

'Favourable' and 'unfavourable' are, in fact, unsuitable words to use in connection with terms of trade, for 'favourable' terms of trade may simply signify that the ratio at which a country's exports are exchanging for imports is the result of the uncompetitiveness of exports: that exports are too highly priced, so that sales abroad are small and there are balance of payments difficulties. On the other hand, a country with 'unfavourable' terms of trade may be exporting so much that it has a substantial balance of payments surplus. The only country which can really afford to have 'favourable' terms of trade is one with a high degree of monopoly over the supply of its more usual exports, for then high export prices can be associated with relatively high sales. The U.K. has not been in this position and despite 'favourable' terms of trade since 1955 the level of exports has generally been too low in relation to her balance of payments needs, just as the level of exports was too low in the first

post-war decade when the terms of trade were unfavourable since the demand for exports was relatively inelastic. Indeed, it seems highly probable that 'favourable' terms of trade are the result of the influence of home demand causing the prices of goods sold in export markets to rise and diminishing the volume of sales.

The composition and volume of British overseas trade

Within any given price structure, the benefits which the United Kingdom derives from overseas trade clearly depend on the composition of her exports, since some types of production confer greater advantages than others. Thus, so long as it is British labour which, in the last resort, exchanges for imports, then the export goods conferring the greatest advantages, or which may be said to have the greatest conversion value, are those with a labour content which is low in relation to the net return. (The net return is measured by the excess of value of the finished product over its import content.) Indirect labour used in making the capital equipment employed in production has of course to be taken into account.

Cotton piece goods are examples of products of high import and high labour content, and profit levels are low as they are marketed under highly competitive conditions. Many of the under-developed but partially industrialized countries are selling these goods very cheaply; and the United Kingdom is forced either to follow suit, getting a very small return for its labour effort, or redistribute its resources to where net returns are higher. At the other extreme there are goods, such as the new engineering products, which have low import and labour contents, but which give high returns to effort. 'Know-how', the term which has come into use to signify the technical knowledge which emanates not only from organized learning (research, development etc.) but from long experience in the same or in related fields of manufacture, plays a significant and highly rewarding part in the manufacture of these newer products, particularly of the newer capital goods exported by the United Kingdom.

In recent years, as we have seen, there has been a considerable change in the pattern of exports: those products generating a low return have diminished in importance, while the newer products bringing in a higher return are becoming more prominent. There is now, for example, less reliance on textiles than at any time in recent British industrial history, though the decline is much more marked in the cheaper than in the high-quality products for which this country has such an excellent reputation and which are still in considerable demand overseas, particularly in the United States and Canada. On the other hand, the industries supported by an advanced technology, which require highly specialized capital equipment and rely on highly trained labour and large technical staffs, have made great progress in the export trade.

Demand conditions in the export market vary greatly. For the simpler finished products, so prominent in British trade, which are sold in competition with very similar foreign products, demand is highly elastic in response to price changes. On many such products the marginal return may be below that of labour catering specifically for home needs. Productivity is thus an important factor, influencing both the volume of the country's exports and its gains from international trade. Considerable progress in improving productivity appears to have been made by the United Kingdom, perhaps more than by any other country except the U.S., between 1938 and 1950 but rather less than by several European countries since 1950.[1]

For goods of a distinctive kind, whether of quality or novelty (for satisfying newly created wants), price is a less important factor in influencing demand: for example, in the sale of the better grades of textiles, chinaware, Scotch whisky and motor-cars the British producer derives considerable monopoly advantages. The price elasticity of demand for such goods is relatively low, but income elasticity is high. If it were not so, British products would not sell, for example, in the American and Canadian markets where high tariff barriers and distribution costs have to be overcome.

In regard to the adjustments believed to be necessary to bring the volume and composition of trade to the optimum, there are differences of opinion. One school of thought believes that this country is exporting too much, with the result that there has been a deterioration in the terms of trade. It therefore advocates less reliance

[1] For further particulars see, for example, *Economic Survey of Europe in 1957* United Nations, 1958.

on international trade, with a greater concentration on home agriculture and on other import-saving measures. An important incidental advantage would be the infusion of greater stability into Britain's international trading position for, as we have seen, the heavy reliance on imports has been a source of instability. The other school of thought, however, believes that the volume of trade ought to be increased.

The terms of trade, according to the first school, are unfavourable to this country, because a high volume of exports can only be achieved by selling cheaply and the large demand for imports can only be satisfied at high prices. A reduction in the British demand for foreign agricultural products would, therefore, it is thought, cause imports to be cheaper, while a reduction in the supply of British manufactured goods would raise the price of her exports. The underlying assumption here is that Britain is doubly a monopolist— a monopolist seller of manufactured goods and a monopolist buyer of agricultural products. As has already been pointed out, the first assumption is undoubtedly partly true in regard to certain of the more distinctive products, but less true in regard to the simpler manufactured products constituting the bulk of the export trade. The United Kingdom's ability to raise export prices is thus limited: the smaller her share of total world trade in manufactures becomes, the smaller her price-influencing power. The second assumption is also partly valid. The British market in agricultural products is undoubtedly important to foreign suppliers, but it seems doubtful whether a reduction in British purchases would appreciably affect the price. Other foreign sales would still be open to the agricultural producers, for the world's need of agricultural products is growing abreast of the growth of world population. Furthermore, as a change in British policy could only occur gradually, foreign producers might reduce supply in step with the reduction in British demand; and there would be little or no consequent fall in price. Britain's power to influence her terms of trade seems, therefore, to be very limited and the outcome of a change in policy to one of greater subsidization of home agricultural production and less manufacturing production would be a matter of conjecture. However, without going into the argument in detail, assuming the terms of trade at their recent level, the transfer of resources from manufacturing to agriculture would have involved a cost of £150 for every extra £100 or so of agricultural output gained.[1] In the short run, greater home production would certainly appear to be relatively more uneconomic as foreign prices would undoubtedly fall. Nevertheless, it cannot be inferred that less home production would have been an advantage, for a greater volume of imports could only be obtained at higher prices, not only on the additional amount but on all the amount imported.

Britain's foreign trade in the future

In the future, in what industries can Britain expect to derive the greatest trading advantages? Because they rely on scientific and technical developments, and generally involve highly specialized capital equipment, the newer industries are unlikely to be capable of transplantation to countries which are only developing their industrial potential, and are obviously of great value and need fostering. Moreover, as we have already noted, when under-developed countries become industrialized they frequently compete with British exports in world markets. To offset this loss of competitive power it has been suggested that the United Kingdom should endeavour to benefit from these countries' processes of industrialization by supplying them with the capital goods they require. A greater concentration during the last few years on the supply of capital goods, the importation of which has received high priority in many developing countries at the expense of imports of consumer goods, would undoubtedly have been beneficial to the United Kingdom's balance of payments position. In the future, exports of capital goods may have to be encouraged, and British manufacturers induced to operate the manufacturing plants in the importing countries and to supply skilled labour, scientists and administrators while the local personnel are trained. The valuable contracts which have been secured by British companies to supply atomic power stations to Japan and Italy are obviously highly beneficial to this country. An

[1] See e.g. D. T. Healey, 'Increased Agriculture or Increased Exports?', *Westminster Bank Review*, May 1955; D. T. Healey, 'Can Agriculture do a Deal with Europe?' *Westminster Bank Review*, August 1958, and note relating to the same article on p. 20 of the same Review, November 1958. Also Austin Robinson, 'The Cost of Agricultural Import Saving', *The Three Banks Review*, December 1958, p. 9.

ever-present need is for British industry to be the innovator and to pioneer new and desirable products: so long as she can maintain this role and keep some steps ahead of the developing countries, a demand for the newer consumer goods and for the more complex items of capital equipment will always exist.

Since 1945 currency blocs and tariff barriers have impeded the free movement of goods, probably to a greater extent than ever before in the world's history. In consequence, Britain's participation in world trade appears to have been both inappropriate in composition and in amount. Of late, however, there have been movements which are in the direction of a gradual relaxation of some of the hindrances to trade. The nations in the free world are nearly all participants in G.A.T.T.[1]—the General Agreement on Tariffs and Trade —and many tariff barriers are being reduced by negotiation.

In Western Europe, since 1950, there has been a considerable liberalization of trade by the gradual elimination of exchange control and quantitative import restrictions. The establishment of the European Payments Union in 1950 (now the European Monetary Agreement), the European Coal and Steel Community (1953) and Euratom (1957) were all movements in this direction, but by far the most important and far-reaching step came in July 1957 when a treaty was signed in Rome bringing the European Economic Community (E.E.C.) into existence. This is a customs and economic union comprising West Germany, France, Italy, Belgium, the Netherlands and Luxembourg, the basic aims of which are threefold. First (starting in January 1959) all customs duties and quotas between the participants are gradually to be abolished over a period of 12 years; at the same time, the several tariff barriers of the members against goods coming in from the outside world are to be replaced by a common tariff—roughly equivalent to the average previously being charged. Secondly, all obstacles to the free movement of persons, services and capital between the member States are to be eliminated. Thirdly, with a view to the harmonization of economic and social conditions, there is to be set up, in certain fields, institutions of a supra-national character, to whose authority each of the member countries must submit. The effective realization of the hopes of this union depend principally on the ability of the members to work together and on the strength of

[1] Thirty-five governments are signatories to the Agreement.

their desire for success. The countries concerned already have a considerable incentive in that the liberalization of trade achieved since 1950 has resulted in a faster growth in production in Western Europe than in any other comparable area in the world. Intra-European trade has certainly been growing much more rapidly than Britain's trade with the Commonwealth: from 1951–9 Western Europe's imports by value rose by some 55%, Britain's by only 3%.

The United Kingdom did not elect to become a founder-member of the E.E.C., partly because she felt unable to accept the political and social integration involved and partly because the substitution of existing British tariffs for those of the new organization and the common agricultural policy was felt to be too high a price to pay. But although at the time neither the Commonwealth nor Great Britain was prepared to abandon Imperial Preference, the United Kingdom was nevertheless very apprehensive of the consequences of remaining outside the Common Market, and she therefore proposed that an industrial Free Trade Area (F.T.A.) should be formed. At the beginning, it was intended that the Common Market countries and the remaining members of O.E.E.C. should constitute the Free Trade Area, but Greece, Iceland, Eire, Portugal and Turkey—all of them primary producing countries—would be unlikely to develop into full participants before 1970. The Free Trade Area was then to consist of the six Common Market countries and another six, the United Kingdom, Denmark, Sweden, Norway, Austria and Switzerland, comprising a population of 240 million people. The new trading system, like the Common Market, would develop gradually to enable industries to adapt themselves to the withdrawal of protection. When fully developed there would be free trade for industrial products within the Area; but, whereas the Common Market countries would operate a common tariff for imports from the rest of the world, the other six members would maintain their individual tariff structures.

The negotiations for the formation of the European Free Trade Area were unsuccessful, but out of them emerged, in an attenuated form, a plan, finalized in Stockholm in July 1959, to set up a Free Trade Association (E.F.T.A.) amongst seven of the more important countries outside the E.E.C.—the U.K., Austria, Denmark, Norway, Portugal, Sweden and Switzerland. Between these countries

—the Outer Seven group so called—the aim of freedom of trade in industrial products is to be achieved over ten years, the first tariff reductions beginning 1 July 1960. Again, as in the case of the proposed F.T.A., members are to retain their own external tariffs, but there are to be certificates of origin for goods traded within E.F.T.A., to prevent the possibility of goods entering one country across a low tariff frontier and then passing duty free to a high tariff member. However, in this case it was found impossible completely to exclude agriculture and a number of bilateral arrangements between member countries relating to agricultural products and fish were included, with the U.K., in particular, obliged to grant a number of concessions.

The formation of E.F.T.A. was but a preparatory step towards the ultimate objective of barrier-less trade among all the members of O.E.E.C. For the U.K., this development was of considerably less significance than would have been the creation of the free trade area, embracing the Six and the Seven. In 1958 the size of population of continental E.F.T.A. was half that of the E.E.C.[1] but econominally the disparity was not so great, as both income per capita and imports per capita were appreciably higher in E.F.T.A. than in the E.E.C. Since that time, however, economic progress has been considerably more pronounced in the E.E.C. than in the E.F.T.A. Indeed, in the course of the last two years it has become increasingly apparent that there would be gains, not only for the U.K. but for the members of both the E.E.C. and E.F.T.A., from the integration of the two trading blocs. Accordingly, after consultation with the other E.F.T.A. members, the U.K. applied for membership of the E.E.C. in August 1961; negotiations for determining the terms on which this country could be admitted and the interests of E.F.T.A. and E.E.C. merged were begun towards the end of 1961 and are still in progress.

In the period 1953–60 industrial production in the U.K. increased by 30% compared with 70% in the E.E.C. and approximately 50% in continental E.F.T.A. The growth in economic activity in Western Europe has been accompanied by a considerable increase in imports. From 1954 to 1960 continental Western Europe increased its total imports by 75% while the U.K.'s imports

[1] The E.E.C. comprises 163 million people and the E.F.T.A. 90 million.

increased by less than 40%. Imports of manufactured products into the former area in fact rose by more than 100%, i.e. proportionately more than all imports. The U.S. participated in this increase to a considerable extent, for Western Europe's imports from U.S.A. increased by 150%, while the U.K. derived less benefit —an increase of less than 50%. During the same period, the volume of the U.K.'s exports increased by 22%, but those to Western Europe increased by 29%.

Thus the U.K., although making less progress in increasing exports to the Continent than the U.S.A., has nevertheless been relatively more successful there, particularly in the E.E.C., than elsewhere. But clearly there is scope for this country to do very much better. In 1960 only 14% of the U.K.'s trade was with the E.E.C. countries, compared with 42% with the Commonwealth and 44% with the rest of the world. *Prima facie* then, the prospects of a marked expansion of exports to Western Europe, particularly to the dynamic E.E.C., are more favourable than those offered by any other trading area in the world.

At the time of writing (June 1962) the outcome of the negotiations is in some doubt. If the U.K. becomes a member of the E.E.C. then the adoption of the Community's Common External Tariff will probably result in the imposition of duty on some raw materials which now enter largely duty-free. Against this, however, some semi-processed and finished goods may enter at reduced cost so that on balance there may be little effect on the price of U.K. exports. But in Europe, at any rate, the effect of any increase would probably be counteracted by the reduced tariffs payable on imports from fellow members of the E.E.C.; this consequent increase in exports to Europe would need to more than offset the reduction in exports to the Commonwealth, likely as a result of the abandonment (or substantial diminution) of Commonwealth Preference and the increase in U.K. imports from Western Europe consequent on the lowering of tariff rates.

In 1957, when it was proposed that the Free Trade Area should be established the Economist Intelligence Unit made a detailed study of its probable implications for British industry.[1] Though this scheme did not materialize the conclusions of the E.I.U. are not without wider significance in that they portray some of the advantages and disadvantages of European economic integration in

[1] *Britain and Europe*, 1957.

general, and are relevant now that negotiations have been renewed on these issues. Assuming, for example, that Britain and the other members of the Outer Seven were eventually to join the E.E.C.—either on their own terms or those of the existing member States—what would be the likely effect on her industrial life. It would seem that the industries most likely to benefit, as judged by the estimated additional increase in output, are motor vehicles, chemicals, wool, electrical and general engineering, rubber manufactures, steel, hosiery and clothing. Likely to be almost as successful are non-ferrous metals, metal manufactures, aircraft, shipbuilding, oil refining, building materials, glass, scientific instruments and sports goods. In contrast to these industries, which are highly efficient and not only are unlikely to suffer any ill effects from the withdrawal of protection but actually likely to gain from the new opportunities in widening markets, there are industries which are almost certain to suffer ill effects. The watch and clock industry, for example—an infant industry now heavily protected—will almost certainly lose ground as also may the cotton fabrics, toys, china and glassware and rayon industries, either because British designs are not entirely to the taste of Continental purchasers or because of the loss of protection in a field where competition is intense. Paper manufactures and leather goods are also likely to suffer. The British machine tool industry, which is already suffering from neglected investment, would seem especially liable to be adversely affected. The remaining industries, in particular railway engineering, jute manufacture and furniture manufacture, would seem unlikely to be affected. The relative importance of these five groups of industries is shown in Table 36. But it is not the position now which is so important as the position which would be reached in fifteen or so years under the stimulus of gradual easement of trading conditions and of gradual intensification of competition. While only a fraction of the labour force in manufacturing industry is likely to be adversely affected, there might nevertheless be some redistribution of the labour force and some frictional unemployment, caused by the less efficient producers in the various industries going out of business as a result of increased competition; but the labour so displaced would seem assured of employment in the more efficient and progressive industries. As the changes would occur over a considerable period, the process of redeployment should take place in the normal course

TABLE 36

LIBERALIZATION OF EUROPEAN TRADE: ANTICIPATED EFFECT ON PRODUCTION AND EMPLOYMENT IN BRITISH MANUFACTURING INDUSTRY

Group of industries	Net value of output in 1950 £ million	Per cent of total net output	Employment in 1955 (000)	Per cent of total employment
1. Gaining	1,897	59	3,809	59
2. Probably gaining	721	22	1,518	23
3. Losing	384	12	624	10
4. Probably losing	94	3	220	3
5. Little affected ..	133	4	321	5
Total ..	3,229	100	6,492	100

Source: Economist Intelligence Unit. *Britain and Europe*, 1957.

of labour turnover—mainly by not replacing workers when they retired.

British agriculture is particularly apprehensive of the outcome of the U.K.'s proposed membership of the E.E.C. Entry would not involve the abandonment by the British Government of the policy of agricultural protection at present followed, since E.E.C. farmers are to continue to receive protection, but the form of protection would have to change. Thus, whereas the main support of the British farmer is subsidization from general taxation, taking the form of deficiency payments should market prices fail to reach a given minimum level, in the E.E.C. agricultural products are sold at 'target' prices, such prices being maintained by the tariff between the Community and the rest of the world, with support-buying by marketing boards. It is not certain, therefore, that the British farmer would suffer any disadvantages from membership of the E.E.C. but the price of food to the British consumer would seem likely to be higher, offset by less pressure on direct-tax payers.

Britain's economic links with the Commonwealth would inevitably change. At present Commonwealth Preference results in mutual advantages to the members of the Commonwealth: there is easier entry for Commonwealth goods to the U.K. and for

British exports to Commonwealth countries. On joining the E.E.C. the U.K. would not be allowed to continue to enjoy the preferences, but the net effect of the elimination or reduction of Commonwealth Preference is difficult to assess; Britain's aim is to safeguard the Commonwealth trading arrangements as far as possible.

Conclusion

British industry and Britain's prosperity in the future, as in the past, depend on her success in exporting her manufactured goods. Not only do exports enable essential imports to be bought, but they also make it possible for the British people and Britain's customers to reap the benefits of the economies of large-scale production and of the international division of labour.

These advantages can be shown, from theoretical considerations, to be greatest when the obstacles to free trade are minimized and there are no currency restrictions, a state of affairs which has not fully existed since the middle of the last century. Nor is anything near to perfect freedom likely to be achieved in the foreseeable future. However, following the establishment of the E.E.C. and E.F.T.A., a considerable measure of liberalization may be expected: for example the United Kingdom now has an interest in 2 large trading areas: in the one—the Sterling Area—the pound sterling would move perfectly freely as now, and in the other—the E.F.T.A. —self-regulating mechanisms working through small movements in exchange rates would bring about equilibrium without an elaborate apparatus of controls, licences and prohibitions. It is true that there may well have to be a re-orientation of the British trade pattern (and even more so if Britain joined the E.E.C.), but insofar as this would mean a greater participation in the trade between industrial countries, with less reliance on traditional markets, the United Kingdom might benefit greatly. In any event, as trade is so vital to her, she has to continue to strive to achieve these benefits.

SUGGESTIONS FOR FURTHER READING

G. C. ALLEN: *British Industries and their Organization*, Longmans, 1959 (4th edition)

G. C. ALLEN: *The Structure of Industry in Britain*, Longmans, 1961.

W. ASHWORTH: *An Economic History of England, 1870–1939*, Methuen, 1960.

D. BURN (ed.): *The Structure of British Industry: a Symposium*, vols. 1 and 2, Cambridge University Press, 1958

C. F. CARTER and B. R. WILLIAMS: *Industry and Technical Progress*, Oxford University Press, 1957

C. F. CARTER and B. R. WILLIAMS: *Investment in Innovation*, Oxford University Press, 1958

P. L. COOK: *Effects of Mergers*, Allen & Unwin, 1958

R. S. EDWARDS and H. TOWNSEND: *Business Enterprise*, Macmillan, 1958

P. EINZIG: *The Economic Consequences of Automation*, Secker & Warburg, 1956

R. EVELY and I. M. D. LITTLE: *Concentration in British Industry*, Cambridge University Press, 1960

P. SARGANT FLORENCE: *The Logic of British and American Industry*, Routledge and Kegan Paul, 1961 (Rev. ed.)

P. SARGANT FLORENCE: *Industry and the State*, Hutchinson University Library, 1957

J. W. GROVE: *Government and Industry in Britain*, Longmans, 1962.

P. H. GUENAULT and J. H. JACKSON: *The Control of Monopoly in the United Kingdom*, Longmans, 1960

J. JEWKES and others: *The Sources of Invention*, Macmillan, 1958

A. E. KAHN: *Great Britain in the World Economy*, Columbia University Press, New York, 1946

W. A. LEWIS: *Economic Survey 1919–1939*, Allen and Unwin, 1949

A. F. LUCAS: *Industrial Reconstruction and the Control of Competition*, Longmans, 1937

P.E.P.: *Government and Industry*, P.E.P., 1952

P.E.P.: *Growth in the British Economy*, Allen and Unwin, 1960.

S. POLLARD: *The Development of the British Economy 1914–1950*, Arnold, 1962.

H. ROSE: *The Economic Background to Investment*, C.U.P., 1960

B. TEW and R. F. HENDERSON (eds.): *Studies in Company Finance*, Cambridge University Press, 1960

INDEX

239